Vagabonding

Changing

Harry Alverson Franck

Alpha Editions

This edition published in 2024

ISBN : 9789362093035

Design and Setting By
Alpha Editions
www.alphaedis.com
Email - info@alphaedis.com

Contents

Contents

FOREWORD

I did not go into Germany with any foreformed hypotheses as a skeleton for which to seek flesh; I went to report exactly what I found there. I am satisfied that there were dastardly acts during the war, and conditions inside the country, of which no tangible proofs remained at the time of my journey; but there are other accusations concerning which I am still "from Missouri." I am as fully convinced as any one that we have done a good deed in helping to overthrow the nefarious dynasty of Hohenzollernism and its conscienceless military clique; I believe the German people often acquiesced in and sometimes applauded the wrong-doings of their former rulers. But I cannot shake off the impression that the more voiceless mass of the nation were under a spell not unlike that cast by the dreadful dragons of their own old legends, and that we should to a certain extent take that fact into consideration in judging them under their new and more or less dragonless condition. I propose, therefore, that the reader free himself as much as possible from his natural repulsion toward its people before setting out on this journey through the Hungary Empire, to the end that he may gaze about him with clear, but unprejudiced, eyes. There has been too much reporting of hearsay evidence, all over the world, during the past few years, to make any other plan worth the paper.

HARRY A. FRANCK.

I
ON TO THE RHINE

For those of us not already members of the famous divisions that were amalgamated to form the Army of Occupation, it was almost as difficult to get into Germany after the armistice as before. All the A. E. F. seemed to cast longing eyes toward the Rhine—all, at least, except the veteran minority who had their fill of war and its appendages for all time to come, and the optimistic few who had serious hopes of soon looking the Statue of Liberty in the face. But it was easier to long for than to attain. In vain we flaunted our qualifications, real and self-bestowed, before those empowered to issue travel orders. In vain did we prove that the signing of the armistice had left us duties so slight that they were not even a fair return for the salary Uncle Sam paid us, to say nothing of the service we were eager to render him. G. H. Q. maintained that sphinxlike silence for which it had long been notorious. The lucky Third Army seemed to have taken on the characteristics of a haughty and exclusive club boasting an inexhaustible waiting-list.

What qualifications, after all, were those that had as their climax the mere speaking of German? Did not at least the Wisconsin half of the 33d Division boast that ability to a man? As to duties, those of fighting days were soon replaced by appallingly unbellicose tasks which carried us still farther afield into the placid wilderness of the S O S trebly distant from the scene of real activity. But a pebble dropped into the sea of army routine does not always fail to bring ripples, in time, to the shore. Suddenly one day, when the earthquaking roar of barrages and the insistent screams of air-raid *alertes* had merged with dim memories of the past, the half-forgotten request was unexpectedly answered. The flimsy French telegraph form, languidly torn open, yielded a laconic, "Report Paris prepared enter occupied territory."

The change from the placidity of Alps-girdled Grenoble to Paris, in those days "capital of the world" indeed, was abrupt. The city was seething with an international life such as even she had never before gazed upon in her history. But with the Rhine attainable at last, one was in no mood to tarry among the pampered officers dancing attendance on the Peace Conference—least of all those of us who had known Paris in the simpler, saner days of old, or in the humanizing times of war strain.

The Gare de l'Est was swirling with that incredible *tohubohu*, that headless confusion which had long reigned at all important French railway stations. Even in the sixteen months since I had first seen Paris under war conditions and taken train at Chaumont—then sternly hidden under the pseudonym of "G. H. Q."—that confusion had trebled. Stolid Britons in khaki and packs clamped their iron-shod way along the station corridors like draft-horses.

Youthful "Yanks," not so unlike the Tommies in garb as in manner, formed human whirlpools about the almost unattainable den of the American A. P. M. Through compact throngs of horizon blue squirmed insistent *poilus*, sputtering some witty *bon mot* at every lunge. Here and there circled eddies of Belgian troopers, their cap-tassels waving with the rhythm of their march. Italian soldiers, misfitted in crumpled and patched dirty-gray, struggled toward a far corner where stood two haughty *carabinieri* directly imported from their own sunny land, stubby rifles, imposing three-cornered hats, and all. At every guichet or hole in the wall waited long queues of civilians, chiefly French, with that uncomplaining patience which a lifetime, or at least a war-time, of standing in line has given a race that by temperament and individual habit should be least able to display patience. Sprightly *grisettes* tripped through every opening in the throng, dodging collisions, yet finding time to throw a coquettish smile at every grinning "Sammy," irrespective of rank. Wan, yet sarcastic, women of the working-class buffeted their multifarious bundles and progeny toward the platforms. Flush-faced dowagers, upholstered in their somber best garments, waddled hither and yon in generally vain attempts to get the scanty thirty kilos of baggage, to which military rule had reduced civilian passengers, aboard the train they hoped to take. Well-dressed matrons laboriously shoved their possessions before them on hand-trucks won after exertions that had left their hats awry and their tempers far beyond the point that speech has any meaning, some with happy, cynical faces at having advanced that far in the struggle, only to form queue again behind the always lengthy line of enforced patience which awaited the good pleasure of baggage-weighers, baggage-handlers, baggage-checkers, baggage-payment receiving-clerks. Now and then a begrimed and earth-weary female porter, under the official cap, bovinely pushed her laden truck into the waiting throngs, with that supreme indifference to the rights and comfort of others which couples so strangely with the social and individual politeness of the French. Once in a while there appeared a male porter, also in the insignia so familiar before the war, sallow and fleshless now in comparison with his female competitors, sometimes one-armed or shuffling on a half-useless leg. It would have been hard to find a place where more labor was expended for less actual accomplishment.

At the train-gate those in uniform, who had not been called upon to stand in line for hours, if not for days, to get passports, to have them stamped and visaed, to fulfil a score of formalities that must have made the life of a civilian without official backing not unlike that of a stray cur in old-time Constantinople, were again specially favored. Once on the platform—but, alas! there was no escaping the crush and goal-less helter-skelter of the half-anarchy that had befallen the railway system of France in the last supreme lunge of the war. The Nancy-Metz express—the name still seemed strange, long after the signing of the armistice—had already been taken by storm.

What shall it gain a man to have formed queue and paid his franc days before for a reserved *place* if the corridors leading to it are so packed and crammed with pillar-like *poilus*, laden with equipment enough to stock a hardware-store, with pack-and-rifle-bearing American doughboys, with the few lucky civilians who reached the gates early enough to worm their way into the interstices left, that nothing short of machine-gun or trench-mortar can clear him an entrance to it?

Wise, however, is the man who uses his head rather than his shoulders, even in so unintellectual a matter as boarding a train. About a parlor-coach, defended by gendarmes, lounged a half-dozen American officers with that casual, self-satisfied air of those who "know the ropes" and are therefore able to bide their time in peace. A constant stream of harried, disheveled, bundle-laden, would-be passengers swept down upon the parlor-car entrance, only to be politely but forcibly balked in their design by the guardsmen with an oily, "Reserved for the French Staff." Thus is disorder wont to breed intrigue. The platform clock had raised its hands to strike the hour of departure when the lieutenant who had offered to share his previous experience with me sidled cautiously up to a gendarme and breathed in his ear something that ended with "American Secret Service." The words themselves produced little more effect than there was truth in the whispered assertion. But the crisp new five-franc note deftly transferred from lieutenant to gendarme brought as quick results as could the whisper of "bakshish" in an Arab ear. We sprang lightly up the guarded steps and along a corridor as clear of humanity as No Man's Land on a sunny noonday. Give the French another year of war, with a few more millions of money-sowing Allies scattered through the length and breadth of their fair land, and the back-handed slip of a coin may become as universal an open sesame as in the most tourist-haunted corner of Naples.

Another banknote, as judiciously applied, unlocked the door of a compartment that showed quite visible evidence of having escaped the public wear and tear of war, due, no doubt, to the protection afforded it by those magic words, "French Staff." But when it had quickly filled to its quota of six, one might have gazed in vain at the half-dozen American uniforms, girdled by the exclusive "Sam Browne," for any connection with the French, staff or otherwise, than that which binds all good allies together. The train glided imperceptibly into motion, yet not without carrying to our ears the suppressed grunt of a hundred stomachs compressed by as many hard and unwieldy packs in the coach ahead, and ground away into the night amid the shouts of anger, despair, and pretended derision of the throng of would-be travelers left behind on the platform.

"Troubles over," said my companion, as we settled down to such comfort as a night in a European train compartment affords. "Of course we'll be hours late, and there will be a howling mob at every station as long as we are in

France. But once we get to Metz the trains will have plenty of room; they'll be right on time, and all this mob-fighting will be over."

"Propaganda," I mused, noting that in spite of his manner, as American as his uniform, the lieutenant spoke with a hint of Teutonic accent. We had long been warned to see propaganda by the insidious Hun in any suggestion of criticism, particularly in the unfavorable comparison of anything French with anything German. Did food cost more in Paris than on the Rhine? Propaganda! Did some one suggest that the American soldiers, their fighting task finished, felt the surge of desire to see their native shores again? Propaganda! Did a French waiter growl at the inadequacy of a 10-per-cent. tip? The *sale Boche* had surely been propaganding among the dish-handlers.

The same subsidized hand that had admitted us had locked the parlor-car again as soon as the last staff pass—issued by the Banque de France—had been collected. Though hordes might beat with enraged fists, heels, and sticks on the doors and windows, not even a corridor lounger could get aboard to disturb our possible slumbers. To the old and infirm—which in military jargon stands for all those beyond the age of thirty—even the comfortably filled compartment of a French *wagon de luxe* is not an ideal place in which to pass a long night. But as often as we awoke to uncramp our legs and cramp them again in another position, the solace in the thought of what that ride might have been, standing rigid in a car corridor, swallowing and reswallowing the heated breath of a half-dozen nationalities, jolted and compressed by sharp-cornered packs and *poilu* hardware, unable to disengage a hand long enough to raise handkerchief to nose, lulled us quickly to sleep again.

The train *was* hours late. All trains are hours late in overcrowded, overburdened France, with her long unrepaired lines of communication, her depleted railway personnel, her insufficient, war-worn rolling-stock, struggling to carry a traffic that her days of peace never attempted. It was mid-morning when we reached Nancy, though the time-table had promised—to the inexperienced few who still put faith in French *horaires*— to bring us there while it was yet night. Here the key that had protected us for more than twelve hours was found, or its counterpart produced, by the station-master. Upon our return from squandering the equivalent of a half-dollar in the station buffet for three inches of stale and gravelly war-bread smeared with something that might have been axle-grease mixed with the sweepings of a shoe-shop, and the privilege of washing it down with a black liquid that was called coffee for want of a specific name, the storm had broken. It was only by extraordinary luck, combined with strenuous physical exertion, that we manhandled our way through the horizon-blue maelstrom that had surged into every available corner, in brazen indifference to "staff" privileges, back to the places which a companion, volunteering for that service, had kept for us by dint of something little short of actual warfare.

From the moment of crossing, not long after, the frontier between that was France in 1914 and German Lorraine things seemed to take on a new freedom of movement, an orderliness that had become almost a memory. The train was still the same, yet it lost no more time. With a subtle change in faces, garb, and architecture, plainly evident, though it is hard to say exactly in what it consisted, came a smoothness that had long been divorced from travel by train. There was a calmness in the air as we pulled into Metz soon after noon which recalled pre-war stations. The platforms were ample, at least until our train began to disgorge the incredible multitude that had somehow found existing-place upon it. The station gates gave exit quickly, though every traveler was compelled to show his permission for entering the city. The aspect of the place was still German. Along the platform were ranged those awe-inspiring beings whom the uninitiated among us took to be German generals or field-officers instead of mere railway employees; wherever the eye roamed some species of *Verboten* gazed sternly upon us. But the iron hand had lost its grip. Partly for convenience sake, partly in retaliation for a closely circumscribed journey, years before, through the land of the Kaiser, I had descended from the train by a window. What horror such undisciplined barbarism would have evoked in those other years! Now the heavy faces under the pseudo-generals' caps not only gave no grimace of protest, presaging sterner measures; not even a shadow of surprise flickered across them. The grim *Verboten* signs remained placidly unmoved, like dictators shorn of power by some force too high above to make any show of feelings worth while.

The French had already come to Metz. One recognized that at once in the endless queues that formed at every window. One was doubly sure of it at sight of a temperament-harassed official in horizon blue floundering in a tempest of *paperasses*, a whirlwind of papers, ink, and unfulfilled intentions, behind the wicket, earnestly bent on quickly doing his best, yet somehow making nine motions where one would have sufficed. But most of the queues melted away more rapidly than was the Parisian custom; and as we moved nearer, to consign our baggage or to buy our tickets, we noted that the quickened progress was due to a slow but methodically moving German male, still in his field gray. He had come to the meeting-place of temperament and *Ordnung*, or system. Both have their value, but there are times and places for both.

Among the bright hopes that had gleamed before me since turning my face toward the fallen enemy was a hot bath. To attain so unwonted a luxury in France was, in the words of its inhabitants, *"toute une histoire"*—in fact, an all but endless story. In the first place, the extraordinary desire must await a

Saturday. In the second, the heater must not have fallen out of practice during its week of disuse. Thirdly, one must make sure that no other guest on the same floor had laid the same soapy plans within an hour of one's own chosen time. Fourthly, one must have put up at a hotel that boasted a bathtub, in itself no simple feat for those forced to live on their own honest earnings. Fifthly—but life is too short and paper too expensive to enumerate all the incidental details that must be brought together in harmonious concordance before one actually and physically got a real hot bath in France, after her four years and more of struggle to ward off the Hun.

But in Germany—or was it only subtle propaganda again, the persistent rumor that hot baths were of daily occurrence and within reach of the popular purse? At any rate, I took stock enough in it to let anticipation play on the treat in store, once I were settled in Germany. Then all at once my eyes were caught by two magic words above an arrow pointing down the station corridor. Incredible! Some one had had the bright idea of providing a means, right here in the station, of removing the grime of travel at once.

A clean bathroom, its "hot" water actually hot, was all ready in a twinkling— all, that is, except the soap. There was nothing in the decalogue, rumor had it, that the Germans would not violate for a bar of soap. Luckily, the hint had reached me before our commissary in Paris was out of reach. Yet, soap or no soap, the population managed to keep itself as presentable as the rank and file of civilians in the land behind us. The muscular young barber who kept shop a door or two beyond was as spick and span as any to whom I remembered intrusting my personal appearance in all France. He had, too, that indefinable something which in army slang is called "snappy," and I settled down in his chair with the genuine relaxation that comes with the ministrations of one who knows his trade. He answered readily enough a question put in French, but he answered it in German, which brought up another query, this time in his mother-tongue.

"*Nein*," he replied, "I am French through and through, 'way back for generations. My people have always been born in Lorraine, but none of us younger ones speak much French."

Yes, he had been a German soldier. He had worn the *feldgrau* more than two years, in some of the bloodiest battles on the western front, the last against Americans. It seemed uncanny to have him flourishing a razor about the throat of a man whom, a few weeks before, he had been in duty bound to slay.

"And do you think the people of Metz *really* like the change?" I asked, striving to imply by the tone that I preferred a genuine answer to a diplomatic evasion.

"*Ja, sehen Sie,*" he began, slowly, rewhetting his razor, "I am French. My family has always looked forward to the day when France should come back to us. *A-aber*"—in the slow guttural there was a hint of disillusionment—"they are a wise people, the French, but they have no *Organizationsinn*—so little idea of order, of discipline. They make so much work of simple matters. And they have such curious rules. In the house next to me lived a man whose parents were Parisians. His ancestors were all French. He speaks perfect French and very poor German. But his grandfather was born, by chance, in Germany, and they have driven him out of Lorraine, while I, who barely understand French and have always spoken German, may remain because my ancestors were born here!"

"Yet, on the whole, Metz would rather belong to France than to Germany?"

Like all perfect barber-conversationalists he spaced his words in rhythm with his work, never losing a stroke:

"We have much feeling for France. There was much flag-waving, much singing of the 'Marseillaise.' But as to what we would *rather* do—what have we to say about it, after all?

"Atrocities? Yes, I have seen some things that should not have been. It is war. There are brutes in all countries. I have at least seen a German colonel shoot one of his own men for killing a wounded French soldier on the ground."

The recent history of Metz was plainly visible in her architecture—ambitious, extravagant, often tasteless buildings shouldering aside the humble remnants of a French town of the Middle Ages. In spite of the floods of horizon blue in her streets the atmosphere of the city was still Teutonic—heavy, a trifle sour, in no way *chic*. The skaters down on a lake before the promenade not only spoke German; they had not even the Latin grace of movement. Yet there were signs to remind one that the capital of Lorraine had changed hands. It came first in petty little alterations, hastily and crudely made—a paper "Entrée" pasted over an "Eingang" cut in stone; a signboard pointing "A Trèves" above an older one reading "Nach Trier." A strip of white cloth along the front of a great brownstone building that had always been the "Kaiserliches Postamt" announced "République Française; Postes, Télégraphes, Téléphones." Street names had not been changed; they had merely been translated—"Rheinstrasse" had become also "Rue du Rhin." The French were making no secret of their conviction that Metz had returned to them for all time. They had already begun to make permanent changes. Yet many mementoes of the paternal government that had so hastily fled to the eastward were still doing duty as if nothing out of the ordinary had happened. The dark-blue post-boxes still announced themselves as "Briefkasten," and bore the fatherly reminder, "Briefmarken und Adresse nicht vergessen" ("Do not forget stamps and address"). At least the simple public could be trusted to write the letter without its attention being called to that necessity. Where crowds were wont to collect, detailed directions stared them in the face, instead of leaving them to guess and scramble, as is too often the case among our lovable but temperamental allies.

A large number of shops were "Consigné à la Troupe," which would have meant "Out of Bounds" to the British or "Off Limits" to our own soldiers. Others were merely branded "Maison Allemande," leaving Allied men in uniform permission to trade there, if they chose. It might have paid, too, for nearly all of them had voluntarily added the confession "Liquidation Totale." One such proprietor announced his "Maison Principale à Strasbourg." *He* certainly was "S. O. L."—which is armyese for something like "Sadly out of luck." In fact, the German residents were being politely but firmly crowded eastward. As their clearance sales left an empty shop a French merchant quickly moved in, and the Boche went home to set his alarm-clock. The departing Hun was forbidden to carry with him more than two thousand marks as an adult, or five hundred for each child—and *der Deutsche Gott* knows a mark is not much money nowadays!—and he was obliged to take a train leaving at 5 A.M.

On the esplanade of Metz there once stood a bronze equestrian statue of Friedrich III, gazing haughtily down upon his serfs. Now he lay broken-headed in the soil beneath, under the horse that thrust stiff legs aloft, as on a battle-field. So rude and sudden had been his downfall that he had carried with him one side of the massive stone-and-chain balustrade that had long protected his pedestal from plebeian contact. Farther on there was a still more impressive sign of the times. On the brow of a knoll above the lake an immense bronze of the late Kaiser—as he fain would have looked—had been replaced by the statue of a *poilu*, hastily daubed, yet artistic for all that, with the careless yet sure lines of a Rodin. The Kaiser's gaze—strangely enough—had been turned toward Germany, and the bombastic phrase of dedication had, with French sense of the fitness of things, been left untouched—"*Errichtet von seinem dankbaren Volke.*" Even "his grateful people," strolling past now and then in pairs or groups, could not suppress the suggestion of a smile at the respective positions of dedication and *poilu*. For the latter gazed toward his beloved France, with those far-seeing eyes of all his tribe, and beneath him was his war slogan, purged at last of the final three letters he had bled so freely to efface—"On les A."

A German ex-soldier, under the command of an American private, rechecked my trunk in less than a minute. The train was full, but it was not overcrowded. Travelers boarded it in an orderly manner; there was no erratic scrambling, no impassable corridor. We left on time and maintained that advantage to the end of the journey. It seemed an anachronism to behold a train-load of American soldiers racing on and on into Germany, perfectly at ease behind a German crew that did its best to make the trip as comfortable and swift as possible—and succeeded far beyond the expectations of the triumphant invaders. In the first-class coach, "Réservé pour Militaires," which had been turned over to us under the terms of the armistice, all was in perfect working order. Half voiceless with a cold caught on the unheated French trains on which I had shivered my way northward from Grenoble, I found this one too hot. The opening of a window called attention to the fact that Germany had been obliged to husband her every scrap of leather; the window-tackle was now of woven hemp. One detail suggested bad faith in fulfilling the armistice terms—the heavy red-velvet stuff covering the seats had been hastily slashed off, leaving us to sit on the burlap undercoverings. Probably some undisciplined railway employee had decided to levy on the enemy while there was yet time for the material of a gown for his daughter or his *Mädchen*. Later journeys showed many a seat similarly plundered.

A heavy, wet snow was falling when we reached Trèves—or Trier, as you choose. It was late, and I planned to dodge into the nearest hotel. I had all but forgotten that I was no longer among allies, but in the land of the enemy. The American M. P. who demanded my papers at the station gate, as his fellows did, even less courteously, of all civilians, ignored the word "hotel" and directed me to the billeting-office. Salutes were snapped at me wherever the street-lamps made my right to them visible. The town was brown with American khaki, as well as white with the sodden snow. At the baize-covered desk of what had evidently once been a German court-room a commissioned Yank glanced at my orders, ran his finger down a long ledger page, scrawled a line on a billeting form, and tossed it toward me.

Beyond the Porta Nigra, the ancient Roman gate that the would-be Romans of to-day—or yesterday—have so carefully preserved, I lost my way in the blinding whiteness. A German civilian was approaching. I caught myself wondering if he would refuse to answer, and whether I should stand on my dignity as one of his conquerors if he did. He seemed flattered that he should have been appealed to for information. He waded some distance out of his way to leave me at the door I sought, and on the way he bubbled over with the excellence of the American soldier, with now and then a hint at the good fortune of Trier in not being occupied by the French or British. When he had left me I rang the door-bell several times without result. I decided to adopt a sterner attitude, and pounded lustily on the massive outer door. At length a window above opened and a querulous female voice demanded, "*Wer ist da?*" To be sure, it was near midnight; but was I not for once demanding, rather than requesting, admittance? I strove to give my voice the peremptoriness with which a German officer would have answered, "American lieutenant, billeted here."

"*Ich komm' gleich hinunter,*" came the quick reply, in almost honeyed tones.

The household had not yet gone to bed. It consisted of three women, of as many generations, the youngest of whom had come down to let me in. Before we reached the top of the stairs she began to show solicitude for my comfort. The mother hastened to arrange the easiest chair for me before the fire; the grandmother doddered toothlessly at me from her corner behind the stove; the family cat was already caressing my boot-tops.

"You must have something to eat!" cried the mother.

"Don't trouble," I protested. "I had dinner at Metz."

"Yes, but that was four hours ago. Some milk and eggs, at least?"

"Eggs," I queried, "and milk? I thought there were none in Germany."

"*Doch,*" she replied, with a sage glance, "if you know where to look for them, and can get there. I have just been out in the country. I came on the same train you did. But it is hard to get much. Every one goes out scouring the country now. And one must have money. An egg, one mark! Before the war they were never so much a dozen."

The eggs were fresh enough, but the milk was decidedly watery, and in place of potatoes there was some sort of jellied turnip, wholly tasteless. While I ate, the daughter talked incessantly, the mother now and then adding a word, the grandmother nodding approval at intervals, with a wrinkled smile. All male members of the family had been lost in the war, unless one counts the second fiancée of the daughter, now an officer "over in Germany," as she put it. When I started at the expression she smiled:

"Yes, here we are in America, you see. Lucky for us, too. There will never be any robbery and anarchy here, and over there it will get worse. Anyhow, we don't feel that the Americans are real enemies."

"No?" I broke in. "Why not?"

"*Ach!*" she said, evasively, throwing her head on one side, "they ... they.... Now if it had been the French, or the British, who had occupied Trier.... At first the Americans were very easy on us—*too* easy" (one felt the German religion of discipline in the phrase). "They arrived on December first, at noon, and by evening every soldier had a sweetheart. The newspapers raged. It was shameful for a girl to give herself for a box of biscuits, or a cake of chocolate, or even a bar of soap! But they had been hungry for years, and not even decency, to say nothing of patriotism, can stand out against continual hunger. Besides, the war—*ach!* I don't know what has come over the German woman since the war!

"But the Americans are stricter now," she continued, "and there are new laws that forbid us to talk to the soldiers—on the street...."

"German laws?" I interrupted, thoughtlessly, for, to tell the truth, my mind was wandering a bit, thanks either to the heat of the porcelain stove or to her garrulousness, equal to that of any *méridionale* from southern France.

"*Nein*, it was ordered by General Pershing." (She pronounced it "Pear Shang.")

Stupid of me, but my change from the land of an ally to that of an enemy had been so abrupt, and the evidence of enmity so slight, that I had scarcely realized it was our own commander-in-chief who was now reigning in Trier. I covered my retreat by abruptly putting a question about the Kaiser. Demigod that I had always found him in the popular mind in Germany, I felt sure that here, at least, I should strike a vibrant chord. To my surprise, she screwed up her face into an expression of disgust and drew a finger across her throat.

"*That* for the Kaiser!" she snapped. "Of course, he wasn't entirely to blame; and he wanted to quit in nineteen-sixteen. But the rich people, the Krupps and the like, hadn't made enough yet. He didn't, at least, need to run away. If he had stayed in Germany, as he should have, no one would have hurt him; no living man would have touched a hair of his head. Our Crown Prince? *Ach!* The Crown Prince is *leichtsinnig* (light-minded)."

"Of course, it is natural that the British and French should treat us worse than the Americans," she went on, unexpectedly harking back to an earlier theme. "They used to bomb us here in Trier, the last months. I have often had to help *Grossmutter* down into the cellar"—*Grossmutter* smirked confirmation—"but that was nothing compared to what our brave airmen did to London and Paris. Why, in Paris they killed hundreds night after night, and the people were so wild with fright they trampled one another to death in trying to find refuge...."

"I was in Paris myself during all the big raids, as well as the shelling by 'Grosse Bertha,'" I protested, "and I assure you it was hardly as bad as that."

"Ah, but they cover up those things so cleverly," she replied, quickly, not in the slightest put out by the contradiction.

"There is one thing the Americans do not do well," she rattled on. "They do not make the rich and the influential contribute their fair share. They make all the people (*das Volk*) billet as many as their houses will hold, but the rich and the officials arrange to take in very few, in their big houses. And it is the same as before the war ended, with the food. The wealthy still have plenty of food that they get through *Schleichhandel*, tricky methods, and the Americans do not search them. Children and the sick are supposed to get milk, and a bit of good bread, or zwiebach. Yet *Grossmutter* here is so ill she cannot digest the war-bread, and still she must eat it, for the rich grab all the better bread, and, as we have no influence, we cannot get her what the rules allow."

I did not then know enough of the American administration of occupied territory to remind her that food-rationing was still entirely in the hands of the native officials. I did know, however, how prone conquering armies are to keep up the old inequalities; how apt the conqueror is to call upon the "influential citizens" to take high places in the local administration; and that "influential citizens" are not infrequently so because they have been the most grasping, the most selfish, even if not actually dishonest.

Midnight had long since struck when I was shown into the guest-room, with a triple "*Gute Nacht. Schlafen Sie wohl.*" The deep wooden bedstead was, of course, a bit too short, and the triangular bolster and two large pillows, taking the place of the French round *traversin*, had to be reduced to American tastes. But the room was speckless; several minor details of comfort had been arranged with motherly care, and as I slid down under the feather tick that does duty as quilt throughout Germany my feet encountered—a hot flat-iron. I had not felt so old since the day I first put on long trousers!

My last conscious reflection was a wonder whether the good citizens of Trier were not, perhaps, "stringing" us a bit with their aggressive show of friendliness, of contentment at our presence. Some of it had been a bit *too* thick. Yet, as I thought back over the evening, I could not recall a word, a tone, a look, that gave the slightest basis to suppose that my three hostesses were not the simple, frank, docile *Volk* they gave every outward evidence of being.

The breakfast next morning consisted of coffee and bread, with more of the tasteless turnip jelly. All three of the articles, however, were only in the name what they purported to be, each being *Ersatz*, or substitute, for the real thing. The coffee was really roasted corn, and gave full proof of that fact by its insipidity. But Frau Franck served me real sugar with it. The bread—what shall one say of German war-bread that will make the picture dark and heavy and indigestible enough? It was cut from just such a loaf as I had seen gaunt soldiers of the Kaiser hugging under one arm as they came blinking up out of their dugouts at the point of a doughboy bayonet, and to say that such a loaf seemed to be half sawdust and half mud, that it was heavier and blacker than any adobe brick, and that its musty scent was all but overpowering, would be far too mild a statement and the comparison an insult to the mud brick. The mother claimed it was made of potatoes and bad meal. I am sure she was over-charitable. Yet on this atrocious substance, which I, by no means unaccustomed to strange food, tasted once with a shudder of disgust, the German masses had been chiefly subsisting since 1915. No wonder they quit! The night before the bread had been tolerable, having been brought from the country; but the three women had stayed up munching that until the last morsel had disappeared.

The snow had left the trees of Trier beautiful in their winding-sheets, but the streets had already been swept. It seemed queer, yet, after sixteen months of similar experience in France, a matter of course to be able to ask one's way of an American policeman on every corner of this ancient German town. In the past eight years I had been less than two in my native land, yet I had a feeling of knowing the American better than ever before; for to take him out of his environment is to see him in close-up perspective, as it were. Even here he seemed to feel perfectly at home. Now and then a group of school-girls playfully bombarded an M. P. with snowballs, and if he could not shout back some jest in genuine German, he at least said something that "got across." The populace gave us our fair half of the sidewalk, some making a little involuntary motion as if expecting an officer to shove them off it entirely, in the orthodox Prussian manner. Street-cars were free to wearers of the "Sam Browne"; enlisted men paid the infinitesimal fare amid much good-natured "joshing" of the solemn conductor, with his colonel's uniform and his sackful of pewter coins.

On railway trains tickets were a thing of the past to wearers of khaki. To the border of Lorraine we paid the French military fare; once in Germany proper, one had only to satisfy the M. P. at the gate to journey anywhere within the occupied area. At the imposing building out of which the Germans had been chased to give place to our "Advanced G. H. Q.," I found orders to proceed at once to Coblenz, but there was time to transgress military rules to the extent of bringing *Grossmutter* a loaf of white bread and a can of condensed milk from our commissary, to repair my damage to the family larder, before hurrying to the station. Yank guardsmen now sustained the contentions of the *Verboten* signs, instead of letting them waste away in impotence, as at Metz. A boy marched up and down the platform, pushing a convenient little news-stand on wheels, and offering for sale all the important Paris papers, as well as German ones. The car I entered was reserved for Allied officers, yet several Boche civilians rode in it unmolested. I could not but wonder what would have happened had conditions been reversed. They were cheerful enough in spite of what ought to have been a humiliating state of affairs, possibly because of an impression I heard one hoarsely whisper to another, "Oh, they'll go home in another six months; an American officer told me so." Evidently some one had been "fraternizing," as well as receiving information which the heads of the Peace Conference had not yet gained.

The *Schnellzug* was a real express; the ride like that from Albany to New York. Now and then we crossed the winding Moselle, the steep, plump hills of which were planted to their precipitous crests with orderly vineyards, each vine carefully tied to its stalk. For mile after mile the hills were terraced, eight-foot walls of cut stone holding up four-foot patches of earth, paths for the workers snaking upward between them. The system was almost exactly that of the Peruvians under the Incas, far apart as they were, in time and place, from the German peasant. The two civilizations could scarcely have compared notes, yet this was not the only similarity between them. But then, hunger and over-population breed stern necessity the world over, and with like necessity as with similar experience, it is no plagiarism to have worked out the problem in the same way. Between the vineyards, in stony clefts in the hills useless for cultivation, orderly towns were tucked away, clean little towns, still flecked with the snow of the night before. Even the French officers beside us marveled at the cleanliness of the towns *en Bochie*, and at the extraordinary physical comforts of Mainz—I mean Mayence—the headquarters of their area of occupation.

Heavy American motor-trucks pounded by along the already dusty road beside us, alternating now and then with a captured German one, the Kaiser's eagles still on its flanks, but driven by a nonchalant American doughboy, its steel tires making an uproar that could be plainly heard aboard the racing express. Long freight-trains rattled past in the opposite direction. With open-work wheels, stubby little cars stenciled "Posen," "Essen," "Breslau," "Brüssel," and the like, a half-dozen employees perched in the cubbyholes on the car ends at regular intervals, they were German from engine to lack of caboose—except that here and there a huge box-car lettered "U. S. A." towered above its puny Boche fellows like a mounted guard beside a string of prisoners. There will still be a market for officers' uniforms in Germany, though their military urge be completely emasculated. Even the brakemen of these freight-trains looked like lieutenants or captains; a major in appearance proved to be a station guard, a colonel sold tickets, and the station-master might easily have been mistaken for a *Feldmarschall*. Some were, in fact. For when the Yanks first occupied the region many of their commanders complained that German officers were not saluting them, as required by orders of the Army of Occupation. Investigation disclosed the harmless identity of the imposing "officers" in question. But the rule was amended to include any one in uniform; we could not be wasting our time to find out whether the wearer of a general's shoulder-straps was the recent commander of the 4th Army Corps or the town-crier. So that now Allied officers were saluted by the police, the firemen, the mailmen—including the half-grown ones who carry special-delivery letters—and even by the "white wings."

Those haughty *Eisenbahnbeamten* took their orders now from plain American "bucks," took them unquestioningly, with signs of friendliness, with a docile, uncomplaining—shall I say fatalism? The far-famed German discipline had not broken down even under occupation; it carried on as persistently, as doggedly as ever. A conductor passing through our car recalled a "hobo" experience out in our West back in the early days of the century. Armed trainmen had driven the summer-time harvest of free riders off their trains for more than a week, until so great a multitude of "boes" had collected in a water-tank town of Dakota that we took a freight one day completely by storm, from cow-catcher to caboose. And the bloodthirsty, fire-eating brakeman who picked his way along that train, gently requesting the uninvited railroad guests to "Give us a place for a foot there, pal, won't you, please?" had the selfsame expression on his face as did this apologetic, smirking, square-headed Boche who sidled so gently past us. My fellow-officers found them cringing, detestably servile. "Put a gun in their hands," said one, "and you'd see how quick their character would change. It's a whole damned nation crying '*Kamerad!*'—playing 'possum until the danger is over."

Probably it was. But there were times when one could not help wondering if, after all, there was not sincerity in the assertion of my guide of the night before:

"We are done; we have had enough at last."

II
GERMANY UNDER THE AMERICAN HEEL

The "Residence City" of Coblenz, headquarters of the American Army of Occupation, is one of the finest on the Rhine. Wealth has long gravitated toward the triangle of land at its junction with the Moselle. The owners—or recent owners—of mines in Lorraine make their homes there. The mother of the late unlamented Kaiser was fond of the place and saw to it that no factory chimneys came to sully its skies with their smoke, or its streets and her tender heart-strings with the wan and sooty serfs of industrial progress. The British at Cologne had more imposing quarters; the French at Mayence, and particularly at Wiesbaden, enjoyed more artistic advantages. A few of our virile warriors, still too young to distinguish real enjoyment from the flesh-pots incident to metropolitan bustle, were sometimes heard to grumble, "Huh! they gave *us* third choice, all right!" But the consensus of opinion among the Americans was contentment. The sudden change from the mud burrows of the Argonne, or from the war-worn villages of the Vosges, made it natural that some should draw invidious comparisons between our long-suffering ally and the apparently unscathed enemy. Those who saw the bogy of "propaganda" in every corner accused the Germans of preferring that the occupied territory be the Rhineland, rather than the interior of Germany, "because this garden spot would make a better impression on their enemies, particularly the Americans, so susceptible to creature comforts." By inference the Boche might have offered us East Prussia or Schleswig instead! It was hard to believe, however, that those splendid, if sometimes top-heavy, residences stretching for miles along the Rhine were built, twenty to thirty years ago in many cases, with any conscious purpose of impressing the prospective enemies of the Fatherland.

It was these creature comforts of his new billeting area that made the American soldier feel so strangely at home on the Rhine. Here his office, in contrast to the rude stone casernes with their tiny tin stoves that gave off smoke rather than heat, was cozy, warm, often well carpeted. His billets scarcely resembled the frigid, medieval ones of France. Now that no colonel can rank me out of it, I am free to admit that in all my travels I have never been better housed and servanted than in Coblenz, nor had a more solicitous host than the staid old judge who was forced to take me in for a mere pittance—paid in the end by his own people. The *Regierungsgebäude*—it means nothing more terrifying than "government building"—which the rulers of the province yielded with outward good grace to our army staff, need not have blushed to find itself in Washington society. To be sure, we were able to dispossess the Germans of their best, whereas the French could only allot us what their own requirements left; yet there is still a margin in favor of the Rhineland for material comfort.

I wonder if the American at home understands just what military occupation means. Some of our Southerners of the older generation may, but I doubt whether the average man can visualize it. Occupation means a horde of armed strangers permeating to every nook and corner of your town, of your house, of your private life. It means seeing what you have hidden in that closet behind the chimney; it means yielding your spare bed, even if not doubling up with some other member of the family in order to make another bed available. It means having your daughters come into constant close contact with self-assertive young men, often handsome and fascinating; it means subjecting yourself, or at least your plans, to the rules, sometimes even to the whims, of the occupiers.

The Americans came to Coblenz without any of those bombastic formalities with which the imagination imbues an occupation. One day the streets were full of soldiers, a bit slow in their movements and thinking processes, dressed in bedraggled dull gray, and the next with more soldiers, of quick perception and buoyant step, dressed in khaki. The new-comers were just plain fighters, still dressed in what the shambles of the Argonne had left them of clothing. They settled down to a shave and a bath and such comforts as were to be had, with the unassuming adaptability that marks the American. The Germans, seeing no signs of those unpleasant things which had always attended *their* occupation of a conquered land, probably smiled to themselves and whispered that these *Amerikaner* were strangely ignorant of military privileges. They did not realize that their own conception of a triumphant army, the rough treatment, the tear-it-apart-and-take-what-you-want-for-yourself style of von Kluck's pets, was not the American manner. The doughboy might hate a German man behind a machine-gun as effectively as any one, but his hatred did not extend to the man's women and children. With the latter particularly he quickly showed that *camaraderie* for which the French had found him remarkable, and the plump little square-headed boys and the over-blond little girls flocked about him so densely that an order had to be issued requiring parents to keep their children away from American barracks.

But the Germans soon learned that the occupiers knew what they were about, or at least learned with vertiginous rapidity. A burgomaster who admitted that he might be able to accommodate four hundred men in his town, if given time, was informed that there would be six thousand troops there in an hour, and that they must be lodged before nightfall. Every factory, every industry of a size worth considering, that produced anything of use to the Army of Occupation, was taken over. We paid well for everything of the sort—or rather, the Germans did in the end, under the ninth article of the armistice—but we took it. Scarcely a family escaped the piercing eye of the billeting officer; clubs, hotels, recreation-halls, the very schools and churches, were wholly or in part filled with the boyish conquerors from overseas. We commandeered the poor man's drinking-places and transferred them into enlisted men's barracks. We shooed the rich man out of his sumptuous club and turned it over to our officers. We allotted the pompous *Festhalle* and many other important buildings to the Y. M. C. A., and "jazz" and ragtime and burnt-cork jokes took the place of *Lieder* and *Männerchor*. While we occupied their best buildings, the German staff which necessity had left in Coblenz huddled into an insignificant little house on a side-street. Promenading citizens encountered pairs of Yanks patrolling with fixed bayonets their favorite *Spaziergänge*. Day after day throngs of Boches lined up before the back door to our headquarters, waiting hours to explain to American lieutenants why they wished to travel outside our area. Though the lieutenants did not breakfast until eight, that line formed long before daylight, and those who did not get in before noon stood on, outwardly uncomplaining, sometimes munching a war-bread sandwich, until the office opened again at two, taking their orders from a buck private, probably from Milwaukee, with a red band on his arm. A flicker of the M. P.'s eyelid, a flip of his hand, was usually the only command needed; so ready has his lifetime of discipline made the average German to obey any one who has an authoritative manner. Every railway-station gate, even the crude little ferries across the Rhine and the Moselle, were subject to the orders of pass-gathering American soldiers.

The Germans could not travel, write letters, telephone, telegraph, publish newspapers, without American permission or acquiescence. Meetings were no longer family affairs; a German-speaking American sergeant in plain clothes sat in on all of them. We marched whole societies off to jail because they were so careless as to gather about café tables without the written permission required for such activities. When they were arrested for violations of these and sundry other orders their fate was settled, not after long meditation by sage old gentlemen, but in the twinkling of an eye by a cocksure lieutenant who had reached the maturity of twenty-one or two, and who, after the custom of the A. E. F., "made it snappy," got it over with at once, and lost no sleep in wondering if his judgment had been wrong. In the matter of cafés, we touched the German in his tenderest spot by forbidding the sale or consumption of all joy-producing beverages except beer and light wines—and the American conception of what constitutes a strong drink does not jibe with the German's—and permitted even those to be served only from eleven to two and from five to seven—though later we took pity on the poor Boche and extended the latter period three hours deeper into the evening.

Occasional incidents transcended a bit the spirit of our really lenient occupation. We ordered the Stars and Stripes to be flown from every building we occupied; and there were colonels who made special trips to Paris to get a flag that could be seen—could not help being seen, in fact—for fifty kilometers round about. The Germans trembled with fear to see one of their most cherished bad customs go by the board when a divisional order commanded them to leave their windows open at night, which these strange new-comers considered a means of avoiding, rather than abetting, the "flu" and kindred ailments. Over in Mayen a band of citizens, in some wild lark or a surge of "democracy," dragged a stone statue of the Kaiser from its pedestal and rolled it out to the edge of town. There an American sergeant in charge of a stone-quarry ordered it broken up for road material. The Germans put in a claim of several thousand marks to replace this "work of art." The American officer who "surveyed" the case genially awarded them three mk. fifty—the value of the stone at current prices. In another village the town-crier summoned forth every inhabitant over the age of ten, from the burgomaster down, at nine each morning, to sweep the streets, and M. P.'s saw to it that no one returned indoors until the American C. O. had inspected the work and pronounced it satisfactory. But that particular officer cannot necessarily be credited with originality for the idea; he had been a prisoner in Germany. We even took liberties with the German's time. On March 12th all clocks of official standing were moved ahead to correspond to the "summer hour" of France and the A. E. F., and that automatically forced private timepieces to be advanced also. My host declined for a day or two to conform, but he had only to miss one train to be cured of his obstinacy. Coblenz was awakened by the insistent notes of the American reveille; it was reminded of bedtime by that most impressive of cradle-songs, the American taps, the solemn, reposeful notes of which floated out across the Rhine like an invitation to wilful humanity to lay away its disputes as it had its labors of the day.

In the main, for all the occupation, civilian life proceeded normally. Trains ran on time; cinemas and music-halls perpetrated their customary piffle on crowded and uproarious houses; bare-kneed football games occupied the leisure hours of German youths; newspapers appeared as usual, subject only to the warning to steer clear of a few specified subjects; cafés were filled at the popular hours in spite of the restrictions on consumption and the tendency of their orchestras to degenerate into ragtime. Would military occupation be anything like this in, say, Delaware? We often caught ourselves asking the question, and striving to visualize our own land under a reversal of conditions. But the imagination never carried us very far in that direction; at least those of us who had left it in the early days of the war were unable to picture our native heath under any such régime.

Though we appropriated their best to our own purposes, the Germans will find it hard to allege any such wanton treatment of their property, their homes, their castles, and their government buildings, as their own hordes so often committed in France and Belgium. Our officers and men, with rare exceptions, gave the habitations that had temporarily become theirs by right of conquest a care which they would scarcely have bestowed upon their own. The ballroom floor of Coblenz's most princely club was solicitously covered with canvas to protect it from officers' hob-nails. Castle Stolzenfels, a favorite place of doughboy pilgrimage a bit farther up the Rhine, was supplied with felt slippers for heavily shod visitors. The Baedekers of the future will no doubt call the tourist's attention to the fact that such a *Schloss*, that this governor's palace and that colonel's residence, were once occupied by American soldiers, but there will be small chance to insinuate, as they have against the French of 1689 into the description of half the monuments on the Rhine, the charge "destroyed by the Americans in 1919."

How quickly war shakes down! Until we grew so accustomed to it that the impression faded away, it was a constant surprise to note how all the business of life went on unconcerned under the occupation. *Ordnung* still reigned. The postman still delivered his letters punctually and placidly. Transportation of all kinds retained almost its peace-time efficiency. Paper ends and cigarette butts might litter a corner here and there, but that was merely evidence that some careless American soldier was not carrying them to a municipal waste-basket in the disciplined German fashion. For if the Boches themselves had thrown off restraint "over in Germany"—a thing hard to believe and still harder to visualize—there was little evidence of a similar tendency along the Rhine.

Dovetailed, as it were, into the life of our late adversaries on the field of battle, there was a wide difference of opinion in the A. E. F. as to the German character. The French had no such doubts. They admitted no argument as to the criminality of the Boche; yet they confessed themselves unable to understand his psychology. "*Ils sont sincèrement faux*" is perhaps the most succinct summing up of the French verdict. "It took the world a long time to realize that the German had a national point of view, a way of thinking quite at variance with the rest of the world"—our known western world, at least; I fancy we should find the Japanese not dissimilar if we could read deep down into his heart. But the puzzling thing about the German's "mentality" is that up to a certain point he is quite like the rest of us. As the alienist's patient seems perfectly normal until one chances upon his weak spot, so the German looks and acts for the most part like any normal human being. It is only when one stumbles upon the subject of national ethics that he is found widely separated from the bulk of mankind. Once one discovers this sharp corner in his thinking, and is able to turn it with him, it is comparatively easy to comprehend the German's peculiar notions of recent events.

"The Hun," asserted a European editorial-writer, "feels that his army has not been beaten; that, on the contrary, he had all the military prestige of the war. Then he knew that there was increasing scarcity of food at home and, feeling that the Allies were in mortal dread of new drives by the German army and would be only too glad to compromise, he proposed an armistice. Germany expected the world to supply her gladly with all her needs, as a mark of good faith, and to encourage the timorous Allies she offered to let them advance to the Rhine. Now the Germans affect to wonder why Germany is not completely supplied by the perfidious Allies, and why the garrisons, having been allowed to see the beautiful Rhine scenery, do not withdraw. Not only the ignorant classes, but those supposedly educated, take that attitude. They consider, apparently, that the armistice was an agreement for mutual benefit, and the idea that the war was anything but a draw, with the prestige all on the German side, has not yet penetrated to the German mind."

With the above—it was written in January—and the outward show of friendliness for the American Army of Occupation as a text, I examined scores of Germans of all classes, whom our sergeants picked out of the throngs that passed through our hands and pushed one by one into my little office overlooking the Rhine. Their attitude, their answers were always the same, parrot-like in their sameness. Before a week had passed I could have set down the replies, almost in their exact words, the instant the man to be interviewed appeared in the doorway, to click his heels resoundingly while holding his arms stiffly at his sides. As becomes a long-disciplined people, the German is certainly no individualist. Once one has a key to it, one can be just as sure what he is going to do, and how he is going to do it, as one can that duplicates of the shoes one has always worn are going to fit. Yet what did they really think, away down under their generations of discipline? This procession of men with their close-cropped heads and their china-blue eyes that looked at me as innocently as a Nürnberg doll, who talked so glibly with apparent friendliness and perfect frankness, surely has *some* thoughts hidden away in the depths of their souls. Yet one seldom, if ever, caught a glimpse of them. Possibly there were none there; the iron discipline of a half-century may have killed the hidden roots as well as destroyed the plant itself. In contrast with the sturdily independent American, sharply individualistic still in spite of his year or two of army training, these heel-clicking automatons were exasperating in their garrulous taciturnity.

"What most characterizes the German," said Mosers, more than a century ago, "is obedience, respect for force." What probably struck the plain American doughboy even more than mere obedience was their passive docility, their immediate compliance with all our requirements. They could have been so mean, so disobedient in petty little ways without openly disobeying. Instead, they seemed to go out of their road to make our task of occupation easy. Their racial discipline not merely did not break down; it permeated every nook and corner. The very children never gave a gesture, a whisper of wilfulness; the family warning found them as docile as a lifetime of training had left the adults. It was easy to imagine French or American boys under the same conditions—all the bright little Hallowe'en tricks they would have concocted to make unpleasant the life of the abhorred enemy rulers. Was it not perhaps this, from the German point of view, criminally undisciplined character of other races, as much as their own native brutality, that caused the armies of the Kaiser to inflict so many unfair punishments? Any traveler who has noted the abhorrence with which the German looks upon the simplest infraction of the most insignificant order—the mere entering by a "Verbotener Eingang"—that the American would disobey and pay his fine and go his way with a smile of amusement on his face, will not find it difficult to visualize the red rage with which the German soldier beheld any lack of seriousness toward the stern and sacred commands of their armies of occupation.

None of us guessed aright as to Germany's action in case of defeat. Talk of starvation though we will, she did not fight to a standstill, as our South did, for example. She gave proof of a strong faith in the old adage beginning "He who fights and runs away...." She quit when the tide turned, not at the last crag of refuge, and one could not but feel less respect for her people accordingly. But whatever remnant of estimation may have been left after their sudden abandonment of the field might have been enhanced by an occasional lapse from their docility, by a proof now and then that they were human, after all. Instead, we got something that verged very closely upon cringing, as a personal enemy one had just trounced might bow his thanks and offer to light his victor's cigar. It is impossible to believe that any one could be rendered so docile by mere orders from above. It is impossible to believe they had no hatred in their hearts for the nation that finally turned the balance of war against them. It must be habit, habit formed by those with superimposed rulers, as contrasted with those who have their word, or at least fancy they have, in their own government.

That they should take the fortunes of war philosophically was comprehensible. The most chauvinistic of them must now and then have had an inkling that those who live by the sword might some day catch the flash of it over their own heads. Or it may be that they had grown so used to military rule that ours did not bother them. Except to their politicians, their ex-officers, and the like, who must have realized most keenly that some one else was "holding the bag," what real difference is there between being ruled by a just and not ungentle enemy from across the sea and by an iron-stern hierarchy in distant Berlin? Besides, has not Germany long contended that the stronger peoples have absolute rights over the weaker? Why, then, should they contest their own argument when they suddenly discovered, to their astonishment, that their claims to the position of superman were poorly based? The weak have no rights—it is the German himself who has said so. Was it this belief that gave their attitude toward us, outwardly at least, a suggestion of almost Arabic fatalism? It is no such anomaly as it may seem that the German and the Turk should have joined forces; they have considerable in common—"Allah, Il Allah, Thy will be done"!

The last thing the Germans showed toward our Army of Occupation was enmity. Nothing pointed to a smoldering resentment behind their masks, as, for example, with the Mexicans. There was slight difference between an errand of liaison to a bureau of the German staff-officers left in Coblenz and similar commissions to the French or the Italians before the armistice—an atmosphere only a trifle more strained, which was natural in view of the fact that I came to order rather than to cajole. The observation balloon that rode the sky above our area, its immense Stars and Stripes visible even in unoccupied territory, was frequently pointed out with interest, never with any evidence of animosity. There was a constant stream of people, principally young men, through our offices, inquiring how they could most easily emigrate to America. Incidentally we were besieged by scores of "Americans" who spoke not a word of English, who had been "caught here by the war" and had in many cases killed time by serving in the German army, but who now demanded all the privileges which their "citizenship" was supposed to confer upon them. A German major wrote a long letter of application for admission into the American army, with the bland complacency with which a pedagogue whose school had been abolished might apply for a position in another. There was not a sign of resentment even against "German-Americans"—as the Boche was accustomed to call them until he discovered the virtual non-existence of any such anomaly—for having entered the war against the old Fatherland. The government of their adopted country had ordered them to do so, and no one understands better than the German that government orders are issued to be obeyed.

Some contended that the women in particular had a deep resentment against the American soldiers, that they were still loyal to the Kaiser and to the old order of things, that they saw in us the murderers of their sons and husbands, the jailers of their prisoners. On a few rare occasions I felt a breath of frigidity in the attitude of some *grande dame* of the haughtier class. But whether it was a definite policy of conciliation to win the friendship of America, in the hope that it would soften the blow of the Treaty of Peace, as a naughty boy strives to make up for his naughtiness at sight of the whip being taken down from its hook, or a mere "mothering instinct," the vast majority of our hostesses, even though war widows, went out of their way to make our stay with them pleasant. Clothes were mended, buttons sewed on unasked. Maids and housewives alike gave our quarters constant attention. The mass of Americans on the Rhine came with the impression that they would be forced to go heavily armed day and night. Except for the established patrols and sentries, the man or officer who "toted" a weapon anywhere in the occupied area could scarcely have aroused the ridicule of his comrades more had he appeared in sword and armor. There was, to be sure, a rare case of an American soldier being done to death by hoodlums in some drunken brawl, but, for the matter of that, so there was in France.

Now and then one stumbled upon the sophistry that seems so established a trait in the German character. No corporation lawyer could have been more clever in finding loopholes in the proclamations issued by the Army of Occupation than those adherents of the "scrap of paper" fallacy who set out to do so. My host sent up word from time to time for permission to spend an evening with me over a bottle of well-aged Rhine wine with which his cellar seemed still to be liberally stocked. On one occasion the conversation turned to several holes in the ceiling of my sumptuous parlor. They were the result, the pompous old judge explained, of an air raid during the last August of the war. A bomb had carried away the window-shutters, portions of the granite steps beneath, and had liberally pockmarked the stone façade of the house.

"It was horrible," he growled. "We all had to go down into the cellar, and my poor little grandson cried from fright. *That* is no way to make war, against the innocent non-combatants, and women and children."

I did not trouble to ask him if he had expressed the same sentiments among his fellow club-members in, say, May, 1915, for his sophistry was too well trained to be caught in so simple a trap.

Whatever the docility, the conciliatory attitude of our forced hosts, however, I have yet to hear that one of them ever expressed repentance for the horrors their nation loosed upon the world. The war they seemed to take as the natural, the unavoidable thing, just a part of life, as the gambler takes gambling, with no other regret than that it was their bad luck to lose. Like the gambler, they may have been sorry they made certain moves in the game; they may have regretted entering the game at all, as the gambler would who knew in the end that his adversary had more money on his hip than he had given him credit for in the beginning. But it was never a regret for being a gambler. Did not Nietzsche say that to regret, to repent, is a sign of weakness? Unless there was something under his mask that never showed a hint of its existence on the surface, the German is still a firm disciple of Nietzschean philosophy.

There was much debate among American officers as to just what surge of feeling passed through the veins of a German of high rank forced to salute his conquerors. With rare exceptions, every Boche in uniform rendered the required homage with meticulous care. Now and then one carefully averted his eyes or turned to gaze into a shop-window in time to avoid the humiliation. But for the most part they seemed almost to go out of their way to salute, some almost brazenly, others with a half-friendly little bow. I shall long remember the invariable click of heels and the smart hand-to-cap of the resplendent old general with a white beard who passed me each morning on the route to our respective offices.

That there was feeling under these brazen exteriors, however, was proved by the fact that most of the officers in the occupied area slipped quietly into civilian clothes, for no other apparent reason than to escape the unwelcome order. From the day of our entrance no German in uniform was permitted in our territory unless on official business, sanctioned by our authorities. But the term "uniform" was liberally interpreted. A discharged soldier, unable to invest in a new wardrobe, attained civilian status by exchanging his ugly, round, red-banded fatigue-bonnet for a hat or cap; small boys were not rated soldiers simply because they wore cut-down uniforms. Then on March 1st came a new order from our headquarters commanding all members of the German army in occupied territory never to appear in public out of uniform, always to carry papers showing their presence in our area to be officially authorized, and to report to an American official every Monday morning. The streets of Coblenz blossomed out that day with more varieties of German uniforms than most members of the A. E. P. had ever seen outside a prisoner-of-war inclosure.

It was easy to understand why Germans in uniform saluted—they were commanded to do so. But why did every male, from childhood up, in many districts, raise his hat to us with a subservient "'n Tag"; why the same words, with a hint of courtesy, from the women? Was it fear, respect, habit, design? It could scarcely have been sarcasm; the German peasantry barely knows the meaning of that. Why should a section foreman, whose only suggestion of a uniform was a battered old railway cap, go out of his way to render us military homage? Personally I am inclined to think that, had conditions been reversed, I should have climbed a tree or crawled into a culvert. But we came to wonder if they did not consider the salute a privilege.

Only the well-dressed in the cities showed an attitude that seemed in keeping with the situation, from our point of view. They frequently avoided looking at us, pretended not to see us, treated us much as the Chinese take their "invisible" property-man at the theater. At the back door of our headquarters the pompous high priests of business and politics, or those haughty, well-set-up young men who, one could see at a glance, had been army officers, averted their eyes to hide the rage that burned within them when forced to stand their turn behind some slattern woman or begrimed workman. In a tramway or train now and then it was amusing to watch a former captain or major, weather-browned with service in the field, still boldly displaying his kaiserly mustache, still wearing his army leggings and breeches, looking as out of place in his civilian coat as a cowboy with a cane, as he half openly gritted his teeth at the "undisciplined" American privates who dared do as they pleased without so much as asking his leave. But it was no less amusing to note how superbly oblivious to his wrath were the merrymaking doughboys.

The kaiserly mustache of world-wide fame, by the way, has largely disappeared, at least in the American sector. In fact, the over-modest lip decoration made famous by our most popular "movie" star seemed to be the vogue. More camouflage? More "*Kamerad*"? A gentle compliment to the Americans? Or was it merely the natural change of style, the passing that in time befalls all things, human or *kaiserlich*?

Speaking of German officers, when the first inkling leaked out of Paris that Germany might be required by the terms of the Treaty of Peace to reduce her army to a hundred thousand men there was a suggestion of panic among our German acquaintances. It was not that they were eager to serve their three years as conscripts, as their fathers had done. There was parrot-like agreement that no government would ever again be able to force the manhood of the land to that sacrifice. Nor was there any great fear that so small an army would be inadequate to the requirements of "democratized" Germany. The question was, "What on earth can we do with all our officers, if you allow us only four thousand or so?" Prohibition, I believe, raised the same grave problem with regard to our bartenders. But as we visualized our own army reduced to the same stern necessity the panic was comprehensible. What would we, under similar circumstances, do with many of our dear old colonels? They would serve admirably as taxi-door openers along Fifth Avenue—were it not for their pride. They would scarcely make good grocery clerks; they were not spry enough, nor accurate enough at figures. However, the predicament is one the Germans can scarcely expect the Allies to solve for them.

"War," said Voltaire, "is the business of Germany." One realized more and more the fact in that assertion as new details of the thorough militarization of land, population, and industry came to light under our occupancy. Fortifications, labyrinths of secret tunnels, massive stores of everything that could by any possibility be of use in the complicated business of war; every man up through middle age, who had still two legs to stand on, marked with his service in Mars's workshop; there was some hint of militarization at every turn. Not the least striking of them was the aggressive propaganda in favor of war and of loyalty to the war lords. Not merely were there monuments, inscriptions, martial mottoes, to din the military inclination into the simple *Volk* wherever the eye turned. In the most miserable little *Gasthaus*, with its bare floors and not half enough cover on the beds to make a winter night comfortable, huge framed pictures of martial nature stared down upon the shivering guest. Here hung a life-size portrait of Hindenburg; there was a war scene of Blücher crossing the Rhine; beyond, an *"Opfergaben des Volkes,"* in which a long line of simple laboring people had come to present with great deference their most cherished possession—a bent old peasant, a silver heirloom; a girl, her hair—on the altar of their rulers' martial ambition. It is doubtful whether the Germans have any conception of how widely this harvest of tares has overspread their national life. It may come to them years hence, when grim necessity has forced them to dig up the pernicious roots.

But the old order was already beginning to show signs of change. On a government building over at Trier the first word of the lettering "Königliches Hauptzollamt" had been obliterated. In a little town down the Rhine the dingy

HOTEL DEUTSCHER KAISER

Diners 1 mk. 50 und höher

Logis von 2 mk. an

had the word "Kaiser" painted over, though it was still visible through the whitewash, as if ready to come back at a new turn of events.

The adaptability of the German as a merchant has long since been proved by his commercial success all over the world. It quickly became evident to the Army of Occupation that he was not going to let his feelings—if he had any—interfere with business. As a demand for German uniforms, equipment, insignia faded away behind the retreating armies of the Kaiser, commerce instantly adapted itself to the new conditions. Women who had earned their livelihood or their pin-money for four years by embroidering shoulder-straps and knitting sword-knots for the soldiers in field gray quickly turned their needles to making the ornaments for which the inquiries of the new-comers showed a demand. Shop-windows blossomed out overnight in a chaos of divisional insignia, of service stripes, with khaki cloth and the coveted shoulder-pins from brass bars to silver stars, with anything that could appeal to the American doughboy as a suitable souvenir of his stay on the Rhine—and this last covers a multitude of sins indeed. Iron crosses of both classes were dangled before his eager eyes. The sale of these "highest prizes of German manhood" to their enemies as mere pocket-pieces roused a howl of protest in the local papers, but the trinkets could still be had, if more or less *sub rosa*. Spiked helmets—he must be an uninventive or an absurdly truthful member of the new Watch on the Rhine who cannot show visible evidence to the amazed folks at home of having captured at least a dozen Boche officers and despoiled them of their headgear. Those helmets were carried off by truck-loads from a storehouse just across the Moselle; they loaded down the A. E. F. mails until it is strange there were ships left with space for soldiers homeward bound. A sergeant marched into his captain's billet in an outlying town with a telescoped bundle of six helmets and laid them down with a snappy, "Nine marks each, sir."

"Can you get me a half-dozen, too?" asked a visiting lieutenant.

"Don't know, sir," replied the sergeant. "He made these out of some remnants he had left on hand, but he is not sure he can get any more material."

If we had not awakened to our peril in time and the Germans had taken New York, would our seamstresses have made German flags and our merchants have prominently displayed them in their windows, tagged with the price? Possibly. We of the A. E. F. have learned something of the divorce of patriotism from business since the days when the money-grabbers first descended upon us in the training-camps at home. The merchants of Coblenz, at any rate, were quite as ready to take an order for a Stars and Stripes six feet by four as for a red, white, and black banner. What most astonished, perhaps, the khaki-clad warriors who had just escaped from France was the German's lack of profiteering tendencies. Prices were not only moderate; they remained so in spite of the influx of Americans and the constant drop in the value of the mark. The only orders on the subject issued by the American authorities was the ruling that prices must be the same for Germans and for the soldiers of occupation; nothing hindered merchants from raising their rates to all, yet this rarely happened even in the case of articles of almost exclusive American consumption.

"Shoe-shine parlors," sometimes with the added enticement, "We Shine Your Hobnails," sprang up in every block and were so quickly filled with Yanks intent on obeying the placard to "Look Like a Soldier" that the proprietors had perforce to encourage their own timid people by posting the notice, "Germans Also Admitted." Barber shops developed hair carpets from sheer inability to find time to sweep out, and at that the natives were hard put to it to get rid of their own facial stubble. When the abhorred order against photography by members of the A. E. F. was suddenly and unexpectedly lifted, the camera-shops resembled the entrance to a ball-park on the day of the deciding game between the two big leagues. There was nothing timid or squeamish about German commerce. Shops were quite ready to display post-cards showing French ruins with chesty German officers strutting in the foreground, once they found that these appealed to the indefatigable and all-embracing American souvenir-hunter. Down in

Cologne a German printing-shop worked overtime to get out an official history of the American 3d Division. In the cafés men who had been shooting at us three months before sat placidly sawing off our own popular airs and struggling to perpetrate in all its native horror that inexcusable hubbub known as the "American jazz." The sign "American spoken here" met the eye at frequent intervals. Whether the wording was from ignorance, sarcasm, an attempt to be complimentary, or a sign of hatred of the English has not been recorded. There was not much call for the statement even when it was true, for it was astounding what a high percentage of the Army of Occupation spoke enough German to "get by." The French never tired of showing their surprise when a Yank addressed them in their own tongue; the Germans took it as a matter of course, though they often had the ill manners to insist on speaking "English" whatever the fluency of the customer in their own language, a barbaric form of impoliteness which the French are usually too instinctively tactful to commit.

On the banks of the Rhine in the heart of "Duddlebug"—keep it dark! It is merely the American telephone girls' name for Coblenz, but it would be a grievous treachery if some careless reader let the secret leak out to Berlin— there stands one of the forty-eight palaces that belonged to the ex-Kaiser. Its broad lawn was covered now with hastily erected Y. M. C. A. wooden recreation-halls that contrast strangely with the buildings of the surrounding city, constructed to stand for centuries, and which awaken in the German breast a speechless wrath that these irreverent beings from overseas should have dared to perpetrate such a *lèse-majesté* on the sacred precincts. But the *Schloss* itself was not occupied by the Americans, and there have been questions asked as to the reason—whether those in high standing in our army were showing a sympathy for the monarch who took Dutch leave which they did not grant the garden variety of his ex-subjects. The allegation has no basis. Upon his arrival the commander of the Army of Occupation gave the palace a careful "once over" and concluded that the simplest solution was to leave its offices to the German authorities who were being ousted from more modern buildings. As to the residence portion, the wily old caretaker pointed out to the general that there was neither gas, electricity, nor up-to-date heating facilities. In the immense drawing- and throne-rooms there was, to be sure, space enough to billet a battalion of soldiers, but it would, perhaps, have been too typically Prussian an action to have risked a repetition of what occurred at Versailles in 1871 by turning over this mess of royal bric-à-brac and the glistening polished floors to the tender care of a hobnailed band of concentrated virility.

Plainly impressive enough outwardly, the "living"-rooms of the castle would probably be dubbed a "nightmare" by the American of simple tastes. The striving of the Germans to ape the successful nations of antiquity, the

Greeks, and particularly the Romans, in art and architecture, as well as in empire-building, is in evidence here, as in so many of the ambitious residences of Coblenz. The result is a new style of "erudite barbarism," as Romain Rolland calls it, "laborious efforts to show genius which result in the banal and grotesque." The heavy, ponderous luxury and mélange of style was on the whole oppressive. In the entire series of rooms there was almost nothing really worth looking at for itself, except a few good paintings and an occasional insignificant little gem tucked away in some corner. They were mainly filled with costly and useless bric-à-brac, royal presents of chiefly bad taste, from Sultan, Pope, and potentate, all stuck about with a very stiff air and the customary German over-ornateness. The place looked far less like a residence than like a museum which the defenseless owner had been forced to build to house the irrelevant mass of junk that had been thrust upon him. Costly ivory sets of dominoes, chess, table croquet, what not, showed how these pathetic beings, kings and emperors, passed their time, which the misfortune of rank did not permit them to spend wandering the streets or grassy fields like mere human beings.

The old caretaker had some silly little anecdote for almost every article he pointed out. He had taken thousands of visitors through the castle—it was never inhabited more than a month or two a year even before the war—and the only thing that had ever been stolen was one of the carved ivory table-croquet mallets, which had been taken by an American Red Cross nurse. I was forced to admit that we had people like that, even in America. In the royal chapel—now an American Protestant church—the place usually taken by the pipe organ served as a half-hidden balcony for the Kaiser, with three glaring red-plush chairs—those ugly red-plush chairs, no one of which looked comfortable enough actually to sit in, screamed at one all over the building—with a similar, simpler embrasure opposite for the emperor's personal servants. The main floor below was fully militarized, like all Germany, the pews on the right side being reserved for the army and inscribed with large letters from front to rear—"Generalität," "General Kommando," "Offiziere und Hochbeamter," and so on, in careful order of rank. Red slip-covers with a design of crowns endlessly repeated protected from dust most of the furniture in the *salons* and drawing-rooms, and incidentally shielded the eye, for the furniture itself was far uglier than the covering.

The most pompous of *nouveaux riches* could not have shown more evidence of self-worship in their decorations. Immense paintings of themselves and of their ancestors covered half the Hohenzollern walls, showing them in heroic attitudes and gigantic size, alone with the world at their feet, or in the very thick of battles, looking calm, collected, and unafraid amid generals and followers who, from Bismarck down, had an air of fear which the royal central figure discountenanced by contrast. Huge portraits of princes, *Kurfürsten*, emperors, a goodly percentage of them looking not quite intelligent enough to make efficient night-watchmen, stared haughtily from all sides. A picture of the old Hohenzollern castle, from which the family—and many of the world's woes—originally sprang, occupied a prominent place, as an American "Napoleon of finance" might hang in his Riverside drawing-room a painting of the old farm from which he set out to conquer the earth. Much alleged art by members of the royal family, as fondly preserved as Lizzy's first—and last—school drawing, stood on easels or tables in prominent, insistent positions. Presents from the Sultan were particularly numerous, among them massive metal tablets with bits in Arabic from the Koran. One of these read, according to the caretaker, "He who talks least says most." Unfortunately, the Kaiser could not read Arabic, hence the particularly pertinent remark was lost upon him. In an obscure corner hung one of the inevitable German cuckoo clocks, placed there, if my guide was not mistaken, by a former empress in memory of the spot where she plighted her troth. Poor, petty little romances of royalty! Probably it was not so much coquetry as an effort to escape the pseudo-magnificence of those appalling rooms that drove her into the corner. How could any one be comfortable, either in mind or in body, with such junk about them, much less pass the romantic hours of life in their midst? I should much have preferred to have my *Verlobungskuss* in a railway station.

Only the library of the ex-empress, with its German, French, and English novels and its works of piety, showed any sign of real human individuality. Her favorite picture hung there—a painting showing a half-starved woman weeping and praying over an emaciated child, called "The Efficacy of Prayer." No doubt the dear empress got much sentimental solace out of it—just before the royal dinner was announced. The Kaiser's private sleeping-room, on the other hand, was simplicity itself—far less sumptuous than my own a few blocks away. He had last slept there, said the caretaker, in the autumn of 1914, while moving toward the western front with his staff.

"And all this belongs to the state now, since Germany has become a republic?" I remarked.

"Only a part of it," replied my guide. "We are making up lists of the private and crown property, and his own possessions will be returned to the Kaiser."

The outstanding feature of the visit was not the castle itself, however, but the attitude of this lifelong servant of the imperial owner. The assertion that no man is a hero to his valet applies, evidently, clear up to emperors. The caretaker was a former soldier in a Jäger and forestry battalion, born in the Thüringerwald fifty-six years ago, a man of intelligence and not without education. He had been one of hundreds who applied for a position in the imperial household in 1882, winning the coveted place because he came "with an armful of fine references." To him the Kaiser and all his clan were just ordinary men, for whom he evidently felt neither reverence nor disdain. Nor, I am sure, was he posing democracy; he looked too tired and indifferent to play a part for the benefit of my uniform. The many gossipy tales of royalty, semi-nobility, and ignobility with which he spiced our stroll were told neither with ill feeling nor with boastfulness; they were merely his every-day thoughts, as a printer might talk of his presses or a farmer of his crops.

Wilhelm der Erste, the first Kaiser, was a good man in every way, he asserted. He had seen him die. He had been called to bring him his last glass of water. Bismarck and a dozen others were gathered about his bed, most of them kneeling—the picture of Bismarck on his knees was not easy to visualize somehow—"and the emperor died with great difficulty"—my informant demonstrated his last moments almost too realistically. The Kaiser—he who wrecked the Hohenzollern ship—was a very ordinary man, possibly something above the average in intelligence, but he did not have a fair chance in life. There was his useless arm, and then his ear. For forty years he had suffered atrociously from an abscess in his left ear. The caretaker had seen him raging mad with it. No treatment ever helped him. No, it was not cancer, though his mother died of that after inhuman suffering, but it was getting nearer and nearer to his brain, and he could not last many years now. Then there was his arm. No, it was not inherited, but resulted from the criminal carelessness of a midwife. For years he used an apparatus in the hope of getting some strength into that arm, tying his left hand to a lever and working it back and forth with his right. But it never did any good. He never got to the point where he could lift that arm without taking hold of it with the other. He grew extraordinarily clever in covering up his infirmity; when he rode he placed the reins in the useless left hand with the right, and few would have realized that they were just lying there, without any grasp on them at all. He kept that arm out of photographs; he kept it turned away from the public with a success that was almost superhuman. On the whole, he was a man with a good mind. "No one of average intelligence can help being a knowing man if he has Ministers and counselors and all the wise men of the realm coming to him every day and telling him everything." But he had too much power, too much chance to rule. He dismissed Bismarck, "a man such as there is only one born in a century," when he was himself still far too young to be his own Chancellor. He never could take advice; when his Ministers came to him they were not allowed to tell him what they thought; they could only salute and do what he ordered them to do. And he never understood that he should choose his words with care because they made more impression than those of an ordinary man.

It was only when I chanced upon his favorite theme—we had returned to his little lodge, decorated with the antlers and tusks that were the trophies of his happiest days—that the caretaker showed any actual enthusiasm for the ex-Kaiser. I asked if it were true that the former emperor was a good shot. "*Ausgezeichnet!*" he cried, his weary eyes lighting up; "he was a marvelous shot! I have myself seen him kill more than eight hundred creatures in one day—and do not forget that he had to shoot with one arm at that." He did not mention how much better record than that the War Lord had made on the western front, nor the precautions his long experience in the "hunting-field" had taught him to take against any possible reprisal by his stalked and cornered game.

The Crown Prince, he had told me somewhere along the way in the oppressive royal museum, was a very nice little boy, but his educators spoiled him. Since manhood he had been "somewhat *leichtsinnig*"—it was the same expression, the old refrain, that I had heard wherever the Kaiser's heir was mentioned—"and his mind runs chiefly on women." In one of the rooms we had paused before a youthful portrait of Queen Victoria. "I have seen her often," remarked my guide, in his colorless voice. "She came often to visit us, at many of the palaces, and the first thing she invariably called for the moment she arrived was cognac." It may have been merely a little side-slap at the hated English, but there was something in that particular portrait that suggested that the queen would have made a very lively little *grisette*, had fate chanced to cast her in that rôle.

Bismarck was plainly the old servant's favorite among the titled throng he had served and observed. "When the second Kaiser died," he reminisced, "after his very short reign—he was a good man, too, though proud—he gave me a message that I was to hand over to Bismarck himself, in person. The long line of courtiers were aghast when I insisted on seeing him; they stared angrily when I was admitted ahead of them to his private study. I knocked, and there was a noise inside between a grunt and a growl"—some of our own dear colonels, I mused, had at least that much Bismarckian about them—"and after I opened the door I had to peer about for some time before I could see where he was, the tobacco smoke was so thick. He always smoked like that. But he was an easy man to talk to, if you really had a good reason for coming to see him, and I had. When I went out all the courtiers stared at me with wonder, but I just waved a hand to them and said, 'The audience is over, gentlemen!' Ah yes, I have seen much in my day, *aber*," he concluded, resignedly, as he accompanied me to the door of his lodge, "*alle diese gute Zeiten sind leider vorbei.*"

III
THOU SHALT NOT ... FRATERNIZE

The armies of occupation have been credited with the discovery of a new crime, one not even implied in the Ten Commandments. Indeed, misinformed mortals have usually listed it among the virtues. It is "fraternization." The average American—unless his habitat be New England—cannot remain aloof and haughty. Particularly the unsophisticated doughboy, bubbling over with life and spirits, is given to making friends with whatever branch of the human family he chances to find about him. Moreover, he was grateful for the advance in material comfort, if not in friendliness, of Germany as compared with the mutilated portion of France he had known. He did not, in most cases, stop to think that it was the war which had made those differences. It was an every-day experience to hear some simple country boy in khaki remark to his favorite officer in a slow, puzzled voice, "Sa-ay, Lieutenant, you know I like these here Boshies a lot better than them there Frogs." The wrangles and jealousies with their neighbors, on which the overcrowded peoples of Europe feed from infancy, were almost unsuspected by these grownup children from the wide land of opportunity. The French took alarm. There seemed to be danger that the *sale Boche* would win over *les Américains*, at least the sympathy of the men in the ranks, by his insidious "propaganda." As a matter of fact, I doubt whether he could have done so. The Germans rather overdid their friendliness. Particularly when it bore any suggestion of cringing, deliberate or natural, it defeated itself, for, simple as he may be in matters outside his familiar sphere, the American soldier has an almost feminine intuition in catching, eventually, a somewhat hazy but on the whole true conception of the real facts. But our allies were taking no chances. A categorical order—some say it emanated from Foch himself—warned the armies of occupation that there must be "no fraternization."

The interpretation of the order varied. As was to be expected, the Americans carried it out more rigorously than did their three allies along the Rhine. Its application also differed somewhat in separate regions within our own area. At best complete enforcement was impossible. With soldiers billeted in every house, what was to hinder a lovelorn buck from making friends with the private who was billeted in *her* house and going frequently to visit *him*? On cold winter evenings one rarely passed a pair of American sentries beside their little coal-fires without seeing a slouchy youth or two in the ugly round cap without vizor which we had so long associated only with prisoners of war, or a few shivering and hungry girls, hovering in the vicinity, eying the soldiers with an air which suggested that they were willing to give anything for a bit of warmth or the leavings of the food the sentries were gorging.

Whether they merely wanted company or aspired to soap and chocolate, there was nothing to prevent them getting warmer when there were no officers in sight.

The soldiers had their own conception of the meaning of fraternization. Buying a beer, for instance, was not fraternizing; tipping the waiter who served it was—unless he happened to be an attractive barmaid. Taking a walk or shaking hands with a German man was to disobey the order; strolling in the moonlight with his sister, or even kissing her under cover of a convenient tree-trunk, was not. The interrelation of our warriors and the civilian population was continually popping up in curious little details. To the incessant demand of children for "Schewing Kum," as familiar, if more guttural, as in France, the regulation answer was no longer "No compree," but "No fraternize." Boys shrilling "Along the Wabash" or "Over There," little girls innocently calling out to a shocked passer-by in khaki some phrase that is more common to a railroad construction gang than to polite society, under the impression that it was a kindly word of greeting, showed how the American influence was spreading. "Snell" had taken the place of "toot sweet" in the soldier vocabulary. German schools of the future are likely to teach that "spuds" is the American word for what the "*verdammte Engländer*" calls potatoes. When German station-guards ran along the platforms shouting, "*Vorsicht!*" at the approach of a train, American soldiers with a touch of the native tongue translated it into their lingo and added a warning, "Heads up!" The adaptable Boche caught the words—or thought he did—and thereafter it was no unusual experience to hear the arrival of a *Schnellzug* prefaced with shouts of, "Hets ub!" In the later days of the occupation the Yank was more apt to be wearing a "*Gott mit uns*" belt than the narrow web one issued by his supply company, and that belt was more likely than not to be girdled round with buttons and metal rosettes from German uniforms, as the original American wore the scalps of his defeated enemies. Our intelligence police frequently ran down merchants or manufacturers guilty of violating the fraternization order by making or offering for sale articles with the German and the American flags intertwined, pewter rings bearing the insignia of some American division and the iron cross; alleged meerschaum pipes decorated with some phrase expressive of Germany's deep love for America in spite of the recent "misunderstanding." The wiseacres saw in all this a subtle "propaganda," cleverly directed from Berlin. I doubt whether it was anything more than the German merchant's incorrigible habit of making what he can sell, of fitting his supply to his customer's wishes, however absurd these may seem to him.

Up to the 1st of February Americans on detached service in Germany ate where they chose. With the non-fraternization order came the command to patronize only the restaurants run by the army or its auxiliary societies. The purpose was double—to shut another avenue to the fraternizer and to leave to the Germans their own scanty food store. This question of two widely different sources of supply side by side required constant vigilance. When two lakes of vastly different levels are separated only by a thin wall it is to be expected that a bit of water from the upper shall spill over into the lower. A pound can of cocoa cost 50 marks in a German shop—if it could be had at all; a better pound sold for 1 mk. 25 in our commissary. A can of butter for which a well-to-do citizen would gladly have given a week's income was only a matter of a couple of dollars for the man in khaki. A bar of soap, a tablet of chocolate, a can of jam, many of the simple little things that had become unattainable luxuries to the mass of the people about us, cost us no more than they did at home before the war. Even if there was no tendency to profit by these wide discrepancies—and with the vast percentage of our soldiers there was not—the natural tender-heartedness of America's fighting-man moved him to transgress orders a bit in favor of charity. Much as one may hate the Boche, it is hard to watch an anemic little child munch a bare slice of disgusting war-bread, knowing that you can purchase a big white loaf made of genuine flour for a paltry ten cents.

There were curious ramifications in this "fraternization" question. Thus, what of the American lieutenant whose father came over from his home in Düsseldorf or Mannheim to visit his son? By strict letter of the law they should not speak to each other. What advice could one give a Russian-American soldier whose brother was a civilian in Coblenz? What should the poor Yank do whose German mother wired him that she was coming from Leipzig to see him, little guessing that for him to be seen in public with any woman not in American uniform was an invitation to the first M. P. who saw him to add to the disgruntled human collection in the "brig"?

I chanced to be the "goat" in a curious and embarrassing situation that grew quite naturally out of the non-fraternizing order. It was down the river at Andernach, a town which, in the words of the doughboy, boasts "the only cold-water geyser in the world—except the Y. M. C. A." A divisional staff had taken over the "palace" of a family of the German nobility, who had fled to Berlin at our approach. One day the daughter of the house unexpectedly returned, alone but for a maid. She happened to be not merely young and beautiful—far above the average German level in the latter regard—but she had all those outward attractions which good breeding and the unremitting care of trained guardians from birth to maturity give the fortunate members of the human family. She was exactly the type the traveler in foreign lands is always most anxious to meet, and least successful in meeting. On the evening of her arrival the senior officer of the house thought to soften the blow of her unpleasant home-coming by inviting her to dinner with her unbidden guests. The little circle was charmed with her *tout ensemble*. They confided to one another that she would stand comparison with any American girl they had ever met—which was the highest tribute in their vocabulary. She seemed to find the company agreeable herself. As they rose from the table she asked what time breakfast would be served in the morning. Thanks to the uncertainty of her English, she had mistaken the simple courtesy for a "standing invitation."

The officers looked at one another with mute appeal in their eyes. Nothing would have pleased them better than to have their grim circle permanently graced by so charming an addition. But what of the new order against fraternization? Some day an inspector might drift in, or the matter reach the erect ears of that mysterious and dreaded department hidden under the pseudonym of "G-2-B." Besides, the officers were all conscientious young men who took army orders seriously and scorned to use any sophistry in their interpretation. Furthermore, though it hurt keenly to admit such a slanderous thought, it was within the range of possibilities that the young lady was a spy, sent here with the very purpose of trying to ingratiate herself into the circle which had so naïvely opened itself to her. It was known that her family had been in personal touch with the Kaiser; for all her "American manner," she made no secret of being German through and through. What could have been more in keeping with the methods of Wilhelmstrasse than the suggestion that she return to her own home and pass on to Berlin any rumors she might chance to pick up from her unwelcome guests?

Plainly she must be gotten rid of at once. None of the officers, however, felt confidence enough in his German to put it to so crucial a test. Whence, it being my fortune to drop in on a friend among the perplexed Americans just at that moment, I was unanimously appointed to the gentle task of banishing the lady from her own dining-room.

It was at the end of a pleasant little luncheon—the sixth meal which the daughter of the house had graciously attended. The conversation had been enlightening, the atmosphere most congenial, the young lady more unostentatiously beautiful than ever. We reduced the audience to her coming humiliation as low as possible by softly dismissing the junior members, swallowed our throats, and began. Nothing, we assured her, had been more pleasant to us since our arrival in Germany than the privilege of having her as a guest at our simple mess. Nothing we could think of—short of being ordered home at once—would have pleased us more than to have her permanently grace our board. But ... fortunately our stiff uniform collars helped to keep our throats in place ... she had possibly heard of the new army order, a perfectly ridiculous ruling, to be sure, particularly under such circumstances as these, but an army order for all that—and no one could know better than she, the daughter and granddaughter of German high officers, that army orders are meant to be obeyed—wherein Pershing himself commanded us to have no more relations with the civilian population than were absolutely unavoidable. Wherefore we ... we ... we trusted she would understand that this was only the official requirement and in no way represented our own personal inclinations ... we were compelled to request that she confine herself thereafter to the upper floor of the house, as her presence on our floor might easily be misunderstood. Her maid no doubt could prepare her meals, or there was a hotel a few yards up the street....

The charming little smile of gratitude with which she had listened to the prelude had faded to a puzzled interest as the tone deepened, then to a well-mastered amazement at the effrontery of the climax. With a constrained, "Is that all?" she rose to her feet, and as we kicked our chairs from under us she passed out with a genuinely imperious carriage, an icy little bow, her beautiful face suffused with a crimson that would have made a mere poppy look colorless by comparison. We prided ourselves on having been extremely diplomatic in our handling of the matter, but no member of that mess ever again received anything better than the barest shadow of a frigid bow from the young lady, followed at a respectful distance by her maid, whom they so often met on her way to the hotel a few yards up the street.

If it were not within the province of a soldier to criticize orders, one might question whether it would not have been better to allow regulated "fraternizing" than to attempt to suppress it entirely. Our soldiers, permeated through and through, whether consciously or otherwise, with many of those American ideals, that point of view, which we are eager for the German *Volk* to grasp, that there may be no more kaisers and no more deliberately built-up military assaults upon the world, would have been the most effective propaganda in our favor that could have been devised to loose upon the German nation. Merely their naïve little stories of how they live at home would in time have awakened a discontent in certain matters, spiritual rather than material, that would have been most salutary. But we committed our customary and familiar American error of refusing to compromise with human nature, of attempting impossible suppression instead of accepting possible regulation, with the result that those ineradicable plants that might have grown erect and gay in the sunshine developed into pale-faced, groveling monstrosities in the cellars and hidden corners. Our allies in the neighboring areas had the same non-fraternizing order, yet by not attempting to swallow it whole they succeeded, probably, in digesting it better.

There was a simple little way of fraternizing in Coblenz without risking the heavy hand of an M. P. on your shoulder. It was to just have it *happen* by merest chance that the seat of the *Fräulein* who had taken your eye be next your own at the municipal theater. It grew increasingly popular with both officers and enlisted men, that modest little *Stadttheater*. The Germans who, before our arrival, had been able to drift in at the last moment and be sure of a seat, were forced to come early in the day and stand in line as if before a butter-shop. The *Kronloge*, or royal box, belonged now to the general commanding the Army of Occupation—until six each evening, when its eighteen seats might be disposed of to ordinary people, though the occupants even in that case were more likely than not to be girdled by the Sam Browne belt. Some observers make the encouraging assertion that there will be more devotees of opera in America when the quarter-million who kept the watch on the Rhine return home. There was a tendency to drift more and more toward the *Stadttheater*, even on the part of some whom no one would have dared to accuse of aspiring to "high-brow" rating, though it must be admitted that the "rag" and "jazz" and slap-stick to which the "Y" and similar well-meaning camp-followers, steeped in the "tired business man" fallacy, felt obliged to confine their efforts in entertaining "the boys," did not play to empty houses.

The little *Stadttheater* gave the principal operas, not merely of Germany, but of France and Italy, and occasional plays, chiefly from their own classics. They were usually well staged, though long drawn out, after the manner of the German, who can seldom say his say in a few succinct words and be done as can the Frenchman. The operas, too, had a heaviness in spots—such as those, for instance, under the feet of the diaphanous nymphs of one hundred and sixty-five pounds each who cavorted about the trembling stage—which did not exactly recall the Opéra in Paris. But it would be unfair to compare the artistic advantages of a city of eighty thousand with those of the "capital of the world." Probably the performances in Coblenz would have rivaled those in any but the two or three largest French cities, and it would be a remarkable town "back in little old U. S. A." that could boast such a theater, offering the best things of the stage at prices quite within reach of ordinary people. When one stopped to reflect, those prices were astonishing. The best seat in the *Kronloge* was but 5 mk. 50, a bare half-dollar then, only $1.25 at the normal pre-war exchange, and accommodations graded down to quite tolerable places in whatever the Germans call their "peanut gallery" at nine cents! All of which does not mean that the critical opera-goer would not gladly endure the quintupled cost for the privilege of attending a performance at the Opéra Comique at Paris.

The question of fraternization and the ubiquitous one of German food shortage were not without their connection. Intelligence officers were constantly running down rumors of too much sympathy of our soldiers for the hungry population. The assertion that Germany had been "starved to her knees," however, was scarcely borne out by observations in the occupied area. It is true that in Coblenz even the authorized quantities—seven pounds of potatoes, two hundred grams of meat, seven ounces of sugar, and so on per person each week, were high in price and not always available. Milk for invalids and those under seven was easier to order than to obtain. A notice in the local papers to "Bring your egg and butter tickets on Monday and get two cold-storage eggs and forty grams of oleomargarine" was cause for town-wide rejoicing. Poor old horses that had faithfully served the A. E. F. to the end of their strength were easily auctioned at prices averaging a thousand marks each, in spite of the requirement that a certificate be produced within a week showing where they had been slaughtered. There was always a certain *Schleichhandel*, or underhand dealing, going on between the wealthy in the cities and the well-stocked peasants. Rancid butter, to be had of excellent quality before the war at two marks, cost in "underground" commerce anything from fifty marks up which the happy man who found it was in a condition to pay. Contrasted with this picture, the wages of an eight-hour day were seldom over five marks for unskilled, or more than ten for skilled labor. The out-of-work-insurance system, less prevalent in our area than "over in Germany," made it almost an advantage to be unemployed. A citizen of Düsseldorf offered a wanderer in the streets eight marks for a day's work in his stable. Many a man would gladly have done the task for three marks before the war. The wanderer cursed the citizen roundly. "You have the audacity," he cried, "to ask me to toil all day for two marks!" "*Two* marks?" gasped the citizen; "you misunderstood me. I said eight." "I heard you say eight," shouted the workman, "and is not eight just two more than the six we get under the unemployment act? Pest with your miserable two marks! If you want to pay me ten for the day—that is, sixteen in all...." He did not add that by going out into the country with his unearned six marks he could buy up food and return to the city to sell it at a handsome profit, but the citizen did not need to be reminded of that oppressive fact.

It was under such conditions as these that the civilians about us lived while we gorged ourselves on the full army ration in the hotels and restaurants we had taken over. There was always a long and eager waiting line where any employment of civilians by the Americans carried with it the right to army food; in many cases it became necessary to confine the opportunity to war widows or others whose breadwinners had been killed.

THE FORMER CROWN PRINCE IN HIS OFFICIAL FACE, ATTENDING THE FUNERAL OF A GERMAN OFFICER AND COUNT, WHOSE MILITARY ORDERS ARE CARRIED ON THE CUSHION IN FRONT

THE HEIR TO THE TOPPLED THRONE WEARING HIS UNOFFICIAL AND MORE CHARACTERISTIC EXPRESSION

BARGES OF AMERICAN FOOD-STUFFS ON THEIR WAY UP THE RHINE

BRITISH TOMMIES STOWING THEMSELVES AWAY FOR THE NIGHT ON BARGES ANCHORED NEAR THE HOLLAND FRONTIER

A man who rented his motor-boat to our Marine Corps at forty-five marks a day and food for himself brought his brother along without charge, both of them living well on the one ration. The poor undoubtedly suffered. Where haven't they? Where do they not, even in times of peace? So did we, in fact, in spite of our unlimited source of supply. For the barbarous German cooking reduced our perfectly respectable fare to something resembling in looks, smell, and taste the "scow" of a British forecastle. In France we had come to look forward to meal-time as one of the pleasant oases of existence; on the Rhine it became again just a necessary ordeal to be gotten over with as soon as possible. If we were at first inclined to wonder what the chances were of the men who had been facing us with machine-guns three months before poisoning us now, it soon died out, for they served us as deferentially, and far more quickly, with comparative obliviousness to tips, than had the *garçons* beyond the Vosges.

The newspapers complained of a "physical deterioration and mental degeneration from lack of nourishing food that often results in a complete collapse of the nervous system, bringing on a state of continual hysteria." We saw something of this, but there were corresponding advantages. Diabetes and similar disorders that are relieved by the starvation treatment had vastly decreased. My host complained that his club, a regal building then open only to American officers, had lost one-third of its membership during the war, not in numbers, but in weight, an average of sixty pounds each. Judging from his still not diaphanous form, the falling off had been an advantage to the club's appearance, if not to its health. But one cannot always gage the health and resistance of the German by his outward appearance. He is racially gifted with red cheeks and plump form. The South American Indian of the highlands also looks the picture of robust health, yet he is certainly underfed and dies easily. In a well-to-do city like Coblenz appearances were particularly deceiving. The bulk of the population was so well housed, so well dressed, outwardly so prosperous, that it was hard to realize how greatly man's chief necessity, food, was lacking. In many a mansion to open the door at meal-time was to catch a strong scent of cheap and unsavory cooking that recalled the customary aroma of our lowest tenements. Healthy as many of them looked, there was no doubt that for the past year or two the Germans, particularly the old and the very young, succumbed with surprising rapidity to ordinarily unimportant diseases. If successful merchants were beefy and war profiteers rotund, they were often blue under the eyes. An officer of the chemical division of our army who conducted a long investigation within the occupied area found that while the *bulk* of food should have been sufficient to keep the population in average health, the number of calories was barely one-third what the human engine requires.

The chief reason for this was that food had become more and more *Ersatz*—substitute articles, ranging all the way from "something almost as good" to the mere shadow of what it pretended to be. "We have become an *Ersatz* nation," wailed the German press, "and have lost in consequence many of our good qualities. *Ersatz* butter, *Ersatz* bread, *Ersatz* jam, *Ersatz* clothing—everything is becoming *Ersatz*." A firm down the river went so far as to announce an *Ersatz* meat, called "Fino," which was apparently about as satisfactory as the *Ersatz* beer which the new kink in the Constitution is forcing upon Americans at home. Nor was the substitution confined to food articles, though in other things the lack was more nearly amusing than serious. Prisoners taken in our last drives nearly all wore *Ersatz* shirts, made of paper. Envelopes bought in Germany fell quickly apart because of the *Ersatz* paste that failed to do its duty. Painters labored with *Ersatz* daubing material because the linseed-oil their trade requires had become *Ersatz* lard for cooking purposes. Rubber seemed to be the most conspicuous scarcity, at least in the occupied regions. Bicycle tires showed a curious ingenuity; suspenders got their stretch from the weave of the cloth; galoshes were rarely seen. Leather, on the other hand, seemed to be more plentiful than we had been led to believe, though it was high in price. The cobbler paid twenty-five marks a pound for his materials, and must have a leather-ticket to get them; real shoes that cost seven to eight marks before the war ran now as high as seventy. A tolerable suit of civilian clothing, of which there was no scarcity in shop-windows, sold for three or four hundred marks, no more at our exchange than it would have cost on Broadway, though neither the material, color, nor make would have satisfied the fastidious Broadway stroller. After the military stores of field-gray cloth were released this became a favorite material, not merely for men's wear, but for women's cloaks and children's outer garments. Paper was decidedly cheaper than in France; the newspapers considerably larger. The thousand and one articles of every-day life showed no extraordinary scarcity nor anything like the prices of France, far less self-supporting than Germany in these matters. Nor was the miscalled "luxury tax"—never collected, of course, of Americans after the first few exemplary punishments—anything like as irksome as that decreed on the banks of the Seine. That the burden of government on the mass of the people was anything but light, however, was demonstrated by the testimony of a workman in our provost court that he earned an average of seventy-five marks a week and paid one hundred and twenty-five marks a month in taxes!

An *Ersatz* story going the rounds in Coblenz shows to what straits matters had come, as well as disproving the frequent assertion that the German is always devoid of a sense of humor. A bondholder, well-to-do before the war, runs the yarn, was too honest or too lacking in foresight to invest in something bringing war profits, with the result that along in the third year of hostilities he found himself approaching a penniless state. Having lost the habit of work, and being too old to acquire it again, he soon found himself in a sad predicament. What most irked his comfort-loving soul, however, was the increasing *Ersatz*-ness of the food on which he was forced to subsist. The day came when he could bear it no longer. He resolved to commit suicide. Entering a drug-store, he demanded an absurdly large dose of prussic acid— and paid what under other conditions would have been a heartbreaking price for it. In the dingy little single room to which fortune had reduced him he wrote a letter of farewell to the world, swallowed the entire prescription, and lay down to die. For some time nothing happened. He had always been under the impression that prussic acid did its work quickly. Possibly he had been misinformed. He could wait. He lighted an *Ersatz* cigarette and settled down to do so. Still nothing befell him. He stretched out on his sagging bed with the patience of despair, fell asleep, and woke up late next morning feeling none the worse for his action.

"Look here," he cried, bursting in upon the druggist, "what sort of merchant are you? I paid you a fabulous price for a large dose of prussic acid—I am tired of life and want to die—and the stuff has not done me the least harm!"

"*Donner und Blitz!*" gasped the apothecary. "Why didn't you say so? I would have warned you that you were probably wasting your money. You know everything in the shop now is *Ersatz*, and I have no way of knowing whether *Ersatz* prussic acid, or any other poison I have in stock, has any such effect on the human system as does the real article."

The purchaser left with angry words, slamming the door behind him until the *Ersatz* plate-glass in it crinkled from the impact. He marched into a shop opposite and bought a rope, returned to his room, and hanged himself. But at his first spasm the rope broke. He cast the remnants from him and stormed back into the rope-shop.

"You call yourself an honest German," he screamed, "yet you sell me, at a rascally price, a cord that breaks under a niggardly strain of sixty kilos! I am tired of life. I wanted to hang myself. I...."

"My poor fellow," said the merchant, soothingly, "you should have known that all our rope is *Ersatz* now—made of paper...."

"Things have come to a pretty pass," mumbled the victim of circumstances as he wandered aimlessly on up the street. "A man can no longer even put himself out of his misery. I suppose there is nothing left for me but to continue to live, *Ersatz* and all."

He shuffled on until the gnawing of hunger became well-nigh unendurable, turned a corner, and ran into a long line of emaciated fellow-citizens before a municipal soup-kitchen. Falling in at the end of it, he worked his way forward, paid an *Ersatz* coin for a bowl of *Ersatz* stew, returned to his lodging—and died in twenty minutes.

IV
KNOCKING ABOUT THE OCCUPIED AREA

If I have spoken chiefly of Coblenz in attempting to picture the American army in Germany, it is merely because things centered there. My assignment carried me everywhere within our occupied area, and several times through those of our allies. The most vivid imagination could not have pictured any such Germany as this when I tramped her roads fifteen, twelve, and ten years before. The native population, dense as it is, was everywhere inundated by American khaki. The roads were rivers of Yankee soldiers, of trucks and automobiles, from the princely limousines of field-officers and generals to the plebeian Ford or side-car of mere lieutenants, often with their challenging insignia—an ax through a Boche helmet, and the like—still painted on their sides. The towns and villages had turned from field gray to olive drab. Remember we had nine divisions in our area, and an American division in column covers nearly forty miles. American guards with fixed bayonets patrolled the highways in pairs, like the *carabinieri* of Italy and the *guardias civiles* of Spain—though they were often the only armed men one met all day long, unless one counts the platoons, companies, or battalions still diligently drilling under the leafless apple-trees. We made our own speed rules, and though civilians may have ground their teeth with rage as we tore by in a cloud of dust or a shower of mud, outwardly they chiefly ignored our presence—except the girls, the poor, and the children, who more often waved friendly greetings. Of children there were many everywhere, mobs of them compared with France—chubby, red-cheeked little boys, often in cut-down uniforms, nearly always wearing the red-banded, German fatigue bonnet, far less artistic, even in color, than the *bonnet de police* of French boys, and accentuating the round, close-cropped skulls that have won the nation the sobriquet of "square-head." The plump, hearty, straw-blond little girls were almost as numerous as their brothers; every town surged with them; if one of our favorite army correspondents had not already copyrighted the expression, I should say that the villages resembled nothing so much as human hives out of which children poured like disturbed bees. Every little way along the road a small boy thrust out a spiked helmet or a *"Gott mit uns"* belt-buckle for sale as we raced past. The children not only were on very friendly terms with our soldiers—all children are—but they got on well even where the horizon blue of the *poilu* took the place of our khaki.

Farmers were back at work in their fields now, most of them still in the field gray of the trenches, turned into "civies" by some simple little change. Men of military age seemed far more plentiful than along French roads. How clean and unscathed, untouched by the war, it all looked in contrast to poor, mutilated, devastated France. Many sturdy draft-horses were still seen, escaped by some miracle from the maw of war. Goodly dumps of American and French shells, for quick use should the Germans suddenly cease to cry *"Kamerad!"* flashed by. In one spot was an enormous heap of Boche munitions waiting for our ordnance section to find some safe means of blowing it up. There were "Big Bertha" shells, and Zeppelin bombs among them, of particular interest to those of us who had never seen them before, but who knew only too well how it feels to have them drop within a few yards of us. Every little while we sped past peasant men and women who were opening long straw- and earth-covered mounds, built last autumn under other conditions, and loading wagons with the huge coarse species of turnip—rutabagas, I believe we call them—which seemed to form their chief crop and food. In the big beech forest about the beautiful Larchersee women and children, and a few men, were picking up beechnuts under the sepia-brown carpet of last year's leaves. Their vegetable fat makes a good *Ersatz* butter. Wild ducks still winged their way over the *See*, or rode its choppy waves, undisturbed by the rumors of food scarcity. For not only did the game restrictions of the old régime still hold; the population was forced to hand over even its shotguns when we came, and to get one back again was a long and properly complicated process.

The Americans took upon themselves the repair and widening of the roads which our heavy trucks had begun to pound into a condition resembling those of France in the war zone—at German expense in the end, of course; that was particularly where the shoe pinched. It broke the thrifty Boche's heart to see these extravagant warriors from overseas, to whom two years of financial *carte blanche* had made money seem mere paper, squandering his wealth, or that of his children, without so much as an if you please. The labor was German, under the supervision of American sergeants, and the recruiting of it absurdly simple—to the Americans. An order to the burgomaster informing him succinctly, "You will furnish four hundred men at such a place to-morrow morning at seven for road labor; wages eight marks a day," covered our side of the transaction. Where and how the burgomaster found the laborers was no soup out of our plates. We often got, of course, the poorest workmen; men too young or too old for our purposes, men either already broken on the wheel of industry or not yet broken to harness; but there was an easy "come-back" if the German officials played that game too frequently. Once enrolled to labor for the American army, a man was virtually enlisted for the duration of the armistice—save for suitable reasons or lack of work. Strikes, so epidemic "over in Germany," were not permitted in our undertakings. A keen young lieutenant of engineers was in charge of road repairs and sawmills in a certain divisional area. One morning his sergeant at one of the mills called him on the Signal Corps telephone that linked all the Army of Occupation together, with the information that the night force had struck.

"Struck!" cried the lieutenant, aghast at the audacity. "I'll be out at once!"

Arrived at the town in question, he dropped in on the A. P. M. to request that a squad of M. P.'s follow him without delay, and hurried on to the mill, fingering his .44.

"Order that night force to fall in here at once!" he commanded, indicating an imaginary line along which the offending company should be dressed.

"Yes, sir," saluted the sergeant, and disappeared into the building.

The lieutenant waited, nursing his rage. A small boy, blue with cold, edged forward to see what was going on. Two others, a bit older, thin and spindle-shanked, their throats and chins muffled in soiled and ragged scarfs, their gray faces testifying to long malnutrition, idled into view with that yellow-dog curiosity of hookworm victims. But the night force gave no evidence of existence. At length the sergeant reappeared.

"Well," snapped the lieutenant, "what about it? Where is that night shift?"

"All present, sir," replied the sergeant, pointing at the three shivering urchins. "Last night at midnight I ordered them to start a new pile of lumber, and the next I see of them they was crouching around the boiler—it *was* a cold night, sir—and when I ordered them back to work they said they hadn't had anything to eat for two days but some war-bread. You know there's been some hold-up in the pay vouchers...."

A small banquet at the neighboring *Gasthof* ended that particular strike without the intervention of armed force, though there were occasionally others that called for the shadow of it.

In taking over industries of this sort the Americans adopted the practice of demanding to see the receipted bills signed by the German military authorities, then required the same prices. Orders were issued to supply no civilian trade without written permission from the Americans. After the first inevitable punishments for not taking the soft-spoken new-comers at their word, the proprietors applied the rule with a literalness that was typically German. A humble old woman knocked timidly at the lieutenant's office door one day, and upon being admitted handed the clerk a long, impressive legal paper. When it had been deciphered it proved to be a laboriously penned request for permission to buy lumber at the neighboring sawmill. In it Frau Schmidt, there present, certified that she had taken over a vacant shop for the purpose of opening a shoe-store, that said occupation was legal and of use to the community, that there was a hole in the floor of said shop which it was to the advantage of the health and safety of the community to have mended, wherefore she respectfully prayed the Herr Leutnant in charge of the sawmills of the region to authorize her to buy three boards four inches wide and three feet long. In witness of the truth of the above assertions of Frau Schmidt, respectable and duly authorized member of the community, the burgomaster had this day signed his name and caused his seal to be affixed.

The lieutenant solemnly approved the petition and passed it on "through military channels" to the sergeant at the sawmill. Any tendency of *das Volk* to take our occupancy with fitting seriousness was too valuable to be jeopardized by typical American informality.

A few days later came another episode to disprove any rumors that the American heel was being applied with undue harshness. The village undertaker came in to state that a man living on the edge of town was expected to die, and that he had no lumber with which to make him a coffin. The tender-hearted lieutenant, who had seen many comrades done to death in tricky ambuscades on the western front, issued orders that the undertaker be permitted to purchase materials for a half-dozen caskets, and as the petitioner bowed his guttural thanks he assured him: "You are entirely welcome. Whenever you need any more lumber for a similar purpose do not hesitate to call on me. I hope you will come early and often."

The Boche gazed at the speaker with the glass-eyed expressionlessness peculiar to his race, bowed his thanks again, and departed. Whether or not he "got the idea" is not certain. My latest letter from the lieutenant contains the postscript, "I also had the satisfaction of granting another request for lumber for six coffins."

They were singing a familiar old song with new words during my last weeks in Coblenz, the chorus beginning "The Rhine, the Rhine, the Yankee Rhine." For many miles up and down the historic stream it seemed so indeed. I have been in many foreign ports in my day, and in none of them have I seen the American flag so much in evidence as at the junction of the Moselle and "Father Rhine." The excursion steamers—those same side-wheelers on which you rode that summer you turned tourist, on which you ate red cabbage at a table hemmed in by paunchy, gross Germans who rolled their sentimental eyes as the famous cliff roused in them a lusty attempt to sing of the Lorelei with her golden hair—carried the Stars and Stripes at their stern now. They were still manned by their German crews; a resplendent "square-head" officer still majestically paced the bridge. But they were in command of American Marines, "snappy," keen-eyed young fellows who had fought their way overland—how fiercely the Boche himself knows only too well—till they came to water again, like the amphibians that they are. A "leatherneck" at the wheel, a khaki-clad band playing airs the Rhine cliffs never echoed back in former years, a compact mass of happy Yanks packing every corner, they plow placidly up and down the stream which so many of their passengers never dreamed of seeing outside their school-books, dipping their flags to one another as they pass, a rubber-lunged "Y" man pouring out megaphoned tales and legends as each "castled crag," flying the Stars and Stripes or the Tricolor now, loomed into view, rarely if ever forgetting to add that unsuspected little touch of "propaganda," "Burned by the French in 1689." Baedeker himself never aspired to see his land so crowded with tourists and sightseers as it was in the spring of 1919. Now and then a shipload of those *poilus* who waved to us from the shore as we danced and sang and megaphoned our way up through their territory came down past Coblenz, their massed horizon blue so much more tangible than our drab brown, their band playing quite other tunes than ours, the doughboys ashore shrilling an occasional greeting to what they half affectionately, half disdainfully call "the poor Frogs." There was a somewhat different atmosphere aboard these horizon-blue excursion boats than on our own; they seemed to get so much more satisfaction, a contentment almost too deep for words, out of the sight of the *sale Boche* in manacles.

Boatloads of "Tommies" came up to look us over now and then, too, a bit disdainful, as is their nature, but friendly, in their stiff way, for all that, their columns of caps punctuated here and there by the cocked hat of the saucy "Aussies" and the red-banded head-gear of those other un-British Britons from the antipodes who look at first glance so startlingly like our own M. P.'s. Once we were even favored with a call by the sea-dogs whose vigil made this new Watch on the Rhine possible; five "snappy" little submarine-chasers, that had wormed their way up through the canals and rivers of France, anchored down beneath the gigantic monument at the mouth of the Moselle. You have three guesses as to whether or not the Germans looked at them with interest.

It was my good fortune to be able to make two excursions into unoccupied Germany while stationed on the Rhine. Those who fancy the sight of an American uniform beyond our lines was like shaking a red tablecloth in a Spanish bull-ring may be surprised to know that these little jaunts were by no means rare. We went not merely in full uniform, quite without camouflage, but in army automobiles and wholly unarmed—and we came back in a condition which a cockney would pronounce in the same way. The first spin was to Düsseldorf, between two of her Sparticist flurries. Not far above Bonn the landscape changed suddenly from American to British khaki, with a boundary post in charge of a circumspect English sergeant between. Below Cologne, with her swarming "Tommies" and her plump and comely girl street-car conductors and "motormen" in their green-banded Boche caps, we passed scores of the apple-cheeked boy recruits England was sending us to take the place of those who were "fed up with it," and who gazed about them with that wide-eyed interest in every little detail of this strange new land which the traveler would fain keep to the end of his days. It seemed natural to find the British here; one had grown to associate them with the flat, low portions of the country. Far down the river a French post stopped us, but the sentry was so interested in posing before my kodak that he forgot to mention passes, and we were soon speeding on through a narrow horizon-blue belt. The Belgians, who turned the scene to brown again not far beyond, were even less exacting than the *poilus*. At the farther end of the great bridge over the Rhine between Neuss and Düsseldorf they had a score of sentries posted behind barbed-wire entanglements, touching the very edge of the unoccupied city. But our only formality in passing them was to shout over our shoulders, *"Armée américaine!"* that open sesame of western Europe for nearly two years.

Somewhat to our disappointment the atmosphere of Düsseldorf was very little different from that of an occupied city. The ubiquitous small boy surrounded us more densely wherever our car halted; the thronged streets stared at us somewhat more searchingly, but there was little other change in attitude to be noted. Those we asked for directions gave us the same elaborate courtesy and annoying assistance; the shops we entered served us as alertly and at as reasonable prices; the manufacturer we called on listened to our wants as respectfully as any of his fellows in the occupied zone—and was quite as willing to open a credit with the American army. The motto everywhere seemed to be "Business as usual." There was next to nothing to suggest a state of war or siege anywhere within a thousand miles of us— nothing, at least, except a few gaunt youths of the '19 class who guarded railway viaducts and government buildings, still wearing their full trench equipment, including—strange to believe!—their camouflaged iron hats! Postal clerks of the S. O. S. supposed, of course, that all this brand of head-gear had long since crossed the Atlantic. Humanity certainly is quick to recuperate. Here, on the edge of the greatest war in history, with the victorious enemy at the very end of the next street, with red revolution hovering in the air, life went on its even way; merchants sold their wares; street-cars carried their lolling passengers; children homeward bound from school with their books in the hairy cowhide knapsacks we had so often seen doing other service at the front chattered and laughed and played their wayside games.

The return to Coblenz was even more informal than the down-stream trip. Belgian, French, and British guards waved to us to pass as we approached; only our own frontier guard halted us, and from then on our right arms grew weary with returning the salutes that were snapped at us in constant, unfailing succession.

The second trip was a trifle more exciting, partly because we had no permission to carry it as far as we did—playing hooky, which in the army is pronounced "A. W. O. L." keeps its zest all through life—partly because we never knew at what moment the war-battered "Dodge" would fall to bits beneath us, like the old one-horse shay, and leave us to struggle back to our billets as best we could. It was a cold but pleasant Sunday. Up the Rhine to Mainz nothing broke the rhythm of our still robust motor except the M. P. at the old stone arch that separated the American from the broad horizon-blue strip—the two journeys laid end to end made one realize what an enormous chunk of Germany the armistice gave the Allies. We halted, of course, at the cathedral of the French headquarters to see the "Grablegung Christi (1492)," as every one should, listened awhile to the whine of the pessimistic old sexton with his, "Oh, such another war will come again in twenty years or so; humanity is like that," and sped on along a splendid highway to Wiesbaden. The French were making the most of their stay in this garden spot. They let no non-fraternizing orders interfere with enjoying the best the Kurhaus restaurant or cellars, the magnificent, over-ornate opera-house, the beautiful park, even the culture of the better class of German visitors, afforded.

Our pass read Wiesbaden and return, but that would have made a tame day of it. Rejuvenated of heart, if saddened of pocketbook, by the Kurhaus luncheon, we rattled swiftly on to the eastward. In due time we began to pass French outposts, indifferent to our passage at first, then growing more and more inquisitive, until there came one which would not be put off with a flip of the hand and a shouted "*Armée américaine*," but brought us to an abrupt stop with a long, slim bayonet that came perilously near disrupting the even purr of our still sturdy motor. The crucial moment had come. If the French guard could read our pass we were due to turn back forthwith, chagrined and crestfallen. But none of us had ever heard of a French guard who *could* read an American pass, and we presented it with that lofty assurance which only those have not learned who wantonly wasted their time with the A. E. F. in France. The sentry received the pass dubiously, as we expected him to; he looked it over on both sides with an inwardly puzzled but an outwardly wise air, as we knew he would; he called his corporal, as we had foreseen; the corporal looked at the pass with the pretended wisdom of all his kind, handed it back with a courteous "*Bien, messieurs*," as we were certain he would, and we sped on "into Germany."

It was a bland and sunny afternoon. The suburban villages of Frankfurt were waddling about in their Sunday best, the city itself was promenading its less dowdy holiday attire along the wide, well-swept streets. We brought up at a square overlooked by a superbly proportioned bronze gentleman who had lost every stitch of his attire except his "tin hat," where we left the car and mingled with the throng. Passers-by directed us courteously enough to the "Goethehaus." Its door-bell handle dangled loosely, as it had fifteen years before, but a sign informed us that the place was closed on Sunday afternoons. The scattered crowd that had paused to gaze at our strange uniforms told us to come next day, or any other time than Sunday afternoon, and we should be admitted at once. We did not take the trouble to explain how difficult it would be for us to come another day. Instead, we strolled nonchalantly through the thickening throng and fell in with the stream of promenaders along the wide main street. There were four of us—Colonel— but never mind the name, for this one happened to be a perfectly good colonel, and he may still be in the army—and three other officers. We—or, more exactly, our uniforms—attracted a decided attention. The majority stared at us vacantly or with puzzled airs; now and then we saw some man of military age whisper our identity to his companion. No one gave any indication of a desire to molest us. Yet somehow the atmosphere about us was considerably more tense than in Düsseldorf. Twice we heard a *"verdammte"* behind us, but as one of them was followed by the word *"Engländer"* it may have been nothing worse than a case of mistaken identity. Still there was something in the air that whispered we had best not prolong our call beyond the dictates of good taste.

The shop-windows were fully as well stocked as those of Cologne or Coblenz; the strollers, on the whole, well dressed. Their faces, in the expert opinion of the colonel, showed no more signs of malnutrition than the average crowd of any large city. Here and there we passed a sturdy, stern-faced sailor, a heavy Browning or Luger at his side, reminding us that these men of the sea—or of the Kiel Canal—had taken over the police duties in many centers. Otherwise nothing met the eye or ear that one would not have seen in Frankfurt in days of peace.

As we were retracing our steps, one of my companions stepped across the street to ask directions to a fashionable afternoon-tea house. He returned a moment later beside a gigantic, heavily armed soldier-policeman. The fellow had demanded to see our passes, our permission to visit Frankfurt. Now, in the words of the American soldier, we had no more permission to visit Frankfurt "than a rabbit." But this was the last place in the world to betray that fact. The pass to Wiesbaden and return I had left in the car. I showed great eagerness to take the policeman to see it. He gave evidence of a willingness to accept the invitation. We were on the point of starting when a more dapper young soldier-guard, a sergeant, appeared. The giant clicked his heels sharply and fell into the background. The sergeant spoke perfect English, with a strong British accent. He regretted the annoyance of troubling us, but—had we a pass? I showed renewed eagerness to conduct him to the car and show it.

"Not at all. Not at all," he apologized. "As long as you have a pass it's quite all right, you know, quite. Ah, and you have an automobile? Yes, yes, quite, the square where the bronze Hermes is. It's quite all right, I assure you. You will pardon us for troubling you? The Astoria? Ah, it is rather a jaunt, you know. But here is the Café Bauer, right in front of you. You'll find their cakes quite as good, and their music is topping, you know. Not at all. Not at all. It's quite all right, really. So sorry to have troubled you, you know. Good day, sir."

It was with difficulty that we found seats in the crowded café, large as it was. A throng of men and women, somewhat less buoyant than similar gatherings in Paris, was sipping beer and wine at the marble-topped tables. A large orchestra played rather well in a corner. Seidels of good beer cost us less than they would have in New York two years before. The bourgeois gathering looked at us rather fixedly, a bit languidly. I started to light a cigar, but could not find my matches. A well-dressed man of middle age at the next table leaned over and lighted it for me. Two youthful students in their gay-colored caps grinned at us rather flippantly. A waiter hovered about us, bowing low and smirking a bit fatuously whenever we spoke to him. There was no outward evidence to show that we were among enemies. Still there was no wisdom in playing too long with fire, once the initial pleasure of the game had worn off. It would have been hard to explain to our own people how we came to be in Frankfurt, even if nothing worse came of another demand for our passes. Uncle Sam would never suffer for the loss of that "Dodge," but he would be quite apt to show extensive inquisitiveness to know who lost it. The late afternoon promenade at the Kurhaus back in Wiesbaden was said to be very interesting. We paid our reckoning, tipped our tip, and wandered casually back to the square graced by the bronze young man whose equipment had gone astray. To say that we were surprised to find the car waiting where we had left it, the doughboy-chauffeur dozing in his seat, would be putting it too strongly. But we were relieved.

The Kurhaus promenade was not what it was "cracked up to be," at least not that afternoon. But we may have been somewhat late. The opera, beginning at six, was excellent, lacking something of the lightness of the same performance in Paris, but outdoing it in some details, chiefly in its mechanical effects. One looked in vain for any suggestion of under-nourishment in the throng of buxom, "corn-fed" women and stodgy men who crowded the house and the top-heavily decorated foyer during the *entr'actes*. Frenchmen in uniform, from generals to *poilus*, gave color to the rather somber audience and made no bones of "fraternizing" with the civilians—particularly if she chanced to be beautiful, which was seldom the case. American officers were numerous; there were Englishmen, "Anzacs," Belgians, Italians, and a Serb or two. The after-theater dinner at the Kurhaus was sumptuous, except in one detail; neither bribery nor pleading could win us the tiniest slice of the black war-bread that was stintingly served to those with bread-tickets.

Otherwise "wine, women, and song" were as much in evidence as if war had never come to trouble the worldly pleasures of Wiesbaden.

We left after ten, of a black night. Our return trip, by direct route, took us through a strip of neutral territory. We were startled some eight or ten times by a stentorian "*Halte!*" at improvised wooden barriers, in lonely places, by soldiers in French uniforms who were not Frenchmen, and who could neither speak any tongue we could muster nor read our pass. They were French colonials, many of them blacker than the night in which they kept their shivering vigil. Most of them delayed us a matter of several minutes; all of them carried aside their clumsy barriers and let us pass at last with bad grace. Nearing Coblenz, we were halted twice by our own soldiers, stationed in pairs beside their blazing fires, and at three in the morning we scattered to our billets.

Two cartoons always come to mind when I look back on those months with the American Watch on the Rhine. One is French. It shows two *poilus* sitting on the bank of the famous stream, the one languidly fishing, with that placid indifference of the French fisherman as to whether or not he ever catches anything; the other stretched at three-fourths length against a wall and yawning with ennui as he remarks, "And they call this the Army of *Occupation!*" The other drawing is American. It shows Pershing in 1950. He is bald, with a snowy beard reaching to his still soldierly waist, while on his lap he holds a grandson to whom he has been telling stories of his great years. Suddenly, as the erstwhile commander of the A. E. F. is about to doze off into his afternoon nap, the grandson points a finger at the map, demanding, "And what is that red spot in the center of Europe, grandpa?" With one brief glance the old general springs to his feet, crying, "Great Cæsar! I forgot to relieve the Army of Occupation!"

Those two squibs are more than mere jokes; they sum up the point of view of the soldiers on the Rhine. The French, and like them the British and Belgians, only too glad that the struggle that had worn into their very souls was ended at last, had settled down to all the comfort and leisure consistent with doing their full duty as guardians of the strip intrusted to them. The Americans, like a team arriving at a baseball tournament so late that they could play only the last three innings, had gone out on the field to bat up flies and play a practice game to take some of the sting out of the disappointment of finding the contest over before they could make better use of their long and arduous training. It was this species of military oakum-picking that was the second grievance of the American soldier on the Rhine; the first was the uncertainty that surrounded his return to the land of his birth. While the neighboring armies were walking the necessary posts and sleeping many and long naps, our soldiers had scarcely found time to wash the feet that had carried them from the trenches to the Rhine, much less cure them of their blisters, when orders swept over the Army of Occupation calling for long hours of intensive training six days a week. It is said that an English general on an inspection tour of our area watched this mile after mile of frenzied trench-digging, of fake bombing-parties, of sham battles the barrages of which still made the earth tremble for a hundred miles around, of never-ending "Squads east and squads west," without a word, until he came to the end of the day and of his review. Then he remarked:

"Astounding! Extraordinary, all this, upon my word! You chaps certainly have the vim of youth. But ... ah ... er ... if you don't mind telling me, just what are you planning to do? Fight your way back through France?"

V
GETTING NEUTRALIZED

There is an aged saying to the effect that the longest way round is often the shortest way home. It applies to many of the crossroads of life. Toward the end of March I found myself facing such a fork in my own particular footpath. My "duties" with the Army of Occupation had slowed down to a point where I could only write the word between quotation-marks and speak it with a throaty laugh. I suggested that I be sent on a walking trip through unoccupied Germany, whence our information was not so meager as contradictory. It would have been so simple to have dropped into the inconspicuous garb of a civilian right there in Coblenz, and to have slipped noiselessly over the outer arc of our bridgehead. Eventually, I believe, the army would have adopted the suggestion. There were times when it showed an almost human interest in the project. But I am of an intensely selfish, self-centered disposition; I wanted to try the adventure myself, personally. Besides, there was no certainty that my grandson would care for that species of sport. He might be of quite the opposite temperament—a solid, respectable, church-going, respected citizen, and all that sort of thing, you know. Furthermore, I had not yet taken the first preliminary, indispensable step toward acquiring a grandson. Wherefore, in a lucid moment, I recalled the moth-eaten adage above plagiarized, and concluded that the easiest way to get "over into Germany" was to turn my back on the Rhine and return to France.

It may be that my offer to relieve Uncle Sam from the burden of my support caught the authorities napping. At any rate, the application sailed serenely over the reef on which I fully expected to see it hopelessly shipwrecked, and a week later I was speeding toward that village in central France known to the A. E. F. as the "canning factory."

Relieved for the first time in twenty-three months of the necessity of awaiting authority for my goings and comings, I returned a fortnight later to Coblenz. It would not have been difficult to sneak directly over our line into unoccupied territory. I knew more than one forest-hidden loophole in it. But that would scarcely have been fair to my erstwhile colonel—and with all his faults the colonel had been rather decent. Besides, while that would have been the more romantic thing, it might not have led to as long and unhampered a stay in Germany as a more orderly and gentlemanly entrance.

Of the two neutralizing points, that to the north was reputed the more promising. The express to Cologne sped across white fields that belied the calendar and gave the heavily blossomed cherry- and apple-trees the appearance of being laden with clinging snow. The more brassy British khaki took the place of our own, the compartment groups changed gradually from American to English officers. The latter were very young, for the most part, and one scarcely needed to listen to their almost childish prattle of their work and things warlike to know that they were not veterans. Long freight-trains crowded with still younger Britishers, exuding the extreme callowness of the untraveled insular youth, rattled into town with us from a more northern direction, happy to take the place of the grim and grizzled warriors that were being demobilized. In the outskirts of the city Germans of both sexes and all ages were placidly yet diligently toiling in their little garden patches into the twilight of the long spring day.

The British, rating me a correspondent, billeted me in a once proud hotel in the shadow of the great cathedral. In the scurry of pursuing passport and visées in Paris I had found no time to change my garb to the kind that flaps about the ankles. In consequence my evening stroll was several times broken by as many of England's boyish new guardsmen, their bayonets overtopping them by several inches in some cases, who pounded their rifle-butts on the pavement in salute and stage-whispered a bit tremulously:

"Officers is not to walk about too much by theirselves, sir."

My query at the first warning had been answered with a:

"Three of them was badly cut up last night, sir."

There were no outward signs of any such serious enmity, however; on the contrary, the populace seemed almost friendly, and at the officers' club guests were checking their side-arms with the German doorman.

The tall and hearty Irish guardsman in charge of British Rhine traffic readily granted my request to go down the river in one of the daily steamers carrying troops back to "Blighty" for demobilization. That day's boat floundered under the simple little name of *Ernst Ludwig Gross Herzog von Hessen und bei Rhein*! I believe the new owners called it *Louie*. A score of German girls came down to the wharf to wave the departing "Tommies" farewell. All day we passed long strings of barges flying the triangular flag of the Food Commission, bearing supplies for the Army of Occupation and the civilian population of the occupied region. The time was but a few weeks off when the arteries of the Third Army flowing through France would be entirely cut off. The food on board the *Louie* was not unlike our own army ration; the bunks supplied the officers were of a sort that would have moved our own more exacting wearers of the "Sam Browne" to start a Congressional investigation. The most noticeable differences between this Blighty-bound multitude and our own doughboys were three in number—their lack of inventiveness in amusing themselves, their lower attitude toward women, and the utter lack of care of the teeth, conspicuous even among the officers.

We should have been hard put to it, however, to find a higher type than the youthful captains and lieutenants in charge of the steamer.

At five we halted for the night beside several huge barges anchored well out in the stream, their holds filled with very passable bunks—as soldiering goes. While the Tommies, pack-laden, clambered down the half-dozen narrow hatches to their light quarters, I dropped in on the families that dwelt in the stern of each. Those who have never paid a similar call might be surprised to find what homelike comfort reigns in these floating residences. Outwardly the barges are of the plainest and roughest, coal-carriers for the most part, with all the smudge and discomfort of such occupation. As the lower house door at the rear opens, his eyes are prepared to behold something about as inviting as the forecastle of a windjammer. Instead they are all but dazzled by the immaculate, housewifely cleanliness, the orderly comfort of the interior. The Rhine-plying dwelling is a close replica of a "lower middle-class" residence ashore—a half-dozen rooms, carpeted, lace-curtained, the walls decorated with family portraits, elaborate-framed mottoes and over-colored statuettes of the Catholic faith, a great square bed of inviting furnishings in the parental room, smaller though no less attractive ones in the other sleeping-chambers, easy-chairs, the latest thing in kitchen ranges, large lamps that are veritable chandeliers suspended from the ceiling—nothing was missing, down to the family cat and canary.

It was noticeable that though the barges had been commandeered by their army and they never lost sight of the fact that their owners were "the enemy," the English officers were meticulously courteous in requesting permission to enter the family cabins. Your Britisher never forgets that a man's home is his castle. One could not but wonder just what the attitude of a German officer would have been under reversed conditions, for the same motto is far less deeply ingrained in the Teuton character. The barge nearest the steamer was occupied by a family with five children, the oldest aged fourteen, all born on board, at as many points of the vessel's constant going and coming between Rotterdam and Mannheim. Two of them were at school in the town in which the family was registered as residents, where the parental marriage was on record, where the father reported when the order of mobilization called him to arms. The oldest had already been entered as "crew," and was preparing to follow in his father's footsteps—if the expression be allowed under the circumstances.

When they had arranged themselves for the night, the "Tommies" returned on board the steamer for a two-hour entertainment of such caliber as could be aroused from their own midst. There were several professional barn-storming vaudeville performers among them, rather out of practice from their long trench vigils, but willing enough to offer such talents as they still possessed. Nor were the amateurs selfish in preserving their incognito. It was simple fare, typified by such uproarious jokes as:

"'Ungry, are you? Well, 'ene, 'ere's a piece of chalk. Go draw yourself a plate of 'am an' eggs."

But it all served to pass the endless last hours that separated the war-weary veterans from the final ardently awaited return to "the old woman an' the kids."

The tramp of hundreds of hobnailed shoes on the deck over our heads awoke us at dawn, and by the time we had reached the open air Germany had been left behind. It needed only the glimpse of a cart, drawn by a dog, occupied by a man, and with a horse hitched behind—a genuine case of the cart before the horse—trotting along an elevated highway, sharp-cut against the floor-flat horizon, to tell us we were in Holland. Besides, there were stodgy windmills slowly laboring on every hand, to say nothing of the rather unprepossessing young Dutch lieutenant, in his sickly gray-green uniform, who had boarded us at the frontier, to confirm the change of nationality of Father Rhine. The lieutenant's duties consisted of graciously accepting an occasional sip of the genuine old Scotch that graced the sideboard of the youthful commanding officer, and of seeing to it that the rifles of the Tommies remained under lock and key until they reached their sea-going vessel at the mouth of the river—a task that somehow suggested a Lilliputian sent to escort a regiment of giants through his diminutive kingdom.

In the little cluster of officers on the upper deck the conversation rarely touched on war deeds, even casually, though one knew that many a thrilling tale was hidden away in their memories. The talk was all of rehabilitation, rebuilding of the civilian lives that the Great Adventure had in so many cases all but wholly wrecked. Among the men below there was more apathy, more silent dreaming, interspersed now and then by those crude witticisms with which their class breaks such mental tension:

"These 'ere blinkin' Dutch girls always makes me think as 'ow their faces 'ave been mashed by a steam-roller an' their bloomin' legs blowed up with a bicycle pump, so 'elp me!"

The remark might easily be rated an exaggeration, but the solid *Jongvrouws* who clattered their wooden-shod way along the banks could not in all fairness have been called delicate.

I was conscious of a flicker of surprise when the Dutch authorities welcomed me ashore without so much as opening my baggage—particularly as I was still in uniform. The hotel I chose turned out to be German in ownership and personnel. Steeped in the yarns of the past five years, I looked forward to at least the excitement of having spies go through my baggage the moment

I left it unguarded. Possibly they did; if so, they were superhumanly clever in repacking the stuff as they found it.

If I had been so foolish as to suppose that I could hurry on at once into Germany I should have been sadly disappointed. The first of the several duties before me was to apply to the police for a Dutch identity card. Without it no one could exist at liberty in nor leave the flat little kingdom. As usually happens in such cases, when one is in a hurry, the next day was Sunday. The chief excitement in Rotterdam on the day of rest was no longer the Zoo, but the American camp, a barbed-wire inclosure out along the wharves about which the Dutchman and his wife and progeny packed a dozen rows deep to gaze at doughboys tossing baseballs or swinging boxing-gloves, with about as much evidence of the amusement as they might show before a Rembrandt or a Van Dyck painting. Naturally so hilarious a Sabbath passes swiftly for a man eager to be elsewhere!

There were, of course, the window displays of the closed shops, of unfailing interest to any one long familiar only with warring lands. No wonder these placid Dutchmen looked so full-cheeked and contented. Though a tradesman may have found some things missing, to the casual eye there were apparently none of the material good things of life that could not be had in superabundance. Butter, eggs, cakes, bonbons, fat bacon, meat of every species, sweets of all kinds, soap as good and as cheap as before the war, cigarettes, cigars, and tobacco enough to have set all France to rioting, all those little dainties which the gormands of the belligerent countries had ceased even to sigh for, were here tantalizingly spread out for block after block, street after street. Restaurants ostentated menu-cards offering anything a hungry man could pay for; milk was to be had every few yards at ten Dutch cents a glass. One had something of the sensation that would come from seeing diamonds and gold nuggets strewn along the way just around the corner from the abode of a band of unsuccessful yeggmen. With the caution bred of nineteen months in France I had filled the interstices of my baggage with chocolate and cigars. It was like carrying gloves to Grenoble. Nothing was more abundantly displayed in the windows of Rotterdam than those two articles.

A closer inspection, however, showed that Holland had not entirely escaped the secondary effects of the war. The milk that still sold so cheaply showed a distinct evidence now of too close an alliance between the herd and the pump. If the restaurants were fully supplied from *hors-d'œuvre* to coffee, the aftermath was a very serious shock to the financial system. There seemed, moreover, to be no place where the average rank and file of laboring humanity could get its wholesome fill for a reasonable portion of its income. The bonbons were a trifle pasty; the cigars not only as expensive as across the Atlantic—which means manyfold more than the old Dutch prices—they were far more inviting behind a plate-glass than when burning in front of the face. The clothing that was offered in such abundance usually confessed frankly to membership in the shoddy class. Suspenders and garters had all but lost their elasticity; shoes—except the more popular Dutch variety—had soared to the lofty realms to which all articles of leather have ascended the world over. Bicycles, the Dutchman's chief means of locomotion, however, seemed as easily within reach as if the far-spread "rubber crisis" had never discovered this corner of Europe.

Yet on the whole these happy, red-cheeked, overfed Dutchmen did not seem to have a care in the world. Their attitude toward the American uniform appeared to be cold, at best not above indifference, though the new doughboy weekly credited them with genuine friendliness. One got the impression that they were pro-Ally or pro-Boche interchangeably, as it served their own interests—which after all is quite in keeping with human nature the world round. The most serious task of the American detachment was to prevent the supplies destined for hungry Europe beyond from dwindling under the hands of the Dutch stevedores who transhipped them. It would, perhaps, be unfair to call the stodgy little nation a war profiteer, yet there were suggestions on all sides that it had not always scorned to take advantage of the distress of its neighbors. I may be prejudiced, but I did not find the Hollanders what the Spaniards calls *simpático*, not even so much as I had fifteen years before. If I may so express it, the kingdom left the same impression one feels upon meeting an old classmate who has amassed wealth in some of the quicker, less laborious methods our own land affords. One rejoices, in a way, at his prosperity, yet one feels more in tune with the less "successful" old-time friend who has been mellowed by his fair share of adversities.

Monday, though it was the last day of April, shivered under a ragged blanket of wet snow. The line-up at the police station was international and it was long. Furthermore, the lieutenants behind the extemporized wickets were genuinely Dutch; they neither gossiped nor loafed, yet they did not propose to let the haste of a disorderly outside world disturb their racial serenity or jar their superb penmanship. They preserved the same sense of order amid the chaos that surrounded their tight little land as the magnificent policemen directing traffic in the main streets outside, who halted the stranger inadvertently following the wrong sidewalk with a courteous but exceedingly firm "You are taking a valk on the *rhight* side of the street, pleasse." In the course of two hours I reached a wicket—only to find that I needed two photographs. By the time I had been mugged and reached the head of the international line again another day had drifted into the irredeemable past.

It was not easy to get the Hollander to talk of the war and its kindred topics, even when one found him able to speak some better-known tongue than his own. He seemed to hold the subject in some such abhorrence as cultured persons do the latest scandal, or, more exactly, perhaps, to look upon it as a highly successful soap manufacturer does the plebeian commodity on which his social superstructure is erected. Americans who had been in the country long enough to penetrate a bit below the surface were inclined to think that, if he had any other feeling than pro-Dutch, he leaned a little to the eastward. Especially, however, was he interested in seeing to it that both sides were given an equal opportunity of eating undisturbed at his table—and paying well for the privilege. In a mild way a clean and orderly hotelkeeper housing two rival football teams would have displayed the same attitude.

But gibes at either side were not wholly tabooed. At an alleged "musical comedy" in a local theater the scene that produced the most audible mirth depicted the erstwhile Kaiser and Crown Prince—excellently mimed down to the crippled arm of the one and the goat-face of the other—enjoying the bucolic hospitality of their land of refuge. The father, dressed in one of the most gorgeous of his innumerable uniforms, stood at a convenient block, splitting kindling with a one-handed hatchet; the son, in wooden shoes and a Zuyder Zee cap, sat on a pierhead serenely fishing. Above their heads stood a road-sign pointing in opposite directions to:

"PARIS—45,000 kilometers; CALAIS—75,000 kilometers."

Their extended quarrel on who started the war, and why, brought no evidence of pro-German sympathy from the audience. It was easy to imagine the horrified protest from the German Legation which such a skit would have brought down upon the producer's head a year before. A scene that caused little less mirth showed a Dutch frontier guard so hoary with service that their clothing had sprouted toadstools and their feet barnacles.

The more widely I inquired the more unlikely seemed the possibility of getting into Germany. This was in keeping with my experiences in other lands, had I stopped to think of it, where it had always proved simpler to dash forward on a difficult trip first and make inquiries afterward. Our consulate in Rotterdam had no suggestions to offer and advised me to see our Legation at The Hague. An excellent train, showing no evidence that the world had ever been at war, set me down at the Dutch capital an hour later.

"You want to get into Germany?" queried the Legation, with elevated eyebrows. "Well, all we can say is God bless you!"

A deeper probing, however, showed that this was only the official voice speaking.

"Personally," continued the particular secretary to whom I had appealed, with a decided accent on the word, "I would suggest that you see the German Legation. Officially, of course, we do not know that any such place exists, but—I have heard—quite unofficially—that there is a Herr Maltzen there who.... But of course you could not call on him in American khaki...."

I came near making the *faux pas* of asking where the German Legation was situated. Of course the secretary could not have known officially. The first passer-by outside, however, readily pointed it out to me—just around the corner. By the time I had returned to Rotterdam and outfitted myself in civilian garb carefully adjusted to pass muster at so exacting a function as a German official visit and at the same time not to suggest wealth to fellow-roadsters should I succeed in entering the Empire, another day had been added to my debit column.

On the train to The Hague next morning I tested the disguise which exceedingly European clothing, a recently acquired mustache, and the remnants of a tongue I had once spoken rather fluently afforded by playing German before my fellow-passengers. To all outward appearances the attempt was successful, but try as I would I saw a German spy in every rosy-cheeked, prosperous Dutchman who turned his bovine eyes fixedly upon me. Herr Maltzen's office hours were not until five in the afternoon. When at last I was ushered into his august presence I summoned my best German accent and laid as much stress as was becoming on some distant relatives who—the past five years willing—still dwelt within the Empire.

"The primary question, of course," pronounced Herr Maltzen, in the precise, resonant language of his calling, "is, are you German or are you an American?"

"American, certainly," I replied.

"Ah, then it will be difficult, extremely difficult," boomed the immaculate Teuton, solemnly. "Up to nine days ago I was permitted to pass personally on the credentials of foreign correspondents. But now they must be referred to Berlin. If you care to make official application...."

"I hereby do so."

"Unfortunately, it is not so simple as that. The application must be in writing, giving references to several persons of the responsible class in Germany, with a statement of your activities during the war, copies of your credentials...."

"And how soon could I expect the answer?"

"With the very best of luck in two weeks, more probably three or four."

I returned to Rotterdam in a somewhat dazed condition, having left Herr Maltzen with the impression that I had gone to think the problem over. Nor was that a false impression. It was more of a problem than even the suave diplomat suspected. It happened that I had a bare six weeks left for a tramp "over in Germany." If I frittered away three-fourths of them among the placid and contented Dutchmen, there would not be much left except the regret of having given up the privilege of returning home—eventually—under army pay and transportation. Moreover, rumblings from Paris indicated that by that time a trip through Germany would be of slight interest. I retired that night more nearly convinced than ever that I was more properly fitted to become a protectorate under the mandate of some benevolent league of managers for irresponsible persons than to attempt to continue as an autonomous member of society.

Some time in the small hours I was rapped on the forehead with a brilliant idea. So extraordinary an experience brought me to a sitting posture and full wakefulness. The Food Commission had a steamer leaving next day for Danzig. What could be more to my purpose than to drop off there and tramp back to Holland? Among my possessions was an elaborately non-committal letter—I had been given the privilege of dictating it myself—from the "Hoover crowd" in Paris, down toward the end of which it was specifically stated that, while I was *not* connected with the Food Commission, they would be glad if any courtesies could be shown me. Carefully read, it would have made a rather satisfactory prelude to the request of a starving and stranded American to be permitted to buy a half-pound of bacon. Carelessly perused, however, it might easily have been mistaken for a document of some importance, particularly as it was decorated with the imposing letterhead of the "Supreme Economic Council." But I had scarcely expected it to be of use until I had succeeded in jimmying my way into unoccupied Germany.

The Rotterdam section of the Food Commission was quite willing that I go to Danzig—or any other place far enough away to make it impossible for me to further disturb their complicated labors. But their duties ceased when they had seen the relief-ships loaded. The ships themselves were under command of the navy. The buck having thus successfully been passed, I waded through a soggy snow-storm to the imposing Dutch building that housed our officers in blue. An exceedingly courteous naval commander gave the false impression that he was extremely sorry not to be able to grant my request, but the already overcrowded boat, the strict orders against carrying civilians.... In short, I should have realized that red tape is not confined to the khaki-clad half of our fighting forces. I shuffled my way back into the heart of the city in my most downcast mood, tempered far beneath by a sneaking little satisfaction that at least if I could not get into Germany I should run no risk of being boiled in oil by the dreadful Sparticists or tickled to death with garden rakes by a grinning band of almond-eyed Bolsheviki.

This would never do. The sun had already begun its last April descent, and I had surrendered nearly three weeks before the privilege of being able to sit idle and still draw a salary. I resolved that May should not catch me supinely squatting in Rotterdam. The chief bridge was soon burned. At the police station my identity card was stamped "out" so quickly as to have given a sensitive person the impression that the country was only too glad to be rid of him. At least I must leave Holland, and if I left in an easterly direction there was only one place that I could bring up. But what of Herr Maltzen? My dime-novel conception of international espionage pictured him as having set a half-dozen of his most trusted agents to dogging my footsteps. I would outwit them! I hastened back to the hotel and wrote the Teuton envoy an elaborate application for permission to enter Germany, with references, copies of credentials, and touching as gently as possible on my unseemly activities during the war. Unfortunately, I could recall the name and address of only one of those distant German relatives of whom I had boasted; the others I was forced to fake, arousing new misgivings in my penny-dreadful conscience. In conclusion I added the subtle misleader that while awaiting his reply I should make the most of my time by journeying about Holland and possibly elsewhere. Then I tossed into a straw suitcase a few indispensable articles, the confiscation of which I felt I could survive, and dashed for the evening train to the eastern frontier.

To carry out still further my movie-bred disguise I took third-class and mingled with the inconspicuous multitude. There was no use attempting to conceal myself in the coal-bin or to bribe the guard to lend me his uniform, for the train did not go beyond the border. On the platform I met an American lieutenant in full uniform, bound for Hamburg as a courier; but I cut our interview as short as courtesy permitted, out of respect for Herr Maltzen's lynx-eyed agents. The lieutenant's suggestion that I ride boldly with him in first-class comfort gave me a very poor impression of his subtlety. Evidently he was not well read in detective and spy literature. However, there was comfort in the feeling of having a fellow-countryman, particularly one of official standing, within easy reach.

Holland lay dormant and featureless under a soggy snow coverlet. Many of her hundreds of fat cattle wore canvas jackets. Every town and village was gay with flags in honor of the tenth birthday of the Dutch princess, a date of great importance within the little kingdom, though quite unnoticed by the world at large. The prosperous, well-dressed workmen in my compartment, having been inconspicuously let into the secret that I was a German, jokingly-seriously inquired whether I was a Sparticist or a Bolshevik. It was evident that they were too well fed to have any sympathy for either. Then they took to complaining that my putative fatherland did not send them enough coal, asserting that thousands had died in Holland for lack of heat during the past few winters. Beyond Utrecht the long stretch of sterile sand-dunes aroused a well-schooled carpenter whose German was fluent to explain why Holland could not agree to any exchange of territory with Belgium. To give up the strip of land opposite Flushing would mean making useless the strong Dutch fortifications there. The piece farther east offered in exchange looked all very well on the map, but it was just such useless heather as this we were gazing out upon. Holland could not accept a slice of Germany—Emden, for instance—instead, because that would be certain sooner or later to lead to war. Of course, he added, teasingly, Holland could beat Germany with wooden shoes now, but ten years hence it would not be so easy. Besides, the Dutch did not care for a part of Belgium, though the Flemish population was eager to join them. They were quite content to remain a small country. Big countries, like rich individuals, had too many troubles, aroused too much envy. He might have added that the citizens of a small country have more opportunity of keeping in close touch with all national questions, but his own speech was a sufficient demonstration of that fact. He knew, for example, just what portions of the Zuyder Zee were to be reclaimed, and marked them on my map. All the southern end was to be pumped out, then two other strips farther north. But the sections north and south of Stavoren were to be left as they were. The soil was not worth the cost of uncovering it and the river Yssel must be left an outlet to the ocean, a viaduct sufficing to carry the railway to the peninsula opposite.

It may have been the waving flags that turned the conversation to the royal family. A gardener who had long worked for them scornfully branded as canards the rumors in the outside world that the German consort was not popular. The prince was quite democratic—royalty radiates democracy nowadays the world over, apparently—and was so genuinely Dutch that he would not speak German with any one who knew any other tongue. He spoke most of the European ones himself, and in addition Tamil and Hindustani. He took no part whatever in the government—unless he advised the Queen unofficially in the privacy of their own chamber—but was interested chiefly in the Boy Scout movement, in connection with which he hoped to visit the United States after the war. They were a very loving couple, quite as much so as if they were perfectly ordinary people.

By this time the short northern night had fallen. With two changes of cars I rattled on into it and brought up at Oldenzaal on the frontier at a late hour. The American lieutenant put up at the same hotel with me and we discussed the pros and cons of my hopes of getting into Germany. They were chiefly cons. The lieutenant was quite willing for me to make use of his presence consistent with army ethics, and I retired with a slightly rosier view of the situation.

In the morning this tint had wholly disappeared. I could not stir up a spark of optimism anywhere in my system. Army life has a way of sapping the springs of personal initiative. To say that I was 99 per cent. convinced that I would be back in Oldenzaal before the day was over would be an understatement. I would have traded my chances of passing the frontier for a Dutch cigar. I bought a ticket on the shuttle train to the first German station in much the same spirit that a poker-player throws his last dollar into a game that has been going against him since the night before.

As a refinement of cruelty the Dutch authorities submitted us to a second customs examination, even more searching than that at our arrival. They relentlessly ferreted out the foodstuffs hidden away in the most unlikely corners of the smallest luggage, and dropped them under the low counter at their feet. An emaciated woman bearing an Austrian passport was thus relieved of seventeen parcels, down to those containing a half-pound of butter or a slice of cheese. In her case not even her midday train lunch escaped. No one could complain that the blockade requirement against Holland reshipping to Germany was being violated at Oldenzaal. As we passed out the door to the platform a soldier ran his hands up and down our persons in search of suspicious lumps and bulges. My Dutch identity card had been taken away from me; I no longer had the legal right to exist anywhere. Once on the train, however, the food blockade proved to have been less watertight than it had seemed. As usual, the "wise ones" had found means of evading it. Several experienced travelers had provided themselves with official authorization to bring in ten or twelve pounds of *Lebensmittel*. A few others aroused the envy of their fellow-passengers—once the boundary was passed—by producing succulent odds and ends from secret linings of their baggage. One loud-voiced individual asserted that there was much smuggling through the forests beside us. It is not likely, however, that the food that escapes the Oldenzaal search brought much relief to the hunger of Germany.

The thin-faced Austrian woman sat hunched in a far corner of the compartment, noiselessly crying. Two middle-aged Germans of the professor-municipal-employee caste whispered cautiously together on the opposite cushion. As we passed the swampy little stream that marks the boundary they each solemnly gave it a military salute, and from that moment on raised their voices to a quite audible pitch. One displayed a sausage he had wrapped in a pair of trousers. The other produced from a vest pocket a tiny package of paper-soap leaves, each the size of a visiting-card. He pressed three or four of them upon his companion. The latter protested that he could not accept so serious a sacrifice. The other insisted, and the grateful recipient bowed low and raised his hat twice in thanks before he stowed the precious leaves away among his private papers. They passed a few remarks about the unfairness of the food blockade, particularly since the signing of the armistice. One spoke scornfully of the attempt of the Allies to draw a line between the German government and the people—there was no such division, he asserted. But by this time we were grinding to a halt in Bentheim, in all probability the end of my German journey.

The passengers and their hand-luggage jammed toward a door flanked by several German non-coms. and a handsome young lieutenant. I pressed closely on the heels of the American courier. He was received with extreme courtesy by the German lieutenant, who personally saw to it that he was unmolested by boundary or customs officials, and conducted him to the outgoing waiting-room toward which we were all striving. Meanwhile a sergeant had studied my passport, quite innocent of the German visé, dropped it into the receptacle of doubtful papers, and motioned to me to stand back and let the others pass, exactly as I had expected him to do. How ridiculous of me to fancy I could bluff my way through a cordon of German officials, as if they had been French or Italian! Would they shut me up or merely toss me back on the Dutch? The last of my legitimate fellow-passengers passed on into the forbidden land and left me standing quite alone in the little circle of German non-coms. One of them rescued my passport and handed it to the handsome young lieutenant as he returned. He looked at me questioningly. I addressed him in German and slipped the weak-kneed Food Commission letter into his hands. Perhaps—but, alas! my last hope gave a last despairing gasp and died; the lieutenant read English as easily as you or I!

"You see," I began, lamely, "as a correspondent, and more or less connected with the Food Commission, I wished to have a glimpse of the distribution from Hamburg—and I can catch one of their ships back from there to Rotterdam. Then as the lieutenant I am with speaks no German, I offered to act as interpreter for him on the way. I ... I...."

I was waiting, of course, to hear the attentive listener bellow the German version of, "You poor fish! do you think you can pull that kind of bull on *me*!" Instead, he bowed slightly in acknowledgment of my explanation and looked more closely at my passport.

"You should have had this stamped at the German Legation in The Hague," he remarked, softly.

"I did not know until shortly before the train left that the lieutenant was coming," I added, hastily, "so there was no time for that. I thought that, with the letter from the Food Commission also...."

Either I am really very simple—in my particular asinine moments I feel the certainty of that fact—or I have been vouchsafed the gift of putting on a very simple face. The German gazed an instant into my innocent eyes, then glanced again at the letter.

"Yes, of course," he replied, turning toward an experience-faced old *Feldwebel* across the room. "Will you be kind enough to wait a moment?"

This gentle-voiced young officer, whom I had rather expected to kick me a few times in the ribs and perhaps knock me down once or twice with the butt of his side-arm, returned within the period specified and handed my papers back to me.

"I have not the authority myself to pass on your case," he explained. "I am only a *Leutnant,* and I shall have to refer it to the *Oberleutnant* at the *Schloss* in town. I do not think, however, that he will make the slightest difficulty."

I thought differently. The *Ober* would almost certainly be some "hard-boiled" old warrior who would subject me to all those brutalities his underling had for some reason seen fit to avoid. Still there was nothing to do but play the game through.

"I shall send a man with you to show the way," continued the lieutenant. "You have plenty of time; the train does not leave for two hours. Meanwhile you may as well finish the other formalities and be ready to go on when you return."

A customs officer rummaged through my hamper.

"No more soap?" he queried, greedily, as he caught sight of the two bars I possessed. Evidently he had hoped to find enough to warrant confiscation. His next dig unearthed three cakes of commissary chocolate. He carefully lifted them out and carried them across the room. My escapade was already beginning to cost me dearly, for real chocolate is the European traveler's most valuable possession in war-time. He laid the precious stuff on a pair of scales, filled out a long green form, and handed it to me as he carefully tucked the chocolate back in my hamper.

"Forty-five pfennigs duty," he said.

At the current exchange that was nearly four cents!

A second official halted me to inquire how much German money I had in my possession. I confessed to twenty-five hundred marks, and exhibited the thick wad of brand-new fifty-mark *Scheine* I carried like so much stationery in a coat pocket. There was no use attempting to conceal it, for just beyond were the little cabins where passengers were submitted to personal search. Luckily I had left some money behind in Rotterdam, in case they confiscated *all* of this. But the official was making out a new form.

"This," he said, handing it to me, "is a certificate for the amount you are bringing in with you. When you leave Germany take this to any branch of the Reichsbank and get another permitting you to take out with you again whatever is left. Otherwise you can take only fifty marks."

In the cabin next the one I entered a man was buttoning his trousers. Stories of skins being treated to a lemon massage to detect secret writing surged up in my memory. I had no concealed valuables, but I have never learned to submit cheerfully to the indignity of personal search. I turned a grim visage toward the not immaculate soldier who had entered with me.

"Hollander?" he asked, as I prepared to strip.

"American," I admitted, for once regretfully. He would no doubt make the most of that fact.

"Indeed!" he said, his eyes lighting up with interest. "Have you any valuables on your person?" he continued, stopping me by a motion from removing my coat.

"None but the money I have declared," I replied.

"Thank you," he said, opening the door. "That is all. Good day."

A thin soldier with a greenish-gray face and hollow eyes, dressed in field gray that had seen long service, was assigned to conduct me to the *Schloss*. Twice on the way he protested that I was walking too fast for him. A long alleyway of splendid trees led to the town, the population of which was very noticeably thinner and less buoyant of step than the Hollanders a few miles behind. At the foot of an aged castle on a hillock the soldier opened the door of a former lodge and stepped in after me. The military office strikingly resembled one of our own—little except the *feldgrau* instead of khaki was different. A half-dozen soldiers and three or four non-coms. were lounging at several tables sprinkled with papers, ink-bottles, and official stamps. Two typewriters sat silent, a sheet of unfinished business drooping over their rolls. Three privates were "horse-playing" in one corner; two others were loudly engaged in a friendly argument; the rest were reading newspapers or humorous weeklies; and all were smoking. The *Feldwebel* in charge laid his cigarette on his desk and stepped toward me. My guide sat down like a man who had finished a long day's journey and left me to state my own case. I retold my story. At the word "American" the soldiers slowly looked up, then gradually gathered around me. Their faces were entirely friendly, with a touch of curiosity. They asked a few simple questions, chiefly on the subject of food and tobacco conditions in Allied territory. One wished to know how soon I thought it would be possible to emigrate to America. The *Feldwebel* looked at my papers, sat down at his desk with them, and reached for an official stamp. Then he seemed to change his mind, rose, and entered an inner office. A middle-aged, rather hard-faced first lieutenant came out with him. The soldiers did not even rise to their feet. The *Ober* glanced at me, then at my papers in the hands of the *Feldwebel*.

"I see no objection," he said, then turned on his heel and disappeared.

When the *Feldwebel* had indorsed my passport I suggested that he stamp the Food Commission also. A German military imprint would give it the final touch within the Empire, at least for any officials who did not read English well. The under-officer carried out the suggestion without comment, and handed the papers back to me. I had permission to go when I chose.

Before I had done so, thanks to the continued curiosity of the soldiers, the *Oberleutnant* sent word that he wished to see me. I kicked myself inwardly for not having gone while the going was good, and entered his private office. He motioned me to a chair, sat down himself, and fell to asking me questions. They were fully as disconnected and trivial as many an interrogation of prisoners I had heard from the lips of American officers. My respect for the stern discipline and trained staff of the German army was rapidly oozing away. Like his soldiers, the C. O. of Bentheim seemed chiefly interested in the plenitude and price of food and tobacco in France and Belgium. Then he inquired what people were saying in Paris of the peace conditions and how soon they expected them to be ready.

"*Sie kriegen keinen Frieden*—they'll get no peace!" he cried suddenly, with considerable heat, when I had mumbled some sort of answer. Then he abruptly changed the subject, without indicating just what form the lack of peace would take, and returned again to food.

"What will Wilson do about his Fourteen Points?" he interrupted, somewhat later.

"All he can," I answered evasively, having had no private tip on the President's plans.

"Yes, but what *can* he," demanded the German, "against that other pair? We shall all be swamped with Bolshevism—America along with the rest of us!

"Luckily for you the train comes in the morning," he concluded, rising to indicate that the interview was at an end. "You would not have found us here this afternoon. May first is a national holiday this year, for the first time. We are a republic now, with socialistic leanings," he ended, half savagely, half sneeringly.

An hour later I was speeding toward Berlin on a fast express. I had always found that a dash at the heart of things was apt to be surer than a dilly-dallying about the outskirts. Once in the capital, I could lay my plans on a sounder foundation than by setting out on my proposed tramp so near the border. To be sure, I had not ventured to buy a ticket to Berlin at a wicket surrounded by a dozen soldiers who had heard me assert that I was going to Hamburg. But—Dame Fortune seeming to have taken me under her wing for the day—a Dutch trainman with whom I fell into conversation chanced to have such a ticket in his pocket, which he was only too glad to sell. As a matter of fact, I doubt whether the open purchase of the bit of cardboard would have aroused any comment, much less created any difficulties. Looking back on it now from the pinnacle of weeks of travel in all parts of the German Empire, by every possible means of locomotion, that teapot tempest of passing the frontier seems far more than ridiculous. It is possible that the combination of circumstances made admittance—once gained— seem easier than it really is. But I cannot shake off the impression that the difficulties were almost wholly within my own disordered brain—disordered because of the wild tales that had been dished out to us by the Allied press. It was, of course, to the advantage of the correspondents fluttering about the dovecote at the head of Unter den Linden to create the impression that the only way to get into Germany was to cross the frontier on hands and knees in the darkest hour of a dark night at the most swampy and inaccessible spot, with a rabbit's foot grasped firmly in one hand and the last will and testament in the other. The *blague* served at least two purposes—perfectly legitimate purposes at that, from a professional point of view—it made "bully good reading" at home, and it scared off competition, in the form of other correspondents, whose timorous natures precluded the possibility of attempting the perilous passage.

Though it sap all the succeeding pages of the "suspense" so indispensable to continued interest, I may as well confess here as later that I moved about Germany with perfect freedom during all my stay there, far more freely than I could have at the same date in either Allied or neutral countries, that neither detectives nor spies dogged my footsteps nor did policemen halt me on every corner to demand my authority for being at large. Lest he hover menacingly in the background of some timorous reader's memory, embittering any dewdrops of pleasure he may wring from this tale, let me say at once that I never again heard from or of the dreadful Herr Maltzen. Indeed, the castle of Bentheim had scarcely disappeared below the wet green horizon of a late spring when I caught myself grumbling that these simple Germans had wrecked what should have been a tale to cause the longest hair to stand stiffly erect and the most pachydermous skin to develop goose-flesh. Saddest of all—let us have the worst and be done with it—they continued that exasperating simplicity to the end, and left me little else for all my labors than the idle vaporings of a summer tourist.

Contrary to my expectations, the train was an excellent *Schnellzug*, making rare stops and riding as easily as if the armistice conditions had not so much as mentioned rolling-stock. The plush covering of several seats was missing, as beyond the Rhine, but things were as orderly, the trainmen as polite and diligently bent on doing their duty as if they had been under the military command of an exacting enemy. In our first-class compartment there were two American lieutenants in uniform, yet there was not so much as a facial protest that they should be occupying seats while German men and women stood in the corridor. There was, to be sure, a bit of rather cold staring, and once what might have been called an "incident." At Osnabrück we were joined by a cropped-headed young German, wearing the ribbon of the Iron Cross in the lapel of his civilian clothing, but whom a chance word informed us was still a captain, accompanied by two older men. They sat in expressionless silence for a time; then one of the older men said, testily:

"Let's see if we can't find a more congenial compartment. Here there is too much English spoken." And the trio disappeared. As a matter of fact, the English they heard was being chiefly spoken by a Dutch diplomat who had fallen in with us. I could not reflect, however, that to have spoken German in a French train at that date would have been positively dangerous. The lieutenants and the diplomat asserted that they had never before seen any such evidence of feeling among the defeated enemy, and it is the only strained situation of the kind that I recall having witnessed during all my German journey. When we changed cars at Löhne soldiers and civilians gazed rather coldly, as well as curiously, at the lieutenants, yet even when people chatted and laughed with them there was no outward evidence of protest.

There were very few cattle and almost no laborers in the fields, though the holiday may have accounted for the absence of the latter. The landscape looked everywhere well cultivated and there were no signs that any except purposely pasture lands had been allowed to lie fallow. Near Hanover, with its great engine-works, stood hundreds of rusted locomotives which had been refused by the Allies. Among them were large numbers that the Germans had drawn from Russia and which were now useless even to the Teutons, since they were naphtha-burners, and naphtha was no longer to be had within the Empire. Acres upon acres of cars, both passenger and freight, filled another yard—cars from Posen, from Breslau, from München, and from Königsberg, from every corner of Germany. At Nauen the masts of the great wireless station from which we had picked up most of our German news during the war loomed into the evening sky, and beyond were some immense Zeppelin hangars bulking above the flat landscape like distant mountains. We reached Berlin on time and before dark. May-day had brought all city transportation to a standstill; neither taxi, carriage, nor tramcar was to be found—though it was reported that this first official national holiday had been the tamest in years. Farmers' carts and beer wagons had been turned into carryalls and transported a score of passengers each, seated precariously on loose boards, from station to station. Hotels were as packed as they seem to be in all capitals in war-time. The magnificent Adlon, housing the Allied commissions, laughed in my face. For two hours I canvassed that section of the city and finally paid eleven marks for accommodation in a hotel of decayed gentility at the door of which an old sign read: "Fine rooms on the garden, two marks and upward." To be sure, the rate of exchange made the difference considerably less than it seemed— to those who had purchased their marks in the foreign market.

VI
THE HEART OF THE HUNGARY EMPIRE

In many districts of Germany the traveler's eye was frequently drawn, during the hectic spring of 1919, to a large colored poster. It showed two men; the one cold, gaunt, and hungry, huddled in the rags of his old uniform, was shuffling through the snow, with a large, dismally gray city in the background; the other, looking well nourished and cheerful, wearing a comfortable new civilian suit, was emerging from a smoke-belching factory and waving gaily in the air a handful of twenty-mark notes. Under the picture ran the device: "DON'T GO TO BERLIN! There every one is hungry and you will find no work. Instead, go to the nearest government employment office"—the address of the most convenient being added.

Despite this and many similar efforts on the part of the authorities and private agencies, people kept crowding into the capital. Not even a personal appeal from his new "Reichspräsident" Ebert to the ordinarily laborious and persistent German to remain at home and keep at work, rather than to try to better his lot by this vain pilgrimage, succeeded in shutting off the Berlinward stream of discontented humanity. War and social disorders seem always to bring this influx into the national metropolis, the world over. It is man's nature to wander in search of happiness when he is not happy, seldom recognizing that he is carrying his unhappiness with him and that it is but slightly dependent upon the particular spot he inhabits. In this case the general misery was largely due to the gnawings of hunger, and surely Berlin, in the year of grace 1919, was the last place in all Germany in which to seek alleviation from that particular misfortune. Yet the quest of the rainbow end went hopefully on, until the tenements of the capital were gorged with famished provincials and her newspapers teemed with offers of substantial rewards to any one who would furnish information of rooms, apartments, or dwelling-houses for rent.

That Berlin was hungry was all too evident, so patent, in fact, that I feel it my duty to set down in a place apart the gruesome details of famine and warn the reader to peruse them only in the presence of a full-course dinner. But the overcrowding was at first glance less apparent. Indeed, a superficial glimpse of the heart of Prussianism showed it surprisingly like what it had been a decade before. The great outdoor essentials were virtually unaltered. Only as one amassed bit by bit into a convincing whole the minor evidences of change, as an experienced lawyer pieces together the scattered threads of circumstantial proof, did one reach the conclusion that Berlin was no longer what she used to be. Her great arteries of suburban railways, her elevated and underground, pulsated regularly, without even that clogging of circulation that threatened the civic health of her great temperamental rival to the west.

Her shops and business houses seemed, except in one particular, well stocked and prosperous; her sources of amusement were many and well patronized. Her street throngs certainly were not shabby in appearance and they showed no outward signs of leading a hampered existence. True, they were unusually gaunt-featured—but here we are encroaching on ground to be explored under more propitious alimentary circumstances.

Of the revolution, real or feigned, through which it had recently passed, the city bore surprisingly few scars. Three or four government buildings were pockmarked with bullet-holes that carried the mind back to "election" days in the capitals of tropical America; over in Alexanderplatz the bricks and stones flaunted a goodly number of shrapnel and machine-gun wounds. But that was all, or almost all, the proof of violence that remained. The palaces of the late Kaiser stood like abandoned warehouses; the Reichstag building was cold and silent, testifying to a change of venue for the government on trial, if not of régime. Yet it could not, after all, have been much of a "revolution" that had left unscathed those thirty-two immense and sometimes potbellied images of the noble Hohenzollerns, elaborately carved in stone, which still oppressed the stroller along the Sieges Allee in the otherwise pleasant Tiergarten. The massive wooden Hindenburg at the end of it, a veritable personification of brute strength from cropped head to well-planted feet, stared down upon puny mankind as of yore, though, to be sure, he looked rather neglected; the nailing had never been completed and the rare visitors passed him by now without any attempt to hammer home their homage. Farther on that other man of iron gazed away across the esplanade as if he saw nothing in this temporary abandonment of his principles to cause serious misgivings.

But perhaps all this will in time be swept away, for there were signs pointing in that direction. The city council of Berlin had already decreed that all pictures and statues of the Hohenzollerns, "especially those of the deposed Kaiser," must be removed from the public halls and schoolrooms. That of itself would constitute a decided change in the capital. In these first days of May several hundred busts and countless likenesses of Wilhelm II and his family had been banished to the cellars of municipal buildings, not, be it noted, far enough away to make restoration difficult. "Among the busts," said one of the local papers, "are some of real artistic value"—I cannot, of course, vouch for the esthetic sense of the editor—"as for example the marble ones of Kaiser Wilhelm I and of Kaiser Friedrich III, which for many years have adorned the meeting-place of the Municipal Council itself." For all this there was no lack of graven images of the discredited War Lord and his tribe still on exhibition; the portraits "adorning" private residences alone could have filled many more cellars. It would be difficult to eradicate in a few brief months a trade-mark which had been stamped into every article of common or uncommon use.

In return for these artistic losses the city was taking on new decorations, in the form of placards and posters unknown in kaiserly days. To begin with, there were the violent representations in color of what the Bolshevists were alleged to perpetrate on the civil population that fell under their bloody misrule, which stared from every conspicuous wall unprotected by the stern announcement that bill-posting was *verboten*. These all ended with an appeal for volunteers and money to halt "the menace that is already knocking at the eastern gates of the Fatherland." Then there were the more direct enticements to recruits for newly formed *Freicorps*—"the protective home guard," their authors called it—usually named for the officer whose signature as commander appeared at the bottom of the poster. Even the newspapers carried full-page advertisements setting forth the advantages of enrolling in the independent battalion of Major B—— or the splendid regiment of Colonel S——, a far cry indeed from the days of universal compulsory service. "If you will join my company," ran these glowing promises, after long-winded appeals to patriotism, "you will be commanded by experienced officers, such as the undersigned, and you will be lodged, fed, and well paid by the government. What better occupation can you find?" These were the *freiwillige* bands that composed the German army of 1919, semi-independent groups, loosely disciplined, and bearing the name of some officer of the old régime. They may not constitute an overpowering force, but there is always the possibility that some man of magnetism and Napoleonic ambition may gather them all together and become a military dictator. Besides, there is still the trickery of militaristic Germany to be reckoned with, genius for subterfuge that will cover up real training under the pretense of police forces, of turnvereins and of "athletic unions."

Thus far these omnipresent appeals did not seem to have met with overwhelming success. The soldiers guarding Berlin were virtually all boys of twenty or under; the older men were probably "fed up with it." Nor did the insolent Prussian officer of former days any longer lord it over the civilian population. He had laid aside his saber and in most cases his uniform, and perhaps felt safer in his semi-disguise of "civies" as he mingled with the throng. Military automobiles carrying stiff-necked generals or haughty civilians in silk hats still occasionally blasted their way down Unter den Linden as commandingly as ever did the Kaiser, but they were wont to halt and grow very quiet when the plebeian herd became dense enough to demand its right of way.

Before we leave the subject of posters, however, let us take a glimpse at those appealing for aid to the *Kriegs und Zivilgefangenen* which inundated the city. The picture showed a group of German prisoners, still in their red-banded caps and in full uniform—as if the ravages of time and their captors had not so much as spotted a shoulder-strap—peering sadly out through a wire barricade. It was plain to see that some German at home had posed for the artist, the beings he depicted were so pitifully gaunt and hungry in appearance. I have seen many thousand German prisoners in France, and I cannot recall one who did not look far better nourished than his fellow-countrymen beyond the Rhine, more full of health, in fact, than the civilian population about the detention camps. They may regret leaving comparative abundance for their hungry Fatherland, when the day of exodus finally comes. But the Germans at home were greatly wrought up about their eight hundred thousand prisoners. Many had convinced themselves that they would never be returned; the general impression of their sad lot brought continuous contributions to the boys and girls who rattled money-cans in the faces of passers-by, even those who wore an Allied uniform, all over Berlin. Stories of the mistreatment of prisoners were quite as current and fully as heartrending in Germany as they were on the other side of the battle-line. Apparently captives are always mishandled—by the enemy, and too well treated on the side of the speaker, a phenomenon even of our own Civil War. I have no personal knowledge of the lot of Allied prisoners of war in Germany, but this much is certain of those wearing the field gray—that the French neglected them both as to food and work; that the British treated them fairly in both matters, and that the Americans overfed and underworked them. But it was a hopeless task to try to convince their fellow-countrymen that they were not one and all suffering daily the tortures of the damned.

Perhaps the greatest surprise that Berlin had in store for me was the complete safety which her recent enemies enjoyed there. With German delegates to the Peace Conference closely guarded behind barbed wire in Versailles, and German correspondents forbidden even to talk to the incensed crowds that gathered along those barriers, it was astounding to find that American and Allied officers and men, in full uniform, wandered freely about the Prussian capital at all hours. Doughboys were quite as much at home along Unter den Linden as if they had been strolling down Main Street in Des Moines. Young Germans in iron hats guarded the entrance to the princely Adlon, housing the various enemy missions, but any one who chose passed freely in or out, whatever his nationality, his business or lack thereof, or his garb. Olive drab attracted no more attention in Berlin than it did in Coblenz. German chauffeurs drove *poilus* and their officers about the streets as nonchalantly as if they had been taxi-drivers in Paris. To be sure, most uniformed visitors stuck rather closely to the center of town, but that was due either to false impressions of danger or to lack of curiosity—and perhaps also to the dread of getting out of touch with their own food-supply. For as a matter of experience they were fully as safe in Berlin as in Paris or New York—possibly a trifle more so—they seemed to run less risk of being separated, legally or forcibly, from their possessions. The hair-raising tales which correspondents poured out over the wires *via* Copenhagen were chiefly instigated by their clamoring editors and readers at home. Let a few random shots be fired somewhere in the city and the scribes were at ease for another day—and the world gasped once more at the bloody anarchy reigning in Berlin, while the stodgy Berliner went on about his business, totally oblivious of the battle that was supposed to be seething about him.

In January, 1919, a group of American officers entered one of the principal restaurants of Berlin and ordered dinner. At that date our olive drab was rare enough in the capital to attract general attention. A civilian at a neighboring table, somewhat the worse for bottled animosity, gave vent to his wrath at sight of the visitors. Having no desire to precipitate a scene, they rose to leave. Several German officers sprang to their feet and begged them to remain, assuring them that the disturber would be silenced or ejected. The Americans declined to stay, whereupon the ranking German apologized for the unseemly conduct of an ill-bred fellow-countryman and invited the group to be his guests there the following evening.

Now I must take issue with most American travelers in Germany during the armistice that the general attitude of courtesy was either pretense, bidding for favor, or "propaganda" directed by those higher up. In the first place, a great many Germans did not at that date admit that the upstarts who had suddenly risen to power were capable of directing their personal conduct. Moreover, I have met scores of persons who were neither astute enough nor closely enough in touch with those outlining national policies to take part in any concerted plan to curry favor with their conquerors. I have, furthermore, often successfully posed as a German or as the subject of a friendly or neutral power, and have found the attitude toward their enemies not one whit different under those circumstances than when they were knowingly speaking to an enemy.

There were undoubtedly many who deliberately sought to gain advantage by wearing a mask of friendliness; but there were fully as many who declined to depart from their customary politeness, whatever the provocation.

Two national characteristics which revolution had not greatly altered were the habit of commanding rather than requesting and of looking to the government to take a paternal attitude toward its subjects. The stern *Verboten* still stared down upon the masses at every corner and angle. It reminded one of the sign in some of our rougher Western towns bearing the information that "Gentlemen will not spit on the floor; others *must* not," and carrying the implication that the populace cannot be intrusted to its own instincts for decency. If only the German could learn the value of moral suasion, the often greater effectiveness of a "Please" than of an iron-fisted "Don't"! Perhaps it would require a new viewpoint toward life to give full strength to the gentler form among a people long trained to listen only to the sterner admonition. The great trouble with the *verboten* attitude is that if those in command accidentally overlook *verboting* something, people are almost certain to do it. Their atrophied sense of right and wrong gives them no gage of personal conduct. Then there is always the man to be reckoned with who does a thing simply because it *is verboten*—though he is rarely a German.

It is in keeping with this commanding manner that the ruling class fails to give the rank and file credit for common horse sense. Instead of the Anglo-Saxon custom of trusting the individual to take care of himself, German paternalism flashes constantly in his face signs and placards proffering officious advice on every conceivable subject. He is warned to stamp his letters before mailing them, to avoid draughts if he would keep his health; he is *verboten* to step off a tramcar in motion, lest he break his precious neck, and so on through all the possibilities of earthly existence, until any but a German would feel like the victim of one of those motherly women whose extreme solicitude becomes in practice a constant nagging. The Teuton, however, seems to like it, and he grows so accustomed to receiving or imparting information by means of placards that his very shop-windows are ridiculously littered with them. Here an engraved card solemnly announces, "This is a suit of clothes"; there another asserts—more or less truthfully— "Cigars—to smoke." One comes to the point of wondering whether the German does not need most of all to be let alone until he learns to take care of himself and to behave of his own free will. Then he might in time recognize that liberty is objective as well as subjective; that there is true philosophy in the Anglo-Saxon contention that "every man's home is his castle." Perhaps he is already on his way to that goal. There were promising signs that Germany is growing less *streng* than she used to be, more easy-going, more human—unless what seemed to be that was the merely temporary apathy of under-nourishment.

The war had made fewer changes in the public and business world of the Fatherland than in Allied countries. Pariserplatz and Französischestrasse retained their names. Down in Munich the finest park was still the Englische Garten. Most American stocks were quoted in the newspapers. One might still get one's mail—if any arrived—through the American Express Company, though its banking business was in abeyance. The repertoire of the once Royal Opera included the works of Allied composers, given only in German, to be sure, but that was the custom even before the war. Shopkeepers of the tourist-baiting class spoke English or French on the slightest provocation—often with provoking insistence. I found myself suddenly in need of business cards with which to impress the natives, and the first printing-shop furnished them within three hours. When I returned to the capital from one of my jaunts into the provinces with a batch of films that must be developed and delivered that same evening, the seemingly impossible was accomplished. I suggested that I carry them off wet, directly after the hypo bath, washing and drying them in my hotel room in time to catch a train at dawn. Where a Frenchman or an Italian would have thrown up his hands in horror at so unprecedented an arrangement, the amenable Teuton agreed at once to the feasibility of the scheme. Thus commerce strode aggressively on, irrespective of the customer's nationality, and with the customary German adaptability.

Some lines of business had, of course, been hard hit by the war. There was that, for instance, of individual transportation, public or private. Now and then an iron-tired automobile screamed by along Unter den Linden, but though the government was offering machines as cheaply as two thousand marks each, the scarcity and prohibitive price of "benzine" made purchasers rare. In the collections of dilapidated outfits waiting for fares at railway stations and public squares it was a question whether horse, coachman, or carriage was nearest to the brink of starvation. The animals were miserable runts that were of no military use even before the scarcity of fodder reduced them to their resemblance to museum skeletons. The sallow-faced drivers seemed to envy the beasts the handful of bran they were forced to grant them daily. Their vagabond garb was sadly in keeping with the junk on wheels in which they rattled languidly away when a new victim succumbed to their hollow-eyed pleading. Most of Berlin seemed to prefer to walk, and that not merely because the legal fares had recently been doubled. Taxis might have one or two real rubber tires, aged and patched, but still pumpable; the others were almost sure to be some astonishing substitute which gave the machine a resemblance to a war victim with one leg—or, more exactly, to a three-legged dog. The most nearly successful *Ersatz* tires were iron rims with a score of little steel springs within them, yet even those did not make joy-riding popular.

On this subject of *Ersatz*, or far-fetched substitutes for the real thing, many pages might be written, even without trespassing for the moment on the forbidden territory of food. The department stores were veritable museums of *Ersatz* articles. With real shoes costing about sixty dollars, and real clothing running them a close race, it was essential that the salesman should be able to appease the wrathful customer by offering him "something else—er—*almost* as good." The shoe substitutes alone made the shop-windows a constant source of amazement and interest. Those with frankly wooden soles and cloth tops were offered for as little as seven marks. The more ambitious contraptions, ranging from these simple corn-torturers improved with a half-dozen iron hinges in the sole to those laboriously pieced together out of scraps of leather that suggested the ultimate fate of the window-straps missing from railway carriages, ran the whole gamut of prices, up to within a few dollars of the genuine article. Personally, I have never seen a German in *Ersatz* footwear, with the exception of a few working in their gardens. But on the theory of no smoke without some fire the immense stocks displayed all over the country were *prima-facie* evidence of a considerable demand. Possibly the substitutes were reserved for interior domestic use—fetching styles of carpet slippers. On the street the German still succeeded somehow in holding his sartorial own, perhaps by the zealous husbanding of his pre-war wardrobe.

Look where you would you were sure to find some new *Ersatz* brazenly staring you in the face. Clothing, furniture, toys, pictures, drugs, tapestries, bicycles, tools, hand-bags, string, galoshes, the very money in your pocket, were but imitations of the real thing. Examine the box of matches you acquired at last with much patience and diplomacy and you found it marked, "Without sulphur and without phosphorus"—a sad fact that would soon have made itself apparent without formal announcement. The wood was still genuine; thanks to their scientific forestry, the Germans have not yet run out of that. But many of their great forests are thinned out like the hair of the middle-aged male—and the loss as cleverly concealed. There has been much Teutonic boasting on this subject of *Ersatz*, but since the armistice, at least, it had changed to wailing, for even if he ever seriously believed otherwise the German had discovered that the vast majority of his laborious substitutes did not substitute.

As we are carefully avoiding the mention of food, the most grievous source of annoyance to the rank and file of which we can speak here is the lack of tobacco. In contrast with the rest of the country there were plenty of cigars in Berlin—apparently, until one found that the heaps of boxes adorning tobacconists' windows were placarded "*Nur leere Kisten*," or at best were filled with rolls of some species of weed that could not claim the most distant relationship to the fragrant leaf of Virginia. I indulged one day, before I had found the open sesame to the American commissary, in one of the most promising of those mysterious vegetables, at two marks a throw. The taste is with me yet. American officers at the Adlon sometimes ventured to leave food-supplies in the drawers of their desks, but their cigars they locked in the safe, along with their secret papers and real money. In the highest-priced restaurant of Berlin the shout of, "Waiter, bring two cigarettes!" was sure to focus all eyes on the prosperous individual who could still subject his fortune to such extravagance. Here and there along Friedrichstrasse hawkers assailed passers-by with raucous cries of "English and American tobacco!" Which proved not only that the German had lost all national feeling on this painful subject, but that the British Tommy and the American doughboy had brought with them some of the tricks they had learned in France.

These street-corner venders, not merely of the only real tobacco to be publicly had in Berlin, but of newspapers, post-cards, and the like, were more apt than not to be ex-soldiers in field gray, sometimes as high in rank as *Feldwebels*. Many others struggled for livelihood by wandering like gipsies from one cheap café to another, playing some form of musical instrument and taking up collections from the clients, often with abashed faces. Which brings us to the question of gaiety in Berlin. Newspapers, posters, and blazing electric signs called constant attention to countless café, cabaret, cinema, and theater entertainments. Every one of them I visited was well filled, if not overcrowded. On the whole they were distinctly immoral in tone or suggestion. Berlin seems to be running more and more to this sort of thing. There is something amiss in the country whose chief newspaper carries the conspicuous announcement: "NAKEDNESS! Fine artistic postals now ready to be delivered to the trade," or with the city where scores of street-corners are adorned by crowds of men huddled around a sneaking vender of indecent pictures. Similar scenes offend the eye in most large cities the world over, of course, but something seemed to suggest that Berlin was unusually given to this traffic. The French claim that theirs is at heart the moral race and that the Boche is a leader in immorality, and they cite many instances of prisoners found in possession of disgusting photographs as one of the proofs of their contention. Peephole shows were not the least popular of the Berliner's evening amusements. His streets, however, were far freer of the painted stalkers by night than those of Paris, and the outcasts less aggressive in their tactics. Gambling, and with it the police corruption that seems to batten best under the democratic form of government, was reported to be growing apace, with new "clubs" springing up nightly. Under the monarchy these were by no means lacking, but they were more "select," more exclusive—in other words, less democratic. Even the government had taken on a Spanish characteristic in this respect and countenanced a public lottery, ostensibly, at least, for the benefit of "sucklings."

At the middle-class theaters the same rarely musical and never comic inanities that hamper the advancement of histrionic art in other countries still held sway, with perhaps an increasing tendency toward the *risqué*. The crowd roared as of yore, munched its black-bread sandwiches between the acts, and seemed for the moment highly satisfied with life. In contrast there were always seats to be had at the performances of literary merit and at the opera, though the war does not seem to have subjected them to any special hardships. The investment of a ticket at the house of song brought high interest—particularly to the foreigner, for the best orchestra seats were still eight marks at matinées and twelve in the evening, a mere sixty cents or a dollar at the armistice rate of exchange. I remember with especial pleasure excellent performances of "Eurydice" and of "Martha." The audience was a plain, bourgeois gathering, with evening dress as lacking as "roughnecks." In the foyer buffet, in contrast to Paris, prices were exceedingly reasonable, but the most popular offerings, next to the watery beer, were plates of potatoes, bologna, pickled fish, and hard-boiled eggs, for, though I should not mention it here, the German theater-goer of these days is as constantly munching as an Arab. In the gorgeous Kaiser's box sat one lone lieutenant and his wife, while a cold-eyed old retainer in livery kept guard outside the locked door as if he were still holding the place for his beloved emperor.

Though ostensibly the same, German prices were vastly lower for visitors than for the native residents. For the first time I had something of the sensation of being a millionaire—cost was of slight importance. The marks I spent in Germany I bought at an average of two for fifteen cents; had I delayed longer in exchanging I might have had them still cheaper. In some lines, notably in that we are for the moment avoiding, prices, of course, had increased accordingly, sometimes outdistancing the advantages of the low rate of exchange. But the rank and file still clung to the old standards; it was a hopeless task to try to make the man in the street understand that the mark was no longer a mark. He went so far as to accuse the American government of profiteering, because the bacon it was indirectly furnishing him cost 7.50 marks a pound, which to him represented, not fifty-seven cents, but nearly two dollars. The net result of this drop in mark value was that the populace was several degrees nearer indigence. Those who could spend money freely were of three classes—foreigners, war profiteers, and those who derived their nourishment, directly or indirectly, at the public teat. Not, of course, that even those spent real money. There was not a penny of real money in circulation in all Germany. Gold, silver, and copper had all long since gone the way of other genuine articles in war-time Germany, and in their place had come *Ersatz* money. Pewter coins did service in the smallest denominations; from a half-mark upward there were only "shin-plasters" of varying degrees of raggedness, the smaller bills a constant annoyance because, like most of the pewter coins, they were of value only in the vicinity of the municipality or chamber of commerce that issued them. Even the larger notes of the Reichsbank were precarious holdings that required the constant vigilance of the owner, lest he wake up some morning to find that they had been decreed into worthless paper.

But I am getting far ahead of my story. Long before I began to peer beneath the surface of Berlin I had to face the problem of legalizing even my superficial existence there. On the very morning after my arrival I hastened to grim-sounding Wilhelmstrasse, uncertain whether my next move would be toward some dank underground dungeon or merely a swift return to the

Dutch border. The awe-inspiring Foreign Office consisted of several adult school-boys and the bureaucrat-minded underlings of the old régime. A Rhodes scholar, who spoke English somewhat better than I, greeted my entrance with a formal heartiness, thanked me for adding my services to the growing band that was attempting to tell a long-deceived world the truth about Germany, and dictated an *Ausweis* which, in the name of the Foreign Office backed by all the authority of the new national government, gave me permission to go when and where I chose within the Empire, and forbade any one, large or small, to put any difficulties whatever in my way. Like a sea monster killed at the body, but with its tentacles still full of their poisoning black fluid, Wilhelmstrasse seemed to have become innocuous at home long before its antennæ, such as the dreadful Herr Maltzen at The Hague, had lost their sting.

If it had been a great relief to see the eyes of passers-by fade inattentively away at sight of me in my civilian garb, after two years of being stared at in uniform, it was doubly pleasant to know that not even the minions of the law could now question my most erratic wandering to and fro within the Fatherland. With my blanket *Ausweis* I was not even required to report to the police upon my arrival in a new community, the *Polizeiliche Anmeldung* that is one of the banes of German existence. I was, of course, still expected to fill out the regulation blank at each hotel or lodging-house I occupied, but this was a far less troublesome formality than the almost daily quest for, and standing in line at, police stations would have been. These hotel forms were virtually uniform throughout the Empire. They demanded the following information of each prospective guest: Day of arrival; given and family name; single, married, or widowed; profession; day, month, year, town, county, and land of birth; legal residence, with street and number; citizenship (in German the word is *Staatsangehörigkeit*, which sounds much more like "Property of what government?"); place of last stay, with full address; proposed length of present stay; whether or not the registering guest had ever been in that particular city or locality before; if so, when, why, and how long, and residence while there. But under the new democracy hotelkeepers had grown somewhat more easy-going than in years gone by, and their exactions in this respect never became burdensome.

It was soon evident that the man in the street commonly took me for a German. In Berlin I was frequently appealed to for directions or local information, not to mention the requests for financial assistance. To my surprise, my hearers seldom showed evidence of detecting a foreign accent, particularly when I spoke with deliberate care. Even then I was usually considered a German from another province, sometimes a Dane, a Hollander, or a Scandinavian. Now and again I assumed a pose out of mere curiosity, and often "got away with it." "You are from ———" (the next town)?

was a frequent query, with a tinge of doubt in the tone. "No, I am from Mechlenburg"—or some other distant corner of Germany, I sometimes answered; to which the response was most likely to be, "Ah yes, I noticed that in your speech." Now and again I let a self-complacent inquirer answer for me, as was the case with a know-it-all waiter in a Berlin dining-room, who proved his infallible ability to "size up" guests with the following cocksure assumptions, which he solemnly set down in his food-ticket register: "*Sie sind Holländer, nicht?*" "*Jawohl.*" "*Kaufmann?*" "*Jawohl.*" "*Aus Amsterdam?*" "*Jawohl.*" "*Unverheiratet?*" "*Jawohl,*" and so on to the end of the list. It is never good policy to peeve a man by showing him up in public. During my first few days in unoccupied Germany I fancied it the part of wisdom to at least passively disguise my nationality, but the notion soon proved ridiculous, and from then on, with only exceptions enough to test certain impressions, I went out of my way to announce my real citizenship among all classes and under all circumstances.

You can learn much of a country by reading its "Want Ads." Thus the discovery that the most respectable newspaper of Rio de Janeiro runs scores of notices of "Female Companion Wanted," or "Young Lady Desires Protector," quickly orientates the moral viewpoint in Brazil. In Berlin under the armistice the last pages of the daily journals gave a more exact cross-section of local conditions than the more intentional news columns. There were, of course, countless pleas for labor of any description, the majority by ex-soldiers. Then came offers to sell or exchange all manner of wearing apparel, "A REAL SILK HAT, still in good condition"; "A black suit of real peace-time cloth"; "A second-hand pair of boots or shoes, such a size, of REAL LEATHER!" "Four dress shirts, NO WAR WARES, will be exchanged for a working-man's blouse and jumper," was followed by the enticement (here, no doubt, was the trail of the war profiteer), "A pair of COWHIDE boots will be swapped for a Dachshund of established pedigree." Farther down were extraordinary opportunities to buy *Leberwurst, Blutwurst, Jagdwurst, Brühwürstchen,* and a host of other appetizing garbage, without meat-tickets. But the most persistent advertisers were those bent on recouping their fortunes by marrying money. It is strange if any new war millionaire in Germany has not had his opportunity to link his family with that of some impoverished one of noble lineage. In a single page of the *Berliner Tageblatt,* which carries about one-tenth the type of the same space in our own metropolitan dailies, there were eighty-seven offers of marriage, some of them double or more, bringing the total up to at least one hundred. Many of them were efforts, often more pathetic than amusing, by small merchants or tradesmen, just returned from five years in uniform, to find mates who would be of real assistance in re-establishing their business. But a considerable number aroused amazement that the wares offered had not been snapped up long ago. I translate a few taken at random:

MERCHANT, 38 years, Christian, bachelor, idealist, lover of nature and sports, fortune of 300,000 marks, wishes to meet a like-minded, agreeable young lady with corresponding wealth which is safely invested. Purpose: MARRIAGE.

FACTORY OWNER, Ph.D., Evangelical, 31, 1 meter 75, fine appearance, reserve officer, sound, lover of sports, humorous and musical, 400,000 marks property, seeks a LIFE COMPANION of like gifts and property in *safe* investments.

Intelligent GENTLEMAN, handsome, splendid appearance, blond, diligent and successful merchant, winning personality, Jewish, etc....

Will a BEAUTIFUL, prominent, artistic, musical, and property-loving woman in her best years make happy an old man (Mosaic) of wealth?

This modest old fellow had many prototypes. Now and then a man, and the women always, were offered by third parties, at least ostensibly, half the insertions beginning, "For my sister"; "For my daughter"; "For my beautiful niece of twenty-two"; "For my lovely sister-in-law"; and so on. Some looked like the opportunity of a lifetime:

I seek for my house physician, aged 55, a secure existence with a good, motherly woman of from 30 to 50....

A neat little BLONDE of 19 with some property seeks gentleman (Jewish) for the purpose of later marriage....

For a BARONESS of 23, orphan, ¾-MILLION property, later heiress of big real estate....

If the demands of my calling had not kept me so busy I should have looked into this splendid opportunity myself; or into the next one:

Daughter of a BIG MERCHANT, 22, ONE MILLION Property....

But, after all, come to think of it, what is a mere million marks nowadays?

MERCHANT'S DAUGHTER, 24, tall and elegant appearance, only child of one of the first Jewish families; ,000 dowry, later large inheritances....

A young widow (Jewish), 28 years, without property, longs for another happy home....

Some did not care how much they spent on advertising. For instance:

I SEEK FOR MY FRIEND, a free-thinking Jewess, elegant woman in the fifties, looking much younger, widow, owner of lucrative wholesale business, a suitable husband of like position. The lady is of beautiful figure, lovable temperament, highly cultured, distinguished, worldly wise, and at the same time a good manager and diligent business woman. [This last detail was plainly a tautology, having already been stated in the ninth word of the paragraph.] The gentleman should be a merchant or a government official of high rank. Chief condition is good character, distinguished sentiments, affectionate disposition. No photographs, but oral interview solicited. Offers addressed, etc....

This last vacancy should have found many suitable candidates, if there was truth in the violently pink handbills that were handed out in the streets of Berlin during one of the "demonstrations" against the peace terms. For the sake of brevity I give only its high lights:

END OF MILITARISM

BEGINNING OF JEW RULE!

Fifty months have we stood at the Front honorably and undefeated. Now we have returned home, ignominiously betrayed by deserters and mutineers! We hoped to find a free Germany, with a government of the people. What is offered us?

A GOVERNMENT OF JEWS!

The participation of the Jews in the fights at the Front was almost nil. Their participation in the new government has already reached 80 per cent.! Yet the percentage of Jewish population in Germany is only 1½ per cent.!

OPEN YOUR EYES!

COMRADES, YOU KNOW THE BLOODSUCKERS!

COMRADES, WHO WENT TO THE FRONT AS VOLUNTEERS?

WHO SAT OUT THERE MOSTLY IN THE MUD? WE!

WHO CROWDED INTO THE WAR SERVICES AT HOME? THE JEWS!

WHO SAT COMFORTABLY AND SAFELY IN CANTEENS AND OFFICES?

WHICH PHYSICIANS PROTECTED THEIR FELLOW-RACE FROM THE TRENCHES?

WHO ALWAYS REPORTED US "FIT FOR DUTY" THOUGH WE WERE ALL SHOT TO PIECES?

These are the people who rule us. [Here followed a long list of names and blanket accusations.] Even in the Soldiers' Councils the Jews have the big word! Four long years these people hung back from the Front, yet on

November 9th they had the courage, guns in hand, to tear away from us soldiers our cockades, our shoulder-straps, and our medals of honor!

Comrades, we wish as a free people to decide for ourselves and be ruled by men of OUR race! The National Assembly must bring into the government only men of OUR blood and OUR opinions! Our motto must be:

GERMANY FOR GERMANS!

German people, rend the chains of Jewry asunder! Away with them! We want neither Pogrom nor Bürgerkrieg! We want a free German people, ruled by free German men! We will *not* be the slaves of the Jews!

ELECTORS

Out of the Parties and Societies run by Jews! Elect no Jews! Elect also no baptized Jews! Elect also none of the so-called "confessionless" Jews! Give your votes only to men of genuine German blood!

DOWN WITH JEWRY!

Though it is violating the chronological order of my tale, it may be as well to sum up at once the attitude of Berlin upon receipt of the peace terms. Four separate times during my stay in Germany I visited the capital, by combinations of choice and necessity. On the day the terms of the proposed treaty were made public apathy seemed to be the chief characteristic of the populace. If one must base conclusions on visible indications, the masses were far less interested in the news from Versailles than in their individual struggles for existence. The talk one heard was not of treaty terms, but of food. Not more than a dozen at a time gathered before the windows of the *Lokal Anzeiger* on Unter den Linden. They read the bulletins deliberately, some shaking their heads, and strolled on about their business as if they had been Americans scanning the latest baseball scores, a trifle disappointed, perhaps, that the home team had not won. There was no resemblance whatever to the excited throngs of Teuton colonists who had surged about the war maps in Rio de Janeiro during August, 1914. One could not but wonder whether this apathy had reigned in Berlin at that date. Scenes of popular excitement and violence had been prophesied, but for two days I wandered the streets of the capital, mingling with every variety of group, questioning every class of inhabitant, without once hearing a violent word. A few individuals asserted that their opinion of America had been sadly shocked; one or two secretaries of Allied correspondents haughtily resigned their positions. But the afternoon tea at the Adlon showed the same gathering of sleek, well-dressed Germans of both sexes, by no means averse to genial chats with enemy guests in or out of uniform. There was no means of forming definite conclusions as to whether the nation had been stunned with the immensity of the tragedy that had befallen it or whether these taciturn beings had some secret cause for satisfaction hidden away in their labyrinthine minds.

Later I was assured that many had stayed up all night, waiting for the first draft of the terms. Südermann explained the apparent apathy with, "We Germans are not like the French; we mourn in the privacy of our homes, but we do not show our sorrow in public." Certainly the Boche has none of the Frenchman's sense of the dramatic, nor his tendency to hysteria. An observer reported that the "epoch-making first meeting of the National Assembly at Weimar opened like the unfinished business of a butchers' lodge." Once, during my absence from the capital, there was a flurry of excitement, but nothing to cause me to regret my presence elsewhere. The "demonstration" against the Ally-housing Adlon proved upon my return to have been serious chiefly in the foreign press. At the most genuinely German restaurant the head waiter had on the same date informed an American woman that her guests would no longer be welcome if they came in Allied uniforms, and that English would not be spoken—then took her whispered order in that language behind a concealing palm. Dodgers were dropped from airplanes on the capital one day, protesting against a half-dozen articles of the treaty, demanding the immediate return of German prisoners, and ending with the query, "Shall noble Germans be judged by Serb murderers, Negro states, Japs, Chinese, Siamese?..." Billboards blossomed out with highly colored maps showing the territory that was being "stolen" from the Empire. But the populace seemed to give little attention to these appeals. Ludendorff called the Allied correspondents together and broke the record for short interviews with, "If this is what they mean by Wilson's Fourteen Points, our enemies can go to hell." Up to date they have not fully complied with the general's proposal. Haughty Richard Strauss declined to waste words on his Allied fellow-guests at the Adlon. On May 9th several of the Berlin dailies admitted at last, "We are conquered." Had their staffs been more efficient they might have shared that news with their readers several months earlier. On the third Sunday in May, when the subject would long since have grown cold among less phlegmatic peoples, I attended a dozen meetings of protest against the peace terms in as many parts of the city. Nothing could have been more ladylike, silent, orderly, and funereal, with the possible exception of the processions that formed after the meetings were over and plodded noiselessly down the shaded length of Unter den Linden.

In the first heat of despair a *Trauerwoche*, or week of mourning, was decreed throughout the Empire, with the cast-iron fist of dreaded Noske to enforce it, but the nation took it less seriously than its forcible language warranted:

In the time between May 10th and 16th, inclusive, must be postponed:

All public theater and musical representations, plays and similar jovialities, so long as there is not in them a higher interest for art or for science, and unless they bear a serious character. Especially are forbidden:

Representations in music-halls, cabarets, and circuses, musical and similar entertainments in inns and taverns.

All joyful public dances (*Tanzlustbarkeiten*), as well as social and private dance entertainments in public places or taverns.

All dramatic representations and gaieties in the public streets, roads, squares, and other public places.

Cinematographic entertainments which do not bear witness to the earnestness of the times; all horse-races and similar public sporting activities.

Gambling clubs are to close, and to remain closed also after the 16th until further notice.

There was no clause demanding that Germany fast or reduce her consumption of food to the minimum; she had long been showing that evidence of national sorrow without the necessity of a formal command.

VII
"GIVE US FOOD!"

Now then, having fortified ourselves for the ordeal, let us take a swift, running glance at the "food situation" in Berlin. That we have escaped the subject thus far is little short of miraculous, for it is almost impossible to spend an hour in the hungry capital without having that burning question come up in one form or another. The inhabitants of every class, particularly the well-to-do, talked food all the time, in and out of turn. No matter what topic one brought up, they were sure to drift back to that. Their best anecdotes were the stirring adventure of getting a pound of butter or ('Sh!) where they had found a half-pound of cocoa for sale. The women were always discussing some kind of *Ersatz* food, how it tasted or how nearly it comes to tasting, how to make it up in the least unappetizing manner, where (Now, keep this strictly to yourself!) one could get it for only a few times at a fair price. It is curious how one's thoughts persist in sticking to food when one hasn't enough of it. I soon found myself thinking of little else, and I am by no means a sybarite or an epicurean. Most of Germany was hungry, but Berlin was so in a superlative degree. No one seemed to escape comparative famine or to have strength of will enough to avoid discussion of the absorbing topic of the hour. When I called on Südermann at his comfortable residence in the suburb of Grunewald he could not confine his thoughts to drama or literature, or even to the "atrocious" peace terms for more than a sentence or two before he also drifted back to the subject of food—how hungry he had been for months; how he had suffered from lack of proper nourishment during a recent convalescence; how he had been forced to resort to *Schleichhandel* to keep himself and his sick daughter alive.

Loose-fitting clothing, thin, sallow faces, prominent cheekbones, were the rule among Berliners; the rosy complexions and the fine teeth of former days were conspicuous by their scarcity. The prevailing facial tint in the city was a grayish-yellow. "Why, how thin you are!" had become taboo in social circles. Old acquaintance meeting old friend was almost sure to find his collar grown too large for him. Old friend, perhaps, did not realize that sartorial change in his own appearance, his mirror pictured it so gradually, but he was quick to note a similar uncouthness in the garb of old acquaintance. In the schoolroom there were not red cheeks enough to make one pre-war pair, unless the face of a child recently returned from the country, shining like a new moon in a fog, trebled the pasty average. Every row included pitiful cases of arrested development, while watery eyes turned the solemn, listless gaze of premature old age on the visitor from every side. The newspapers of Berlin were full of complaints that pupils were still required to attend as many hours and otherwise strive to attain pre-war standards. It was "undemocratic," protested many parents, for it gave the few children of those wealthy enough to indulge in *Schleichhandel* an unfair advantage over the underfed youngsters of the masses. Even adults condoled with one another that their desire and ability to work had sunk to an incredibly low level. "Three hours in my office," moaned one contributor, "and my head is swirling so dizzily that I am forced to stretch out on my divan, dropping most pressing affairs. Yet before the war I worked twelve and fourteen hours a day at high pressure, and strode home laughing at the idea of fatigue."

It was perfectly good form in Berlin for a man in evening dress to wrap up a crust of black bread and carry it away with him. Even in the best restaurants waiters in unimpeachable attire ate all the leavings—in the rare cases that there were any—on their way back to the kitchen. I have already mentioned the constant munching of wretched lunches by theater audiences. The pretense of a meal on the stage was sure to turn the most uproarious comedy into a tear-provoking melodrama. Playwrights avoided such scenes in recent works; managers were apt to "cut them out" when offering the older classics. The Berliner suffered far more from the cold than in the bygone days of plenitude. Two or three raw spells during the month of May, which I scarcely felt myself, found thousands buttoned up in one and even two overcoats, and wrapped to their noses in mufflers. The newspapers were constantly publishing "hunger sketches"; the jokesters found the prevailing theme an endless source of sad amusement. "There are many children of four who have never tasted butter," remarked one paragrapher; "some hardly know what meat is; no one of that age has ever tasted real bread." A current joke ran: "How old is your sister?" "I don't know," replied the foil, "but she can still remember how bananas taste." A cartoonist showed a lean and hollow-eyed individual standing aghast before a friend whose waistcoat still bulged like a bay-window—where he found him in Berlin is a mystery—with the caption, "*Mein lieber Karl*, you must have been getting some of that famous American bacon!" Those food-supplies from America, so incessantly announced, were a constant source both of amusement and of wrath in Germany, not wholly without reason, as I shall show before I have done with this distressing subject.

There was a suggestion of the famine victims of India in many German faces, particularly among the poor of large cities and in factory districts. In a social stampede such as that surging through Germany for the past year or two those who get down under the hoofs of the herd are the chief sufferers. The poor, the sick, whether at home or in hospitals, the weak, the old, the less hardy women, and the little children showed the most definite evidence of the efficiency of the blockade and of the decrease in home production. On the streets, especially of the poorer districts, the majority of those one passed looked as if they ought to be in bed, though many a household included invalids never seen in public. Flocks of ragged, unsoaped, pasty-skinned children swarmed in the outskirts. Even such food as was to be had by those in moderate circumstances contained slight nourishment, next to none for weaklings and babies; while the most hardy found next morning that very little of it had been taken up by the body. Hasty visitors to Berlin, well supplied with funds, who spent a few days in the best hotels, often with the right to draw upon the American or Allied commissaries, or with supplies tucked away in their luggage, were wont to report upon their return that the hunger of Germany was "all propaganda." Those who lived the unfavored life of the masses, even for as short a time, seldom, if ever, confirmed this complacent verdict. There were, of course, gradations in want, from the semi-starvation of the masses to the comparative plenty of the well-to-do; but the only ones who could be said to show no signs whatever of under-nourishment were foreigners, war profiteers, and those with a strangle-hold on the public purse.

The scarcity of food was everywhere in evidence. Almost no appetizing things were displayed to the public gaze. The windows of food-dealers were either empty or filled with laborious falsehoods about the taste and efficacy of the *Ersatz* wares in them. Slot-machines no longer yielded a return for the dropping of a pewter coin. Street venders of anything edible were almost never seen, except a rare hawker of turnips or asparagus—*Spargel*, for some reason, seemed to be nearly plentiful—who needed not even raise their voices to dispose of their stock in record time. It was no use dropping in on one's friends, for even though the welcome were genuine, their larder was sure to be as scantily garnished as one's own.

The distribution of such food as remained was carried on with the elaborate orderliness for which the German has long been noted. All Berlin bloomed with posters advising those entitled to them where they could get six ounces of marmalade on such a day, or four pounds of potatoes on another date. The newspapers gave up much of their space to the *Lebensmittelkalender*, or "food calendar," of Berlin, the capital being divided into hundreds of sections, or "commissions," for the purposes of distribution:

Until Sunday, in the divisions of the 169, 170, 190, 205, and 207th Bread Commissions, 125 grams of cheese per head are being allowed. During the next week 50 grams of cooking fat for the coupon No. L4 of the new special card for foodstuffs from outside the Empire. A half-pound of foreign white flour, for those previously reporting, in the time between the 4th and the 7th of June, 1919, on the coupon P5 of the new card.

This week, as already stated, there will be given out a new source of nourishment as a substitute for meat. The main rations remain unchanged. In Bread Districts 116, 118, 119, 120, and 209 will be given out 125 grams of marmalade. On the CI and CII cards will be given a can of condensed milk every four days. Children born between May 1, 1913, and May 1, 1917, receive a card for chocolate (though it is not guaranteed that they can find any for sale). On coupon E2 will be given 125 grams of American pork products.

As late as May the long-announced supplies of food from America had not put in an appearance in sufficient quantities to make an appreciable increase in Germany's scanty ration. In the occupied region, where our army kept close tabs on the distribution and prices, and even assisted the municipalities, for the sake of keeping peace in the community, American foodstuffs reached all classes of the population, with the exception of the "self-providing" peasants. But "over in Germany" only tantalizing samples of what might come later were to be had at the time of my visit. This may have been the fault of the Boche himself, though he laid it to the enmity of the Allies, whom he accused of purposely "keeping him starved," of dangling before his hungry nose glowing false promises until he had signed the Peace Treaty. The "Hoover crowd," demanding payment in gold before turning over supplies to the authorities of unoccupied Germany, often had laden ships in port long before the Germans were prepared to pay for the cargo. Moreover, once financially satisfied, they bade the Teutons "take it away," and washed their hands of the matter. There were rumors that large quantities were illegally acquired by the influential. At any rate, the "American food products" publicly for sale or visibly in existence inside Germany were never sufficient, during my stay there, to drive famine from any door. Berlin and the larger cities issued a few ounces of them per week to those who arrived early; in the rest of the country they were as intangible as rumors of life in the world to come.

The *Brotcommissionen* charged with the equal distribution of such food as existed were chiefly run by schoolteachers. Their laborious system of ledgers and "tickets" was typically German, on the whole well done, though now and then their boasted efficiency fell down. Seldom, however, were such swarming mobs lined up before the places of distribution as in France— which implied a better management behind the wicket. Each applicant carried a note-book in which an entry was made in an orderly but brief manner, and was soon on his way again, clutching his handful of precious "tickets."

My own case was a problem to the particular Bread Commission of the ward I first inhabited in Berlin, to which I hastened as soon as Wilhelmstrasse had legalized my existence within the country. But they were not only courteous to a superlative degree, in spite of—or, perhaps, because of—my nationality; they insisted on working out the problem, before which a Latin would probably have thrown up his hands in disgust or despair. There was no difficulty in supplying me with food-tickets during my stay in the capital, nor of transferring my right to eat to any other city in which I chose to make my residence. But what was to be done for a man who proposed to tramp across the country, without any fixed dwelling-place? Apparently the ration system of Germany had neglected to provide for such cases. A long conference of all members of the commission wrestled with the enigma, while the line of ticket-seekers behind me grew to an unprecedented length. A dozen solutions were suggested, only to be rejected as irregular or specifically *verboten*. But a plan was found at last that seemed free from flaws. Tickets of all kinds were issued to me at once for the ensuing week, then the foolscap sheet on which such issue would have been noted weekly, had I remained in the capital, was decorated with the words, in conspicuous blue pencil, "*Dauernd auf Reise*"—"Always traveling." Provincial officials might in some cases decline to honor it, but the commission was of the unanimous opinion that most of them would accept the document as a command from the central government.

Some of the supplies to which the tickets entitled me must be purchased on the spot, in specified shops scattered about the neighboring streets. That was a matter of a few minutes, for the shopkeepers already had them wrapped in tiny packages of the allotted size. There was a half-pound of sugar, coarse-grained, but nearly white; then a bar of sandy soap of the size of a walnut. My week's supply of butter I tucked easily into a safety-match box and ate with that day's lunch. Three coupons on an elaborate card entitled "American Foodstuffs" yielded four ounces of lard (in lieu of bacon), two ounces of what seemed to be tallow, and a half-pound of white flour. The price of the entire collection, being government controlled, was reasonable enough, especially in view of the foreign rate of exchange; a total of two mk. eighty, or less than the butter alone would have cost from "underground" dealers. Fortunately the meat, potato, and bread tickets were good anywhere, sparing me the necessity of carrying these supplies with me. In fact, *Reisebrotmarken*, or "travel bread-tickets," were legal tender throughout the Empire, and were not confined to any particular date or place. Those I had been furnished for a month to come, a whole sheath of them, totaling twenty-five hundred grams. That sounds, perhaps, like a lot of bread, but the fact is that each elaborately engraved fifty-gram coupon represented a thin slice of some black concoction of bran, turnip-meal, and perhaps sawdust which contained little more nourishment and was far less appetizing in appearance than the ticket itself. The potato-tickets were invaluable; without them one was either denied the chief substance of a Berlin meal or forced to pay a painful price for an illegal serving of it; with them one could obtain two hundred and fifty grams for a mere thirty pfennigs. Other vegetables, which were just then beginning to appear on bills of fare, were not subject to ticket regulation.

The white flour left me with a problem equal to that I had been to the *Brotcommissionen*. Obviously I could not afford to waste such a luxury; quite as obviously I could not eat it raw. In the end I turned it over to the head waiter of my hotel, together with the lard, and breakfasted next morning on two long-enduring *Pfannkuchen*. But the go-between charged me a mark for his trouble, three marks for two eggs, without which a German "pancake" is a failure, and a mark for the cooking!

I drifted out to the central market of Berlin one afternoon and found it besieged by endless queues of famished people, not one of whom showed signs of having had anything fit to eat, nor a sufficient quantity of anything unfit, for months. Yet the only articles even of comparative abundance were heaps of beet-leaves. A few fish, a score or so of eels, and certain unsavory odds and ends, all "against tickets," were surrounded by clamoring throngs which only the miracle of the loaves and fishes could have fed even for a day with the quantity on hand. Only the flower-market showed a supply by any means in keeping with the demand, and that only because various experiments had proved flowers of no edible value. The emptiness of these great market-places, often of ambitious architecture and fitted with every modern convenience—except food—the silence of her vast slaughter-house pens, and the idleness of her sometimes immense, up-to-date kitchens, make the genuine hunger of Germany most forcibly apparent.

The efforts of the masses to keep from being crowded over the brink into starvation had given Berlin new customs. Underfed mobs besieged the trains in their attempts to get far enough out into the country to pick up a few vegetables among the peasants. Each evening the elevated, the underground, and the suburban trains were packed with gaunt, toil-worn men, women, and children, the last two classes in the majority, returning from more or less successful foraging expeditions, on fourth-class tickets, to the surrounding farms and hamlets; the streets carried until late at night emaciated beings shuffling homeward, bowed double under sacks of potatoes or turnips. Then there were the *Laubengärten*, or "arbor gardens," that had grown up within the past few years. The outer edges of Berlin and of all the larger cities of Germany were crowded with these "arbor colonists," living in thousands of tiny wooden shacks, usually unpainted, often built of odds and ends of lumber, of drygoods-boxes, of tin cans, like those of the negro laborers along the Panama Canal during its digging. About Berlin the soil is sandy and gives slight reward for the toil of husbandry, yet not an acre escaped attempted cultivation. In most cases a "general farmer" leased a large tract of land and parceled it out in tiny plots, hiring a carpenter to build the huts and an experienced gardener to furnish vegetarian information to the city-bred "colonists." Here the laborer or the clerk turned husbandman after his day's work in town was done, and got at least air and exercise, even though he made no appreciable gain in his incessant struggle for food. Here, too, he might have a goat, "the poor man's cow," to keep him reminded of the taste of milk, and perhaps a pig for his winter's meat-supply.

The great shortage in animal flesh and fats had made the German of the urban rank and file a vegetarian by force. Theoretically every one got the allotted one hundred and twenty-five grams of meat a week; practically many could not even pay for that, and even if they had been able to it would scarcely have ranked them among the carnivorous species. The rich, of course, whether in hotels or private residences, got more than the legal amount, and of a somewhat higher quality, but they paid fabulous prices for it, and they could not but realize that they were cheating their less fortunate fellow-countrymen when they ate it. The war had not merely reduced Germany's cattle numerically; the lack of fodder had made the animals scarcely fit for butchering. They weighed, perhaps, one half what they did in time of peace, and the meat was fiberless and unnourishing as so much dogfish. The best steak I ever tasted in Berlin would have brought a growl of wrath from the habitué of a Bowery "joint." The passing of a gaunt *Schlachtkuh* down a city street toward the slaughter-house was sure to bring an excited crowd of inhabitants in its wake. To bread and potatoes had fallen the task of keeping the mass of the people alive, and the latter were usually, the former always, of low quality.

The resultant gnawings of perpetual hunger had brought to light a myriad of *Ersatz* foods that were in reality no food at all. It was frequently asserted that this consumption of unwholesome imitations of food was responsible for the erratic conduct of many a present-day German, manifesting itself now in morose, now in talkative moods, often in more serious deviations from his moral character. Certainly it had made him less pugnacious. Indirectly it had made him more of a liar—at least on his bills of fare. The best hotel in Berlin made no bones of shredding turnips or beet-roots and serving them as mashed potatoes. Once in a while an honest waiter warned the unsuspecting client, as was the case with one who shattered my fond hopes of an appetizing dish announced on the menu-card he had handed me. "*Venison* your grandmother!" he whispered, hoarsely. "It is horse-meat soaked in vinegar. Take the beef, for at least that is genuine, poor as it is." Milk, butter, and all such "trimmings" as olives, pickles, sauces, preserves, and the like were wholly unknown in public eating-places. Pepper I saw but once in all Germany—as a special luxury in a private household. Coffee might now and then be had, but an imitation of burnt corn and similar ingredients took its place in an overwhelming majority of cases, and cost several times what real coffee did before the war. Beechnut oil, supplied only to those holding tickets, did the duty of butter and lard in cooking processes. The richest and most influential could not get more than their scanty share of the atrocious, indigestible stuff miscalled bread. Bakers, naturally, were mighty independent. But those who could get bread often got cake, for there was always more or less "underground" traffic in forbidden delicacies. One of the most difficult tasks of all was to lay in a lunch for a journey. Before my first trip out of the capital I tramped the streets for more than an hour in quest of something edible to carry along with me, and finally paid six marks for an egg-and-sausage sandwich that went easily into a vest pocket.

Good linen had almost wholly disappeared—at least from sight. It was never seen on dining-tables, having long since been commandeered by the government for the making of bandages—or successfully hidden. Paper napkins and tablecloths were the invariable rule even in the most expensive establishments. Personal linen was said to be in a sad state among rich and poor alike; the *Ersatz* soap or soap-powders reduced it quickly to the consistency and durability of tissue-paper. Many of the proudest families had laid away their best small-clothes, hoping for the return of less destructive wash-days. As to soap for toilet purposes, among German residents it was little more than a memory; such as still existed had absolutely no fat in it, and was made almost wholly of sand. Foreigners lucky or foresighted enough to have brought a supply with them might win the good will of those with whom they came in contact far more easily than by the distribution of mere money.

But we are getting off the all-absorbing topic of food. If the reader feels he can endure it, I wish to take him to a half-dozen meals in Berlin, where he may see and taste for himself. The first one is in a public soup-kitchen, where it will be wiser just to look on, or at most to pretend to eat. Long lines of pitiful beings, women and children predominating, file by the faintly steaming kettles, each carrying a small receptacle into which the attendants toss a ladleful of colored water, sometimes with a piece of turnip or some still more plebeian root in it. The needy were lucky to get one such "hot meal" a day; the rest of the time they consumed the dregs of the markets or things which were fed only to hogs before the war. The school lunch and often the supper of perhaps the majority of the children of Berlin consisted of a thin but heavy slice of war-bread lightly smeared with a colic-provoking imitation of jam. In contrast, one might stroll into the Adlon in the late afternoon and see plump and prosperous war profiteers—"Jews" the Berliners called them, though they were by no means confined to a single race—taking their plentiful "tea" in the midst of, and often in company with, Allied officers.

My own first German meal—for those in the occupied region were rather meals in Germany—was a "breakfast" in a second-class hotel, of the kind with which almost every one began the day in the Fatherland. There was set before me with great formality a cupful of lukewarm water with something in it which made a faint effort to pretend it was coffee, a very thin slice of war-bread, yielded only after long argument because I had as yet no bread-tickets, and a spoonful of a sickly looking purple mess that masqueraded under the name of "marmalade." Where the Germans got their comparative abundance of this last stuff I do not know. Its appearance suggested that it was made of bruised flesh; its taste reminded one of rotten apples. The bill on this occasion was three marks, plus 10 per cent. for service. Begin a few days on that and see how much "pep" you have left; by noon you will know the full meaning of the word hungry.

I took lunch that day in a working-man's restaurant. There I got a filling, though not a very lasting, dinner of beans and potatoes, a "German beefsteak"—resembling our "Hamburger," but possibly made of horse-meat—a slice of what Europe calls bacon, which is really salt pork, and two mugs of weak beer—total, four mk. forty. No bread was asked or given. The clients ranged from small merchants to hackmen.

For supper I investigated a long-established vegetarian restaurant on Friedrichstrasse. An oat soup was followed by a plate of mashed peas, one storage egg (two marks), a cold potato salad, a pint of "white beer," and a pudding that would have been tasteless but for its *Himbeer* sauce, sickly as hair-oil. The check came to seven mk. seventy-five, including the usual tip.

A few blocks farther on along this same chief cross-artery of Berlin is a famous "Tunnel" restaurant below the level of the sidewalk. If you have been in the German capital during this century you have no doubt passed it, though you probably took care not to enter. In 1919 it was one of the chief rendezvous of lost souls. Girls of sixteen, already *passées*, mingled with women of once refined instincts whom the war had driven to the streets. Their male companions were chiefly "tough characters," some of them still in uniform, who might give you a half-insolent, half-friendly greeting as you entered, but who displayed little of that rowdyism so characteristic of their class in our own country. Here no attention was paid to meatless days, and, though the date was plainly written on the bill of fare, it offered, even on Tuesdays and Fridays, several species of beef and veal and many kinds of game—wild duck, marsh fowl, rabbit, mountain goat, and so on, all evidently the real article. The servings were more than generous, the potatoes almost too plentiful. The menu asserted that "Meat, bread, and potatoes were served only against tickets," but for the payment of an extra twenty-five pfennigs the lack of these was overlooked, except in the case of bread. A small glass of some sickly-sweetish stuff called beer cost the same amount; in the more reputable establishments of the capital the average price for a beverage little better was about four times that. Five marks sufficed to settle the bill, after the most nearly satisfying meal I had so far found in Berlin. Here 15 per cent.

was reckoned in for service. Evidently the waiters had scorned a mere 10 per cent. in so low-priced a resort.

While I ate, an old woman wandered in, peddling some sort of useless trinkets. She was chalky in color and emaciated to the last degree, staggering along under her basket as if it had been an iron chest. Several of the habitués got rid of her with a pewter coin. I happened to have no change and gave her instead a few bread-tickets. The result was not exactly what I had expected. So great was her gratitude for so extraordinary a gift, beside which mere money seemed of little or no interest, that she huddled over my table all the rest of the evening. Before the war she had been the wife of a shopkeeper in Charlottenburg. Her husband and both her sons had died in France. Business had dwindled away for lack of both demand and supply until she had been dispossessed, and for nearly two years she had been wandering the night streets of Berlin with her basket. Her story was that of thousands in the larger cities of Germany.

"No, I am not exactly sick," she explained, after all but toppling over upon me, "but my heart is so weak that it gives way when I try to work. I faint in the street every few hours and know nothing about it until I find myself in some shop door or alleyway where passers-by have carried me. The back of my head and my neck have ached for more than a year now, all the time, from the chin clear around. It is lack of food. I know where I could get plenty of meat, if I could pay for it and spend six or seven marks for a coach to get there."

"But you get American bacon now, don't you?" I put in, more out of curiosity to know how she would answer than to get information.

"Bacon!" she coughed. "Yes, indeed, one slice every two weeks! Enough to grease my tongue, if it needed it."

A moment later I chanced to mention Holland. She broke off a mumbling account of the horrors of war suffering at home with:

"Holland! Isn't that where our Kaiser is? Do you think our wicked enemies will do something wrong to his Majesty? Ah me, if only he would come back!"

Like all her class, she was full of apologies for the deposed ruler and longed to bask once more in the blaze of his former glory, however far she was personally removed from it. Nor had her sufferings dimmed her patriotism. An evil-faced fellow at a neighboring table spat a stream of his alleged beer on the floor and shouted above the hubbub of maudlin voices: *"Ein Hundeleben ist das in Deutschland!* A *dog's* life! Mine for a better country as quick as possible."

"Rats always desert a sinking ship," snapped the old woman, glaring at the speaker with a display of her two yellow fangs, "no matter how well they have once fared upon it."

The fifth meal to which the reader is invited was one corresponding to our "business man's lunch." The clients were wholesale merchants, brokers, lawyers, and the like. In its furnishings the place was rather sumptuous, but as much cannot be said of its food. My own luncheon consisted of a turnip soup, roast veal (a mere shaving of it, as tasteless as deteriorated rubber), with one potato, a "German beefsteak," some inedible mystery dubbed "lemon pudding," and a small bottle of water—beer was no longer served in this establishment. The bill, including the customary forced tip, was nineteen mk. eighty, and the scornful attitude of the waiter proved that it was considerably less than the average. Even here the majority of the dishes were some species of *Ersatz*, and the meat itself was so undernourished that it had virtually no nourishment to pass on. Of ten pounds of it, according to the wholesale butcher who sat opposite me, at least five disappeared in the cooking. Finish such a meal at one and you were sure to be ragingly hungry by three. Yet there was less evidence of "profiteering" in establishments of this kind in Berlin than I had expected. The ice-cold bottle of mineral water, for instance, cost forty-five pfennigs, a mere four cents to foreigners. The German does not seem to go over his entire stock daily and mark it higher in price irrespective of its cost to him, as in Paris and, I fear, in our own beloved land.

But there was one restaurant in Berlin where a real meal, quite free from *Ersatz*, could still be had, by those who could pay for it—the famous Borchardt's in Französischerstrasse. Situated in the heart of the capital, in the very shadow of the government that issues those stern decrees against "underground" traffic in foodstuffs, it was protected by the rich and influential, and by the same government officials whose legal duty it was to suppress it. Admittance was only by personal introduction, as to a gambling club. The only laws this establishment obeyed were in the serving of bread and the use of paper in place of table linen. Meatless days meant nothing to its chefs; many articles specifically forbidden in restaurants were openly served to its fortunate guests. It depended, of course, entirely on *Schleichhandel* for its supplies. Among the clients, on the evening in question, were generals out of uniform, a noted dealer in munitions, a manufacturer of army cloth, several high government officials, two or three Allied correspondents, and Bernsdorff's right-hand "man" in several of his American trickeries—in a silky green gown that added to the snaky effect of her serpent-like eyes. It was she who "fixed" so thoroughly the proposed attack on us from Mexico during the early days of 1917.

Four of us dined together, and this is a translation of the bill:

Cover (tablecloth and napkins, or paper)	2.50	Marks
Two bottles of Yquem	90.	
Wine tax on same	18.	
Half-bottle Lafanta (ordinary wine)	13.50	
Tax on same	2.60	
Hors-d'œuvre (radishes, foie gras, etc.)	150.	
Roast veal (very ordinary)	80.	
Potatoes (cost, 1 mark in the market)	12.50	
Asparagus (plentiful in Berlin)	54.	
Charlotte (a tasteless dessert)	20.	
Ice	6.	
Bread (one very thin slice each—black)	.60	
Cigars (three horrible cabbages)	18.	
Butter	4.	
	471.20	
10 per cent. for service	47.15	
Total	518.35	

Thankfully received, May 8, 1919

FRITZ REICH.

At that day's rate of exchange this amounted to something over forty dollars; at the pre-war rate, which was still in force so far as the German clients were concerned, it was about one hundred and twenty-five dollars. Small wonder the clientèle was "select" and limited.

Before we end this round of restaurants let us settle with the waiters. About the time of the revolution the majority of them refused to have their income any longer subject to the whims of clients, a movement which had spread through all the larger cities of unoccupied Germany. In most eating-places a charge of "10 per cent. for service" was now added to the bill; in a few cases it ran as high as 25 per cent. How soon they will be demanding 100 per cent. is a question I cannot answer. There were suggestions that before long they will expect to get free-will tips in addition to the forced contribution, especially after the first flock of American tourists descends upon the Fatherland. In many hotels the bills were stamped "10 per cent. added" so faintly that the unsuspecting new-comer was often overgenerous by mistake. At some establishments the waiter was required to inform the guest that the service fee had been included, but the majority labored under no such compulsion, and those who did frequently whispered the information so hurriedly that only ears sharpened by financial worries could catch it. Another favorite trick was to find it so difficult to make change that the busy client finally stalked out without it. The advantages to the customer of this system were dubious; the waiters, on the whole, seem to like the new arrangement. "We may not get any more," I was assured in a wide variety of cases, "or even as much; but at least we know what we are getting." Some of the clan seemed to do their best, in their quiet, phlegmatic way; others took full advantage of the fact that, like physicians, they got their fees, anyway, no matter how poor the service. As is the tendency among the laboring class the world over, the fellows were inclined greatly to overrate their importance in these new days of "democracy." Formerly they were quite content to be addressed as *"Kellner,"* and their chief answered with alacrity to the call of *"Ober Kellner."* To-day the wise diner summons the most humble of the serving personnel with a respectful, gently modulated *"Herr Ober."*

The question of *Schleichhandel,* or food trickery, had grown disturbing all over Germany, particularly so in Berlin. It is undeniable that those with plenty of money could still get enough to eat, irrespective both of the law and of the general supply, though by so doing they abetted profiteering, hoarding, smuggling, and several other species of rascality. Perhaps it was not worth while for the government to expend its energies in combating the illegal traffic in foodstuffs, which, compared with the whole problem, was a minor matter and might involve a struggle with the most influential citizens. More likely the higher officials feared that an honest inquiry would disclose their own bedraggled skirts. The newspapers of the capital teemed with such paragraphs as the following:

SCHLEICHHANDEL WITH POTATOES

In the past two months not only has underhand dealing become far more prevalent, but the prices of articles affected by it have greatly increased. We now have the common circumstance that wares in no way to be had legally are offered openly for sale in *Schleichhandel*, so that the expression *"Schleich"* (slippery, underground) is no longer true. For instance, every one knows to-day the price of butter in *Schleichhandel*, but very few know the official price. The government has sent out the following notice:

"The *Schleichhandel* in potatoes has taken on an impulse that makes the furnishing of the absolutely necessary potatoes, officially, very seriously threatened. From many communities, especially in the neighborhood of large cities, thousands of hundredweight of potatoes are carried away daily by 'hamsterers.' At present the authorities are chiefly contenting themselves with confiscating the improperly purchased wares, without taking action against the improper purchasers. A bettering of the situation can only be hoped for through a sharper enforcement of the laws and decrees concerning food. The potato-protective law of July 18, 1918, calls for a punishment of a year's imprisonment and 10,000 marks fine, or both. For all illegal carrying off of food—and in this, of course, all *Schleichhandel* is included—the fine must equal twenty times the value of the articles."

Yet for all these threats Borchardt's and similar establishments went serenely on, often feeding, in all probability, the very men who issued these notices.

Of ordinary thievery Germany also had her full share. Every better-class hotel within the Empire displayed the following placard in a prominent position in all rooms:

The honorable guests are warned, on account of the constantly increasing thefts of clothing and footwear, not to leave these articles outside the room, as was formerly the custom, for cleaning, but to hand them over personally for that purpose directly to the employees charged with that service, since otherwise the hotel declines any responsibility for the loss of such articles.

VEREIN OF HOTEL OWNERS.

As to foodstuffs, thefts were constant and attended with every species of trickery, some of them typically German in their complications. Thieves and smugglers on the large scale were particularly fond of using the waterways about the capital. One night the boat-watch on the Spree detected a vessel loaded with fifty hundredweight of sugar slipping along in the shadow of the shore. The two brothers on board, a waiter and a druggist, announced that they had bought their cargo from a ship, and had paid five thousand marks for it, but they were unable to explain how the ship had reached Berlin. They planned to dispose of the sugar privately, "because it would cause fewer complications."

A few days later the papers announced:

The police of Berlin report that not only native foodstuffs, but our foreign imports, are being stolen. American flour disappears in startling quantities. Many arrests of drivers and their helpers show where much of it goes. It is stolen, and later most of it comes into *Schleichhandel*. The drivers who take the flour from the boats to the bakers are too seldom given a guardsman, and even when they are they find friends to act as such and help them in the stealing. Even in the finest weather the driver puts a tarpaulin over the load, and his accomplice hides himself under it. There he fills an empty bag he has brought along by pawing a few handfuls out of each sack of flour and sewing them up again. Then he slips into some tavern along the way. The number of sacks remains the same, and as our bakers are not familiar with the fullness of American flour sacks, hundreds of hundredweight of flour are lost this way daily. In spite of many arrests the stealing continues.

The wildest rumors on the subject of food were current in Berlin. One of the yellow sheets of the capital, for instance, appeared one evening with the blatant head-line, "GOAT SAUSAGE OF CHILD FLESH!" asserting that many Berliners were unconsciously indulging in cannibalism. "Where," shrieked the frenzied article, "are those one hundred and sixty-five children who have disappeared from their homes in Berlin during the past month, and of whom the police have found no trace? Ask the sausage-makers of one of our worst sections of town, or taste more carefully the next 'goat sausage' you buy so cheaply in some of our less reputable shops and restaurants...." To my astonishment, I found no small number of the populace taking this tale seriously.

I have it from several officers of the American shipping board that affairs were still worse along the Kiel Canal and in the northern ports than in Berlin. At Emden, where there were even "vinegar tickets," and along the canal the inhabitants were ready to sell anything, particularly nautical instruments, for which Germany has now so little use, for food—though not for money. Even the seagulls were said to abandon their other activities to follow the American flag when a food-ship came into port. Stevedores sent down into the hold broke open the boxes and ate flour and lard by the handful, washing it down with condensed milk. If German guards were placed over them, the only difference was that the guards ate and drank also. Set American sentries over them and the stevedores would strike and possibly shoot. What remained under the circumstances but to let them battle with their share of the national hunger in their own indigestible manner?

VIII
FAMILY LIFE IN MECHLENBURG

Two or three days after my arrival in Berlin I might have been detected one morning in the act of stepping out of a wabbly-kneed *Droschke* at the Stettiner Bahnhof soon after sunrise. In the northernmost corner of the Empire there lived—or had lived, at least, before the war—a family distantly related to my own. I had paid them a hurried visit ten years before. Now I proposed to renew the acquaintance, not only for personal reasons, but out of selfish professional motives. The exact degree of war suffering would be more easily measured in familiar scenes and faces; moreover, the German point of view would be laid before me frankly, without any mask of "propaganda" or suspicion.

Memories of France had suggested the possible wisdom of reaching the station well before train-time. I might, to be sure, have purchased my ticket in leisurely comfort at the Adlon, but for once I proposed to take pot-luck with the rank and file. First-hand information is always much more satisfactory than hearsay or the dilettante observation of the mere spectator—once the bruises of the experience have disappeared. The first glimpse of the station interior all but wrecked my resolution. Early as I was, there were already several hundred would-be travelers before me. From both ticket-windows lines four deep of disheveled Germans of both sexes and all ages curved away into the farther ends of the station wings. Boy soldiers with fixed bayonets paraded the edges of the columns, attempting languidly and not always successfully to prevent selfish new-comers from "butting in" out of their turn. I attached myself to the end of the queue that seemed by a few inches the shorter. In less than a minute I was jammed into a throng that quickly stretched in S-shape back into the central hall of the station.

We moved steadily but almost imperceptibly forward, shuffling our feet an inch at a time. The majority of my companions in discomfort were plainly city people of the poorer classes, bound short distances into the country on foraging expeditions. They bore every species of receptacle in which to carry away their possible spoils—hand-bags, hampers, baskets, grain-sacks, knapsacks, even buckets and toy wagons. In most cases there were two or three of these to the person, and as no one dreamed of risking the precious things out of his own possession, the struggle forward suggested the writhing of a miscellaneous scrap-heap. Women were in the majority—sallow, bony-faced creatures in patched and faded garments that hung about their emaciated forms as from hat-racks. The men were little less miserable of aspect, their deep-sunk, watery eyes testifying to long malnutrition; the children who now and then shrilled protests at being trodden underfoot were gaunt and colorless as corpses. Not that healthy individuals were lacking, but they were just that—individuals, in a throng which as a whole was patently weak and anemic. The evidence of the scarcity of soap was all but overpowering. Seven women and at least three children either fainted or toppled over from fatigue during the two hours in which we moved a few yards forward, and they were buffeted out of the line with what seemed to be the malicious joy of their competitors behind. I found my own head swimming long before I had succeeded in turning the corner that cut off our view of the pandemonium at the ticket-window.

At eight-thirty this was suddenly closed, amid weak-voiced shrieks of protest from the struggling column. The train did not leave until nine, but it was already packed to the doors. Soldiers, and civilians with military papers, were served at a supplementary window up to the last minute before the departure. The disappointed throng attempted to storm this wicket, only to be driven back at the point of bayonets, and at length formed in column again to await the reopening of the public guichets at noon.

The conversation during that three-hour delay was incessantly on the subject of food. Some of it was good-natured; the overwhelming majority harped on it in a dreary, hopeless grumble. Many of the women, it turned out, were there to buy tickets for their husbands, who were still at work. Some had spent the previous day there in vain. I attempted to ease my wearying legs by sitting on my hamper, but querulous protests assailed me from the rear. The gloomy seekers after food seemed to resent every inch that separated them from their goal, even when this was temporarily unattainable. One would have supposed that the order-loving Germans might have arranged some system of numbered checks that would spare such multitudes the necessity of squandering the day at unproductive waiting in line, but the railway authorities seemed to be overwhelmed by the "crisis of transportation."

From noon until one the struggle raged with double fury. The boy soldiers asserted their authority in vain. A mere bayonet-prick in the leg was apparently nothing compared with the gnawing of continual hunger. Individual fights developed and often threatened to become general. Those who got tickets could not escape from the crushing maelstrom behind them. Women were dragged unconscious from the fray, often feet first, their skirts about their heads. The rear of the column formed a flying wedge and precipitated a free-for-all fracas that swirled vainly about the window. When this closed again I was still ten feet away. I concluded that I had my fill of pot-luck, and, buffeting my way to the outer air, purchased a ticket for the following morning at the Adlon.

A little episode at my departure suggested that the ever-obedient German of Kaiser days was changing in character. The second-class coach was already filled when I entered it, except that at one end there was an empty compartment, on the windows of which had been pasted the word *"Bestellt."* In the olden days the mere announcement that it was "engaged" would have protected it as easily as bolts and bars. I decided to test the new democracy. Crowding my way past a dozen men standing obediently in the corridor, I entered the forbidden compartment and sat down. In a minute or two a seatless passenger put his head in at the door and inquired with humble courtesy whether it was I who had engaged the section. I shook my head, and a moment later he was seated beside me. Others followed, until the compartment was crowded with passengers and baggage. One of my companions angrily tore the posters from the windows and tossed them outside.

"Bestellt indeed!" he cried, sneeringly. "Perhaps by the Soldiers' Council, eh? I thought we had done away with those old favoritisms!"

A few minutes later a station porter, in his major's uniform, appeared at the door with his arms full of baggage and followed by two pompous-looking men in silk hats. At sight of the throng inside he began to bellow in the familiar old before-the-war style.

"This compartment is *bestellt,*" he vociferated, in a crown-princely voice, "and it remains *bestellt!* You will all get out of there at once!"

No one moved; on the other hand, no one answered back. The porter fumed a bit, led his charges farther down the train, and perhaps found them another compartment; at any rate, he never returned. "Democracy" had won. Yet through it all I could not shake off the feeling that if any one with a genuinely bold, commanding manner, an old army officer, for instance, decorated with all the thingamabobs of his rank, had ordered the compartment vacated, the occupants would have filed out of it as silently and meekly as lambs.

The minority still ruled in more ways than one. A placard on the wall, forbidding the opening of a window without the unanimous consent of the passengers within the compartment, was strictly obeyed. The curtains had long since disappeared, as had the leather straps with which one raised or lowered the sash, which must now be manipulated by hand. As in the occupied zone, the seats had been stripped of their velvety coverings, suggesting that this had been no special affront to the Allies, but merely a sign of the scarcity of cloth for ladies' blouses. It was a cloudless Sunday, and railway employees along the way were taking advantage of it to work in their little vegetable gardens, tucked into every available corner. They did not neglect their official duties, however, for all that. At every grade crossing the uniformed guard stood stiffly at attention, his furled red flag held like a rifle at his side, until the last coach had passed.

At Spandau there lay acre upon acre of war material of every species, reddening with rust and overgrowing with grass and weeds. The sight of it aroused a few murmurs of discontent from my companions. But they soon fell back again into that apathetic silence that had reigned since our departure. A few had read awhile the morning papers, without a sign of feeling, though the head-lines must have been startling to a German, then laid them languidly aside. Apparently the lack of nourishing food left them too sleepy to talk. The deadly apathy of the compartment was quite the antithesis of what it would have been in France; a cargo of frozen meat could not have been more uncommunicative.

The train showed a singular languor, due perhaps to its *Ersatz* coal. It got there eventually, but it seemed to have no reserve strength to give it vigorous spells. The station we should have passed at noon was not reached until one-thirty. Passengers tumbled off *en masse* and besieged the platform lunch-room. There were *Ersatz* coffee, *Ersatz* cheese, watery beer, and war-bread for sale, the last only "against tickets." I had not yet been supplied with bread-coupons, but a fellow-passenger tossed me a pair of them and replied to my thanks with a silent nod. The nauseating stuff seemed to give the traveler a bit of surplus energy. They talked a little for the next few miles, though in dreary, apathetic tones. One had recently journeyed through the occupied area, and reported "every one is being treated fairly enough there, especially by the Americans." A languid discussion of the Allies ensued, but though it was evident that no one suspected my nationality, there was not a harsh word toward the enemy. Another advanced the wisdom of "seeing Germany first," insisting that the sons of the Fatherland had been too much given to running about foreign lands, to the neglect of their own. Those who carried lunches ate them without the suggestion of an offer to share them with their hungry companions, without even the apologetic pseudo-invitation of the Spaniard. Then one by one they drifted back to sleep again.

The engine, too, seemed to pick up after lunch—or to strike a down-grade—and the thatched Gothic roofs of Mechlenburg soon began to dot the flat landscape. More people were working in the fields; cattle and sheep were grazing here and there. Groups of women came down to the stations to parade homeward with their returning soldier sons and brothers. Yet after the first greeting the unsuccessful warriors seemed to tire of the welcome and strode half proudly, half defiantly ahead, while the women dropped sadly to the rear.

Where I changed cars, four fellow-travelers reached the station lunch-room before me and every edible thing was *bestellt* when my turn came. With three hours to wait I set out along the broad, well-kept highway. A village hotel served me a huge *Pfannkuchen* made of real eggs, a few cold potatoes, and some species of preserved fruit, but declined to repeat the order. The bill reached the lofty heights of eight marks. Children playing along the way, and frequently groups of Sunday strollers, testified that there was more energy for unnecessary exertion here in the country than in Berlin. The flat, well-plowed land, broken only by dark masses of forest, was already giving promise of a plentiful harvest.

The two women in the compartment I entered at a station farther on gave only one sign of life during the journey. A railway coach on a siding bore a placard reading, "*Übergabe Wagen an die Entente.*" The women gazed at it with pained expressions on their gaunt faces.

"It's a fine new car, too," sighed one of them, at last, "with real leather and window-curtains. *We* don't get any such to ride in—and to think of giving it to *England! Ach!* These are sad times!"

The sun was still above the horizon when I reached Schwerin, though it was nearly nine. There was a significant sign of the times in the dilapidated coach which drove me to my destination for five marks. In the olden days one mark would have been considered a generous reward for the same journey in a spick-and-span outfit. The middle-aged woman who met me at the door was by no means the buxom matron she had been ten years before. But her welcome was none the less hearty.

"*Bist du auch gegen uns gewesen?*" she asked, softly, after her first words of greeting. "You, too, against us?"

"Yes, I was with our army in France," I replied, watching her expression closely.

There was regret in her manner, yet, as I had foreseen, not the faintest suspicion of resentment. The German is too well trained in obedience to government to dream that the individual may make a choice of his own international affairs. As long as I remained in the household there was never a hint from any member of it that the war had made any gulf between us. They could not have been more friendly had I arrived wearing the field gray of the Fatherland.

A brief glance about the establishment sufficed to settle once for all the query as to whether the civil population of Germany had really suffered from the ravages of war and of the blockade. The family had been market-gardeners for generations. Ten years before they had been prosperous with the solid, material prosperity of the well-to-do middle class. In comparison with their neighbors they were still so, but it was a far call from the plenitude of former days to the scarcity that now showed its head on every hand. The establishment that had once been kept up with that pride of the old-fashioned German as for an old family heirloom, which laughs at unceasing labor to that end, was everywhere sadly down at heel. The house was shedding its ancient paint; the ravages of weather and years gazed down with a neglected air; the broken panes of glass in the hotbeds had not been replaced; farm wagons falsely suggested that the owner was indifferent to their upkeep; the very tools had all but outlived their usefulness. Not that the habit of unceasing labor had been lost. The family sleeping-hours were still from ten to four. But the war had reduced the available helping hands and the blockade had shut out materials and supplies, or forced them up to prices which none but the wealthy could reach.

Inside the house, particularly in the kitchen, the family had been reduced to almost as rudimentary a life as the countrymen of Venezuela, so many were the every-day appliances that had been confiscated or shut off by the war-time government, so few the foodstuffs that could be obtained. Though other fuel was almost unattainable, gas could only be had from six to seven, eleven to twelve, and seven to eight. Electricity was turned on from dark until ten-thirty, which at that season of the year meant barely an hour. Petroleum or candles were seldom to be had. All the better utensils had long since been turned in to the government. When I unearthed a bar of soap from my baggage the family literally fell on my neck; the only piece in the house was about the size of a postage-stamp, and had been husbanded for weeks. Vegetables were beginning to appear from the garden; without them there would have been little more than water and salt to cook. In theory each adult member of the household received 125 grams of beef a week; in practice they were lucky to get that much a month. What that meant in loss of energy I began to learn by experience; for a mere three days without meat left me weary and ambitionless. Those who could bring themselves to eat it might get horse-flesh in the markets, without tickets, but even that only in very limited quantities. The bread, "made of potatoes, turnips, and God knows what all they throw into it," was far from sufficient. Though the sons and daughters spent every Sunday foraging the country-side, they seldom brought home enough to make one genuine meal.

The effect of continued malnutrition seemed to have been surprisingly slight on those in the prime of life. The children of ten years before, men and women now, were plump and hardy, though the color in their cheeks was by no means equal even to that of the grandfather—sleeping now in the churchyard—at the time of my former visit. Of the two granddaughters, the one born three years before, when the blockade was only beginning to be felt in these backwaters of the Empire, was stout and rosy enough; but her sister of nine months looked pitifully like the waxen image of a maltreated infant of half that age. The simple-hearted, plodding head of the household, nearing sixty, had shrunk almost beyond recognition to those who had known him in his plump and prosperous years, while his wife had outdistanced even him in her decline.

Business in the market-gardening line had fallen off chiefly because of the scarcity of seeds and fertilizers. Then there was the ever more serious question of labor. Old women who had gladly accepted three marks for toiling from dawn until dark ten years before received eleven now for scratching languidly about the gardens a bare eight hours with their hoes and rakes. Male help had begun to drift back since the armistice, but it was by no means equal to the former standard in numbers, strength, or willingness. On top of all this came a crushing burden of taxation. When all the demands of the government were reckoned up they equaled 40 per cent. of the ever-decreasing income. The war had brought one advantage, though it was as nothing compared to the misfortunes. For generations two or three members of the family had spent six mornings a week, all summer long, at the market-place in the heart of town. Since the fall of 1914 not a sprig of produce had been carried there for sale; clamoring women now besieged the gate of the establishment itself in far greater numbers than the gardens could supply.

The hardship of the past four years was not the prevailing topic of conversation in the household, however, nor when the subject was forced upon them was it treated in a whining spirit. Most of the family, like their neighbors, adroitly avoided it, as a proud prize-fighter might sidestep references to the bruises of a recent beating. Only the mother could now and then be drawn into specifying details of the disaster.

"Do you see the staging around our church there?" she asked, drawing me to a window one morning after I had persisted some time in my questions. "They are replacing with an *Ersatz* metal the copper that was taken from the steeple and the eaves. Even the bells went to the cannon-foundries, six of them, all but the one that is ringing now. I never hear it without thinking of an orphan child crying in the woods after all the rest of its family has been eaten by wolves. *Ach!* What we have not sacrificed in this fight to save the Fatherland from our wolfish enemies! We gave up our gold and our silver, then our nickel and our copper, even our smallest pots and pans, our aluminum and our lead, our leather and our rubber, down to the last bicycle tire. The horses and the cows are gone, too—I have only goats to milk now. Then the struggles I have had to keep the family clothed! Cloth that used to cost fifty pfennigs a meter has gone up to fifteen marks, and we can scarcely find any of that. Even thread is sold only against tickets, and we are lucky to get a spool a month. We are far better off than the *poor* people, too, who can only afford the miserable stuff made of paper or nettles. America also wants to destroy us; she will not even send us cotton. And the wicked *Schleichhandel* and profiteering that go on! Every city has a hotel or two where you can get anything you want to eat—if you can pay for it. Yet our honest tickets are often of no use because rascals have bought up everything at wicked prices. If we do not get food soon even this *Handarbeiter* government will recommence war against France, surely as you are sitting there. The young men are all ready to get up and follow our generals. The new volunteer corps are taking on thousands every day. *Ach!* The sufferings of these last years! And now our cruel enemies expect our poor brave prisoners to rebuild Europe. But then, *I* have no right to complain. At least my dear own boy was not taken from me."

The son, whom we will call Heinrich, I had last seen as a child in knickerbockers. Now he was a powerful, two-fisted fellow of twenty-one, with a man's outlook on life. Having enlisted as a *Freiwilliger* on his sixteenth birthday, at the outbreak of the war, he had seen constant service in Russia, Rumania, and in all the hottest sectors of the western front, had been twice wounded, twice decorated with those baubles with which princes coax men to die for them, and had returned home with the highest non-commissioned rank in the German army. What struck one most forcibly was the lack of opportunity offered such men as he by their beloved Fatherland. In contrast with the positions that would have been open to so promising a youngster, with long experience in the command of men, in America, he had found nothing better than an apprenticeship in the hardware trade, paying forty marks for the privilege and bound to serve three long years without pay. Like nearly all the young men in town, from grocery clerks to bankers' sons, he still wore his uniform, stripped of its marks of rank, not out of pride, but because civilian clothing was too great a luxury to be indulged, except on Sundays. I was surprised, too, at the lack of haughtiness which I had fancied every soldier of Germany felt for his calling. When I made some casual remark about the gorgeous spiked helmet he had worn, with its Prussian and Mechlenburger cockades, which I took for granted he would set great store by to the ends of his days, he tossed it toward me with: "Here, take the thing along, if you want it. It will make a nice souvenir of your visit." When I coaxed him outdoors to be photographed in his two iron crosses, he would not put them on until we had reached a secluded corner of the garden, because, as he explained, the neighbors might think he was boastful.

"I should gladly have died for the Fatherland," he remarked, as he tossed the trinkets back into the drawer full of miscellaneous junk from which he had fished them, "if only Germany had won the war. But not for this! Not I, with no other satisfaction than the poor fellows we buried out there would feel if they could sit up in their graves and look about them."

There were startling changes in the solemn, patriarchal attitude toward life which I had found so amusing, yet so charming, in the simple people of rural Germany at the time of my first visit. The war seemed to have given a sad jolt to the conservative old customs of former days, particularly among the young people. Perhaps the most tangible evidence of this fact was to see the daughters calmly light cigarettes, while the sternly religious father of ten years before, who would then have flayed them for sneezing in church, looked idly on without a sign of protest. They were still at bottom the proper German *Fräuleins* of the rural middle class—though as much could not be said of all the sex even in respectable old Schwerin—but on the surface there were many of these little tendencies toward the *Leichtsinnig*.

When it came to discussions of the war and Germany's conduct of it, I found no way in which we could get together. We might have argued until doomsday, were it fitting for a guest to badger his hosts, without coming to a single point of agreement. Every one of the old fallacies was still swallowed, hook and line. If I had expected national disaster to bring a change of heart, I should have been grievously disappointed. To be sure, Mechlenburg is one of the remotest backwaters of the Empire, and these laborious, unimaginative tillers of the soil one of its most conservative elements. They would have considered it unseemly to make a business of thinking for themselves in political matters, something akin to accepting a position for which they had no previous training. There was that to arouse pity in the success with which the governing class had made use of this simple, unquestioning attitude for its own ends. One felt certain that these honest, straightforward victims of premeditated official lies would never have lent a helping hand had they known that the Fatherland was engaged in a war of conquest and not a war of defense.

Here again it was the mother who was most outspoken toward what she called "the wicked wrecking of poor, innocent Germany." The father and the children expressed themselves more calmly, if at all, though it was evident that their convictions were the same. Apparently they had reached the point where further defense of what they regarded as the plain facts of the situation seemed a waste of words.

"I cried when the armistice was signed," the mother confided to me one day, "for it meant that our enemies had done what they set out to do many years ago. They deliberately planned to destroy us, and they succeeded. But they were never able to defeat our wonderful armies in the field. England starved us, otherwise she would never have won. Then she fostered this Bolshevismus and Spartakismus and the wicked revolution that undermined us at the rear. But our brave soldiers at the front never gave way: they would never have retreated a yard but for the breakdown at home."

She was a veritable mine of stories of atrocities by the English, the French, and especially the Russians, but she insisted there had never been one committed by the Germans.

"Our courageous soldiers were never like that," she protested. "*They* did not make war that way, like our heartless enemies."

Yet in the same breath she rambled on into anecdotes of what any one of less prejudiced viewpoint would have called atrocities, but which she advanced as examples of the fighting qualities of the German troops. There again came in that curious German psychology, or mentality, or insanity, or whatever you choose to call it, which has always astounded the world at large. "Heinie" had seen the hungry soldiers recoup themselves by taking food away from the wicked Rumanians; he had often told how they entered the houses and carried away everything portable to sell to the Jews at a song, that the next battle should not find them unprepared. The officers had just pretended they did not see the men, for they could not let them go unfed. They had taken things themselves, too, especially the reserve officers. But then, war is war. If only I could get "Heinie" to tell some of the things he had seen and heard; how, for instance, the dastardly Russians had screamed when they were pushed back into the marshes, whole armies of them.

I found more interest in "Heinie's" stories of the insuperable difficulties he had overcome as a *Feldwebel* in keeping up the discipline of his men after the failure of the last great German offensive, but I did not press that point in her presence.

"No," she went on, in answer to another question, "the Germans *never* did anything against women. Those are all English lies! Heinie never told me of a single case"—"Heinie" was, of course, no more apt to tell mother such details than would one of the well-bred boys of our own Puritan society, but I kept the mental comment to myself. "Of course there were those shameless Polish girls, and French and Belgian hussies, who gave themselves freely to the soldiers, but...."

"Certainly the Kaiser will come back," she insisted. "We need our Kaiser; we *need* princes, to govern the Empire. What are Ebert and all that crowd? *Handarbeiter*, hand workers, and nothing more. It is absurd to think that they can do the work of rulers. We need our princes, who have had generations of training in governing. *Siehst du*, I will give you an example. We have been *Handelsgärtner* for generations. Hermann knows all about the business of gardening, because he was trained to it as a boy, *nicht wahr?* Do you think a man who had never planted a cabbage could come and do Hermann's work? *Ausgeschlossen!* Well, it is just as foolish for a *Handarbeiter* like Ebert to attempt to become a ruler as it would be for one of our princes to try to run Hermann's garden.

"Germany is divided into three classes—the rulers, the middle class (to which *we* belong), and the proletariat or hand-workers, which includes Ebert and all these new upstarts. It is ridiculous to be getting these distinctions all mixed up. Leave the governing to the princes and their army officers and the Junkers. We use the nickname 'Junker' for our noble gentlemen, von

Bernstorff, for instance, who is well known in America, and all the others who have a real right to use the 'von' before their names, whose ancestors were first highway robbers and then bold warriors, and who are naturally very proud"—she evidently thought this pride quite proper and fitting. "Then our army officers are chosen from the very best families and can marry only in the *gelehrten* class, and only then if the girl has a dowry of at least eight hundred thousand marks. So they preserve all the nobility of their caste down through every generation and keep themselves quite free from middle-class taint— the *real* officers I am speaking of, not the *Reservisten*, who are just ordinary middle-class men, merchants and doctors and teachers and the like, acting as officers during the war. *Those* are the men who are trained to govern, and the only ones who *can* govern."

GERMANS READING THE PEACE-TERMS BULLETINS
BEFORE THE OFFICE OF THE "LOKAL ANZEIGER," ON
UNTER DEN LINDEN

A CORNER OF THE EX-KAISER'S PALACE AFTER THE
SPARTICISTS GOT DONE WITH IT

THE GERMAN SOLDIER IS NOT ALWAYS SAVAGE OF FACE

THE GERMAN'S ARTISTIC SENSE LEADS HIM TO
OVERDECORATE EVEN HIS MERRY-GO-ROUNDS

I knew, of course, that the great god of class was still ruling in Germany, but I confess that this bald statement of that fact left me somewhat flabbergasted. It is well to be reminded now and again, however, that the Teuton regards politics, diplomacy, and government as lifelong professions and not merely as the fleeting pastimes of lawyers, automobile-makers, and unsuccessful farmers; it clarifies our vision and aids us to see his problems more nearly as he sees them.

Several rambles in and about Schwerin only confirmed the impressions I had already formed—that the region was hopelessly conservative and that it had really seriously suffered from the war and the blockade. On the surface there was often no great change to be seen; but scratch beneath it anywhere and a host of social skeletons was sure to come to light. Even the famous old *Schwerinerschloss*, perhaps the most splendid castle in Germany, showed both this conservatism and the distress of the past years. The repairs it was undergoing after a recent fire had ceased abruptly with the flight of the reigning family of Mechlenburg, but the marks of something more serious than the conflagration showed in its seedy outward appearance. Yet not a chair had been disturbed within it, for all the revolution, and guards stationed about it by the Soldiers' Council protected it as zealously as if they, too, were waiting for "our princes" to come back again. Almost the only sign of the new order of things was the sight of a score or more of discharged soldiers calmly fishing in the great *Schwerinersee* about the castle, a crime that would have met with summary vengeance in the old ducal days.

Rumor having it that the peace terms were to be published that afternoon, I hastily took train one morning back to Berlin, that I might be in the heart of the uproar they were expected to arouse. At the frontier of Mechlenburg soldiers of the late dukedom went carefully through passengers' baggage in search of food, particularly eggs, of which a local ordinance forbade the exportation. The quest seemed to be thorough and I saw no tips passed, but there was considerable successful smuggling, which came to light as soon as the train was well under way again. A well-dressed merchant beside me boastfully displayed a twenty-mark sausage in the bottom of his innocent-looking hand-bag, and his neighbors, not to be outdone in proof of cleverness, showed their caches of edibles laboriously concealed in brief-cases, hat-boxes, and laundry-bags.

"The peasants have grown absolutely shameless," it was agreed. "They have the audacity to demand a mark or more for a single egg, and twenty for a chicken"—in other words, the rascals had turned upon the bourgeois some of his own favorite tricks, taking advantage of conditions which these same merchants would have considered legitimate sources of profit in their own business. Wrath against the "conscienceless" countrymen was unlimited, but no one thought of shaming the smugglers for their cheating.

The contrast between the outward courtesy of these punctilious examples of the well-to-do class and their total lack of real, active politeness was provoking. A first-class compartment had been reserved for a sick soldier who was plainly on his last journey, with a comrade in attendance. Travelers visibly able to stand in the corridor crowded in upon him until the section built for six held thirteen, and forced the invalid to crouch upright in a corner. Women were rudely, almost brutally, refused seats, unless they were pretty, in which case they were overwhelmed with fawning attentions.

A discussion of America broke out in the compartment I occupied. It resembled an exchange of opinions on the character of some dear friend of the gathering who had inadvertently committed some slight social breach. There was not a word at which the most chauvinistic of my fellow-countrymen could have taken offense. When I had listened for some time to the inexplicable expressions of affection for the nation that had turned the scales against their beloved Fatherland, I discarded my incognito. My companions acknowledged themselves surprised, then redoubled their assertions of friendliness. Was their attitude a mere pose, assumed on the chance of being heard by some representative of the country they hoped to placate? It seemed unlikely, for they had had no reason to suspect my nationality. I decided to overstep the bounds of veracity in the hope of getting at their real thoughts, if those they were expressing were merely assumed.

"I said I am an American," I broke in, "but do not misunderstand me. We *Chileans* are quite as truly Americans as those grasping Yankees who have been fighting against you."

To my astonishment, the entire group sprang instantly to the defense of my real countrymen as against those I had falsely adopted. All the silly slanders I had once heard in Chile they discarded as such, and advanced proofs of Yankee integrity which even I could not have assembled.

"You Chileans have nothing to fear from American aggression," the possessor of the twenty-mark sausage concluded, reassuringly, as the rumble of the train crossing the Spree set us to gathering our traps together. "The North Americans are a well-meaning people; but they are young, and England and France have led them temporarily astray, though they have not succeeded in corrupting their simple natures."

IX
THUS SPEAKS GERMANY

Lest he talk all the pleasure out of the rambles ahead, let us get the German's opinion of the war cleared up before we start, even if we have to reach forward now and then for some of the things we shall hear on the way. I propose, therefore, to give him the floor unreservedly for a half-hour, without interruption, unless it be to throw in a question now and then to make his position and his sometimes curious mental processes clearer. The reader who feels that the prisoner at the bar is not entitled to tell his side of the story can easily skip this chapter.

Though I did not get it all from any one person—no resident of the Fatherland talked so long in the hungry armistice days—the German point of view averaged about as follows. There were plenty of variations from this central line, and I shall attempt to show the frontier of these deviations as we go along. We shall probably not find this statement of his point of view very original; most of his arguments we have heard before, chiefly while the question of our coming or not coming into the war was seething. Fifteen years ago, when I first visited him at home, I did not gather the impression that every German thought alike. To-day he seems to reach the same conclusions by the same curious trains of thought, no matter what his caste, profession, experience, and to some extent his environment—for even those who remained far from the scene of conflict during all the war seem to have worked themselves into much the same mental attitude as their people at home. But then, this is also largely true of his enemies, among whom one hears almost as frequently the tiresome repetition of the same stereotyped conclusions that have in some cases been deliberately manufactured for public consumption. One comes at times to question whether there is really any gain nowadays in running about the earth gathering men's opinions, for they so often bear the factory-made label, the trade-mark of one great central plant, like the material commodities of our modern industrial world. The press, the cable, the propagandist, and the printer have made a thinking-machine, as Edison has made a talking-machine, and Burroughs a mechanical arithmetic.

The first, of course, if not the burning question of the controversy was, who started the war, and why? The German at home showed a certain impatience at this query, as a politician might at a question that he had already repeatedly explained to his constituents. But with care and perseverance he could usually be drawn into the discussion, whereupon he outlined the prevailing opinion, with such minor variations as his slight individuality permitted; almost always without heat, always without that stone-blind prejudice that is so frequent among the Allied man in the street. Then he fell into apathetic silence or harked back to the ever-present question of food. But let him tell it in his own way.

"The war was started by circumstances. War had become a necessity to an over-prosperous world, as bleeding sometimes becomes necessary to a fat person. Neither side was wholly and deliberately guilty of beginning it, but if there is actual personal guilt, it is chiefly that of the Allies, especially England. We understand the hatred of France. It came largely from fear, though to a great extent unnecessary fear. The ruling party in Russia wanted war, wanted it as early as 1909, for without it they would have lost their power. It was a question of interior politics with them. But with England there was less excuse. In her case it was only envy and selfishness; the petty motives that sprout in a shopkeeper's soul. We were making successful *concurrenz* against her in all the markets of the world—though by our German word '*concurrenz*' we mean more than mere commercial competition; she saw herself in danger of losing the hegemony of Europe, her position as the most important nation on the globe. She set out deliberately to destroy us, to *vernichten*, to bring us to nothing. We hate"—though come to think of it I do not recall once having heard a German use the word hate in describing his own feelings, nor did I run across any reference to the notorious "Hymn of Hate" during all my travels through the Empire—"we dislike, then, we blame England most, for it was she more than any other one party in the controversy who planned and nourished it. How? By making an Entente against us that surrounded us with a steel wall; by bolstering up the *revanche* feeling in France; by urging on the ruling class in Russia; by playing on the dormant brutality of the Russian masses and catering to the natural fanaticism of the French, deliberately keeping alive their desire to recover Alsace-Lorraine. Edward VII set the ball rolling with his constant visits to Paris."

"I had much intercourse and correspondence with Frenchmen before the war," said a German professor of European history, "and I found a willingness among those of my own generation, those between thirty and fifty, to drop the matter, to admit that, after all, Alsace-Lorraine was as much German as French. Then some ten years ago I began to note a change of tone. The younger generation was being pumped full of the *revanche* spirit from the day they started to school; in foreign countries every French text-book incited crocodile tears over the poor statue of Strassburg, with its withered flowers. It was this younger generation that brought France into the war—this and Clemenceau, who is still living back in 1870."

"But the despatches, the official state papers already published, show that England was doing her best to avoid...."

"Oh, you simple Americans! You do not seem to realize that such things are made for foreign consumption, made to sell, to flash before a gaping world, to publish in the school-books of the future, not for actual use, not to be seriously believed by the experienced and the disillusioned. That has been the story of European politics for centuries, since long before you dear, naïve people came into existence. You are like a new-comer dropping into a poker game that has been going on since long before you learned to distinguish one card from another. You do not guess that the deck is pin-pricked and that every kind of underhand trick is tacitly allowed, so long as the player can 'get away with it.' Now if we could get the *really* secret papers that passed back and forth, especially if we could get what went on in private conversation or 'way inside the heads of Grey and the rest of them...."

"Yes, but—you will pardon my naïveté, I am sure—but if England had long deliberately planned a European war, why did she have nothing but a contemp—but a very small army ready when it broke out?"

"Because she expected, as usual, to have some one else do her fighting for her. And she succeeded! When they were almost burned beyond recovery she got America to pull her chestnuts out of the fire—and now America does not even get enough out of it to salve her scorched fingers. But for America we should have won the war, unquestionably. But England has lost it, in a way, too, for she has been forced to let America assume the most important place in the world. You will have a war with England yourselves for that very reason in a few years, as soon as she catches her breath and discovers you at the head of the table, in the seat which she has so long arrogated to herself. You will be her next victim—with Japan jumping on your back the moment it is turned.

"Yes, in one sense Germany did want war. She had to have it or die, for the steel wall England had been forging about her for twenty years was crushing our life out and had to be broken. Then, too, there was one party, the 'Old Germans'—what you call the Junkers—that was not averse to such a contest. The munition-makers wanted war, of course; they always do. Some of our generals"—Ludendorff was the name most frequently heard in this connection; Hindenburg never—"wanted it. But it is absurd to accuse the Kaiser of starting it, simply because he was the figurehead, the most prominent bugaboo, a catchword for the mob. The Hohenzollerns did us much damage; but they also brought us much good. The Kaiser loved peace and did all in his power to keep it. He was the only emperor—we were the only large nation that had waged no war or stolen no territory since 1871. But the English-French-Russian combination drove us into a corner. We had to have the best army in the world, just as England has to have the best navy. We had no world-conquering ambitions; we had no '*Drang nach Osten*' which our enemies have so often charged against us, except for trade. Our diplomats were not what they should have been; Bethmann-Hollweg has as much guilt as any one in the whole affair, on our side. We have had no real diplomats, except von Bülow, since Bismarck. But the Germans as a nation never wanted war. The Kaiser would not have declared it even when he did had he not feared that the Social Democrats would desert him in the crisis if it were put off longer. We had only self-protection as our war aim from the beginning, but we did not dare openly say so for fear the enemy, which had decided on our annihilation, would take it as an admission of weakness."

This whitewashing of the Kaiser was universal in Germany, as far as my personal experience goes. No one, whatever his age, sex, caste, place of residence, or political complexion, accused him of being more than an accessory before the fact. The most rabid—pardon, I never heard a German speak rabidly on any subject, unless it was perhaps the lack of food and tobacco—the most decidedly monarchical always softened any criticism of the ex-emperor with the footnote that he, after all, was not chiefly to blame. His bad counselors, the force of circumstances over which he had little control ... and so on. Then there were those, particularly, though not entirely, in the backwaters of Prussia, the women especially, who gazed after his retreated figure pityingly, almost tearfully, as if he had been the principal sufferer from the catastrophe.

Nor did I ever hear any German, not even a Socialist of the extremest left, not even a Bavarian, admit that Germany was wholly in the wrong. Once only did I hear a man go so far as to assert that Germany had at least half the guilt of the war. He was a stanch-minded, rather conservative Socialist living in the Polish atmosphere of Bromberg. On the other hand, citizens of the Allied countries, who had dwelt in Germany since 1914, were all more or less firm converts to the England-France-Russia theory. Such is the power of environment. An English governess, who had lost a brother in the war and who was returning home for the first time since it began, expressed the fear that she would soon be compelled to return to Germany to preserve her peace of mind. A few laid the blame entirely to Russia; some charged it all to "the Jews," implying a rather extraordinary power on the part of the million or so of that race within the Empire.

Now and then one ran across a simple old countryman who took his opinions wholly and unreservedly as they had been delivered to him, without ever having opened the package. "How did it start? Why, let's see. They killed some prince down in ... somewhere or other, I never can remember these foreign names, and his wife, too, if I remember, and then Russia ..." and so on. He was of the same class as those who asserted, "I don't know when gas was first used, or just where, but it was by the wicked French—or was it the scoundrelly English?" But these simple, swallow-it-whole yokels were on the whole more rare than they would have been in many another land. However much we may sneer at her *Kultur*, the Kaiser régime brought to the most distant corners of the Empire a certain degree of instruction, even if it was only of a deliberately Teutonic brand. In the great majority of cases one was astounded at the clear, comprehensive, and, within limits, unprejudiced view of all the field of European politics of many a peasant grubbing out his existence on a remote hillside. More than one of them could have exchanged minds with some of our national officials to the decided advantage of the latter. My memory still harks back to the tall, ungainly farmer in whose lowly little inn I spent the last night of my German tramp, a man who had lived almost incessantly in the trenches during all the war, and returned home still a "simple soldier," who topped off a sharp, clear-cut exposé of the politics of Europe for the past half-century with: "Who started it? Listen. Suppose a diligent, sober, hard-working mechanic is engaged on the same job with an arrogant, often careless, and sometimes intoxicated competitor. Suppose the competitor begins to note that if things go on as they are the sober mechanic will in time be given all the work, for being the more efficient, or that there will come a time when, thanks to his diligence, there will be no work left for either of them. If the rowdy suddenly strikes his rival a foul blow in the back when he is not looking and the hard-worker drops his tools and strikes back, who started it?"

On the conduct of the war there was as nearly unanimity of opinion as on its genesis. "The Russians and the French, secretly sustained by England, invaded Germany first. William"—they call him that almost as often as the Kaiser now—"who was the only important ruler who had not declared war in more than forty years, gave them twelve hours to desist from their designs; they refused, and the war went on. Had we planned to go to war we should certainly have passed the tip to the millions of Germans in foreign lands in time for them to have reached Germany. You yourself have seen how they poured down to the ports when they heard of the Fatherland's danger, and how regretfully they returned to their far-off duties when it became apparent that England was not going to let them come home. Then we went through Belgium. We should not have done so, of course, but any people would have done the same to protect its national existence. Besides, we offered to do so peacefully; the stubborn Belgians would not have suffered in the slightest. And Belgium had a secret treaty with the Entente that would have permitted them to attack us from that side ..." and so on.

"Moral guilt? Not the slightest. As we feel no guilt whatever for starting the war—because we did not start it—so we feel none for any of the ways in which we waged it. The U-boats? What was our drowning of a few silly passengers who insisted on traveling compared with what the British were doing in starving our women and children, our entire nation?" (The old specious argument about the warning not to take the *Lusitania* was still frequently heard.) "We had to use U-boats or starve. A hysterical world blamed us for the more dramatic but by far the less wicked of two weapons.

Drowning is a pleasant death compared with starvation. War is war. But it was a very stupid mistake on the part of old fool Tirpitz." (The admiral probably had his whiskers pulled more often, figuratively, than any other man in the Empire. True, he was almost the only German left who felt capable of still nourishing so luxurious an adornment. But the U-boat policy had very few partizans left.) "Moral guilt, most certainly not. But it was the height of asininity. If he had had ten times as many U-boats, yes, by all means. But not when it brought in America and still failed to break the blockade. If the U-boat fans had not insisted on their program the war would have been over in 1916. But America would probably have come in, anyway; there were her loans to the Allies, and the munitions she furnished them. America, we suspect, was chiefly interested in her interest."

To all charges of unfair methods of warfare, of tyranny over the civilian population, of atrocities, Germany replied with an all-embracing: "You're another." "If we first used gas"—which by no means all Germans admitted—"think of those dreadful tanks! If we bombed London and Paris, see how our dear brethren along the Rhine suffered from your airmen. If we were forced to be stern with the population of the occupied regions, go hear what the Russians did in our eastern provinces. You make martyrs of your Cavells and Fryatts; we can name you scores of Germans who suffered worse far more unjustly. As to accusing us of wanton atrocities, that has become one of the recognized weapons of modern warfare, one of the tricks of the game, this shouting of calumnies against your gagged enemy to a keenly listening audience not averse to feeding on such morbid morsels. It was accepted as a recognized misdeal in the political poker game as far back as the Boer War, when the science of photography first reached the advanced stage that made it possible to show English soldiers catching on their bayonets babies that had never been within a hundred miles of them. Like all the underhand moves, it was immensely improved or perfected during this long life-and-death struggle. That was one of the things we somewhat neglected, first from lack of foresight, later because of the impossibility of making ourselves heard by the audience, of getting it across the footlights, while our enemies screened the whole front of the stage. Ninety per cent. of the so-called atrocities were made out of whole cloth, or out of very slight remnants. We admit the cleverness of the other side in 'getting away with it,' but now that it has served its purpose we expect him, if he is the fair sportsman he pretends, to acknowledge it was only a trick, at least as soon as the smoke and heat of action have cleared a bit." (This view was widely held among citizens of Allied nations who have traveled in Germany since the signing of the armistice, though few of them admitted it except in private conversation.) "There were, of course, things that should not have been. There are in all armies; there have been in all wars, and always will be. But if some of our soldiers forgot themselves, if our reserve officers were not always of the high standard their position called for, let us tell you of some of the horrible things the Russians perpetrated in our eastern provinces"— somehow Germany always seemed to flee eastward when this question of atrocities came up.

"One of our greatest mistakes was the failure to realize the value of *réclame*, of publicity, propaganda, advertising, or whatever you choose to call it, until it was too late." (Berlin was showing one of our great "Hun" pictures in her principal cinemas at the time of my visit, partly for the amusement of seeing themselves as others see them, but chiefly as an example of how they "missed a bet" in not discovering how the "movies" could also be "mobilized" for war ends.) "The United States was finally led astray and brought into the war chiefly because England and France made skilful use of propaganda, because they controlled the great avenues of the transmission of news. It looks like a silly, childish little trick for the Allies to take our cables away from us—along with our milch cows—but it is really very important, for they keep on telling unrefuted lies about us as long as it serves their purposes. Now that they have a clear field, they will discolor the facts more than ever. They censored, doctored their public prints far more than we did. See how they dare not even yet publish the terms of the treaty that was handed us at Versailles; yet we have had them here in Germany for days. Even the French Chamber and the American Senate got them first from our papers. Open diplomacy indeed! There never was a time during the war that French and English and, when we could get them, American papers could not be bought at any kiosk in our larger cities. Look at Haase, who publishes daily the strongest kind of attacks on the government, quite openly, while the newspapers of Paris are still sprinkled with the long white hoofprints of the censor.

"We admit our fault—and we are now paying for it. This publicity was one of the 'perfectly legitimate' moves in the crooked game of war, one of the cleverest of the tricks, and we overlooked it, thanks to the thick heads of our diplomats! It was perhaps the deciding factor. The English with their shopkeeper souls; the French, crudely materialistic under their pretended love of art; the traitorous Italians—were not equal all together to downing us. But when they succeeded in talking over America, a great big healthy child overtopping them all, naïve, inexperienced, rather flattered at being let into a man's game, somewhat hysterical"—I am putting things a bit more baldly than I ever heard them stated, but that is what was meant—"we might have known it was all over with us. Now we are in a pretty predicament. We have no national wealth left, except our labor, for we have given up everything else. We cannot even emigrate—except to Russia. My children will see a great combination with them, unless this Bolshevism sweeps all before it now while the bars are down.

"But we were never defeated militarily. *Ausgeschlossen!* We won the war—on the field of battle, such a war as was never before waged against a nation in all history. That is what makes our real defeat so bitter. America did it, with her unlimited flood of materials, her endless resources, plus the hunger blockade. With the whole world against us and starvation undermining us at the rear, what was left for us? But we still held our front; our line never cracked. The German army was the best in the world—to-day the American is—its discipline was strict, but there was a reason, centuries of experience, behind every command. But the war lasted too long; we got overtrained, went stale and...."

No German, from the mouth of the Elbe to the mountains of Bavaria, admitted for an instant that his army was defeated. Whatever their other opinions, the Boches insisted on hugging to themselves the cold conviction that they were beaten from within, never by a foreign enemy. They seemed almost fond of boasting that it took America with her boundless resources to turn the scales against them. But they were not always consistent in this view, for they admitted that with the failure of the last offensive they knew the game was up; they admitted that Hindenburg himself asserted that the side that succeeded in bringing up the last half-million fresh troops would win the war. In this connection it may be of interest to hear what the German Staff (American Intelligence Section) thought of the American army. "The United States enlisted men," runs their statement, "were excellent soldiers. They took battle as an adventure and were the best shock troops of the war when it ended. Their officers were good up to and sometimes through battalion commanders; above that they were astonishingly weak."

Throughout all Germany the proposed peace terms were received in much the same spirit they had been in Berlin. Outwardly they were greeted with surprising calmness, almost apathy. But one could find protests and to spare by knowing where to listen. "This peace is even less open and fair than that of the Congress of Vienna," came the first returns. "We expected to lose some territory in the east, perhaps, but that Alsace-Lorraine should be allowed to vote which of us she cared to join, that 'self-determination' of which Wilson has spoken so much. Both of those provinces always belonged to Germany, except for the hundred years between the time Louis XIV stole them from us and Bismarck won them back; they belonged to Germany just as much as Poland ever did to the Poles. Lorraine may want to be French; Alsace certainly does not, and never did."

It seemed to be the old men who resented most the loss of territory, as the women were most savage in their expressions. Probably grandfather would miss the far corner lot more than would the younger members of the family, who had not been accustomed to seeing it so long. When one could get the Germans to specify, they rated the proposed terms about as follows: "The loss of the Saar is the worst; the losses in the east, second; the loss of our colonies, third." But they reminded one of a man who has just returned home and found his house wrecked—the farther he looks the more damage he discovers; at each new discovery he gasps a bit more chokingly, and finally stands dumb before the immensity of the catastrophe that has befallen him, for some time undecided just what his next move shall be. "We would rather pay any amount of indemnity than lose territory," they went on, at last. "It is a crime to occupy the Rhineland, the richest, most taxable, the most freedom-loving part of Germany. And now they are trying to steal that from us in addition! The Allies are trying to Balkanize us. They do not want money from us; they want to *vernichten* us, to destroy us completely. The immense majority of the people of the Rhineland do not want to abandon us; they are loyal to the Empire. But the French have the upper hand now; they protect the few self-seekers who are riding it over the loyal masses; the British are willing and the Americans are simple enough to believe that the republic that is to have its capital in Coblenz represents the desires of the majority. Never! The Catholics and the capitalists combined to form the Rhine Republic, with the aid of the French—because they could thus both have more power for themselves." (How true this statement may be I can only judge from the fact that a very small minority of those I questioned on the subject while with the Army of Occupation expressed any desire to see the region separated from Germany, and that I found virtually *no* sentiment for abandoning the Empire in any portion whatever of unoccupied Germany.)

"Then these new frontiers in the east were set by men who know the conditions there only from books, not from being on the spot, or at best by men who were misinformed by the stupid or biased agents they sent. Thus many towns almost wholly inhabited by Germans are now to be given to the Poles, and *vice versa*." As to the proposed punishment of the Kaiser, though there seemed to be very little love and no great loyalty—except in acquitting him on the score of beginning the war—left for him among the great mass of the people, this clause aroused as great wrath as any. The German saw in it a matter of national honor.

Such anger as the peace terms aroused was, of course, chiefly poured out upon President Wilson. "We believed in Wilson and he betrayed us," protested a cantankerous old man. "Wilson told us that if we chased the Hohenzollerns out he would 'treat us right'; we did so, and now look what he has gone and done to us! He has led us to slaughter, and all the time we thought he was leading us out of the wilderness. He has grossly betrayed us. People put too much faith in him. *I* never did, for I always considered his lean face the mask of hypocrisy, not the countenance of justice and idealism. We Germans, with few exceptions, believed him to be a noble character, whereas he is operated by strings in the hands of the American capitalists, like the puppets the children at the Guignol mistake for living people." "Only the capitalists," cried a motorman, "led by Wilson, had any say in this treaty. Your Wilson and his capitalists are far worse tyrants than the Kaiser ever aspired to be in his wildest moments." "Wilson leads the capitalists of the world against Socialism, against socialistic Germany, which they fear far more than they ever did a military Germany," asserted the Majority-Socialist papers.

On the other hand there were Germans who stanchly defended Wilson, taking an unprejudiced, scientific view of the entire question, as they might of the fourth dimension or of the Bacon-Shakespeare controversy. These were apt to bring their fellow-countrymen up with a round turn by asserting that Wilson never promised to make peace with Germany based on his Fourteen Points. Ah, those Fourteen Points! If they had been bayonets I should have resembled a sieve long, long before my journey was ended.

"We Germans can look at the problem from both sides," insisted one such open-minded professor, "because we are more liberal than the Allies, because we travel, we do business in all parts of the world. We have advanced beyond the stage of melodrama, of believing that all right, all good is on one side and the contrary on the other. The Frenchman rarely leaves home, the Englishman never changes his mind when he does—he has it set in cement for safety's sake before he starts. The American is too young to be able to look frankly at a question from both sides."

"Militarism," said a mason who had one crippled leg left, yet who chatted with me in an equally friendly manner both before and after he had learned my nationality, "was our national sport, as football is in England, and whatever you play most is in America. Now we have discovered that it is not a very pleasant sport. We have a nose full of it! Yet we cannot sign this peace. If a man has a thousand marks left and a footpad says to him: 'I am going to take this away from you. Kindly sign this statement to the effect that you are giving it to me freely. I shall take it, anyway, but we will both be better off if I have your consent,' what would you expect the man to do? Let the Allies come to Berlin! We cannot go to war again, but—the people must stand behind the government!"

Just what he meant by the last assertion was not entirely clear; but at least the first half of the assertion was frequently borne out by little hints that all but escaped the eye. Thus, a large bookstore in Berlin bore the meaningful placard, "War Literature at Half Price!"

"From this date" (May 8th), gasped an important Berlin daily, "we drop to a fourth-rate power, along with Spain." (There were, to be sure, some Spanish suggestions in the uncleanliness, the apathy, the run-down condition of buildings that had suffered five years of disrepair, in the emaciated beggars one occasionally saw in the Germany of 1919.) "With this 'peace' we are down and out; we can never get on our feet again. There is not wealth enough in all Germany to pay this indemnity and still save ourselves. We can never recover because we can never buy the raw materials we must have to do so. There is nothing left in the country with which to pay for these raw stuffs except our labor, and we cannot set to work because we have no raw stuffs to work with. We are caught in the whirlpool! It is a fallacy to think that we shall save money on our army. The army we have to-day costs us far more than the one we had when the armistice was signed. If we are required to have an army of volunteers only and pay them as good wages as they now require ... to-day one soldier costs us more than thirty did under the old system! And what soldiers! We shall not be able to compete with the world, first of all because the exchange on the mark will make our raw materials cost us three times what they do our rivals, and then we have these new eight-hour laws and all the rest of the advance socialistic program, which they do not have in other countries. The Allies should have hunted out the guilty individuals, not punish us all as a nation, as an incompetent captain punishes his entire company because he is too lazy or too stupid to catch the actual wrong-doers. In twenty years Germany will have been completely destroyed. All the best men will have emigrated. If we try to spend anything for *Kultur*— that excellent heritage of the old régime which our enemies so falsified and garbled—for working-men's insurance, new schools, municipal theaters, even for public baths, the Allies will say, 'No, we want that money ourselves; you owe us that on the old war game you lost.' In that case all we can do is to resort to passive resistance"—a strange German occupation indeed!

The little blond German "ace of aces," credited with bringing down some twoscore Allied airmen, hoped to come to America and play in a circus. He put little faith in the rumor that he might not be received there, and thought that if there really was any opposition it could easily be overcome by getting one of our large "trusts" to take a financial interest in his case. In fact, the chief worry of many Germans seemed to be whether or not and how soon they would be allowed to come to America—North or South. "Rats desert a sinking ship." One man whose intelligence and experience warranted attention to his words assured me that he belonged to a party that had been working for some time in favor of, and that they found a strong sentiment for—making Germany an American colony! I regret the inability to report any personal evidence to support his statements.

But if the general tone was lacrymose, notes of a more threatening timbre were by no means lacking. "With this 'peace,'" was one assertion, "we shall have another Thirty Years' War and all Europe will go over the brink into the abyss." "We Germans got too high," mused a philosophic old innkeeper accustomed to take advantage of his profession as a listening-post. "He who does is due for a fall, and we got it. But France is the haughty one now, and she is riding to a cropper. She will rue her overbearing manner, for the *revanche* is here already—on our side this time. And if French and Germans ever go to war again there will be no prisoners taken!" "If the Germans are forced to sign this 'peace,'" cried a fat Hollander who had lived much in Germany, "there will be another war within ten years, and all Europe will be destroyed, Holland with the rest, France certainly, for she is tottering already. If they do not sign, we shall all be plunged into anarchy." "We had looked to Wilson to bring an end to a century-old situation that had grown intolerable," moaned a Berlin merchant. "Now we must drill hatred into our children from their earliest age, so that in thirty years, when the time is ripe...."

What does Germany plan to do with herself, or what is left of her, now? Does she wish to remain a republic, to return to the Hohenzollerns, or to establish a new monarchy under some other less sinister dynasty? As with so many of the world's problems, the answer depends largely on the papers one, or those of whom one made inquiries, read. The replies ran the entire gamut. Some asserted that even the heads of the socialistic parties have lost only the symbols of kaiserism, that the masses still keep even those. A majority of the peasant class is probably monarchical, when they are not wholly indifferent to anything beyond their own acres and the price of beer. They seem to like the distant glamour of a glittering pageantry, a ruler to whom they can attribute superman or demigod qualities—so long as the cost thereof is not extracted too openly from their pockets. The Junkers, the old robber barons from Borussia, of course still want a monarchy, probably of Hohenzollern complexion, though the present heir to that bankrupt estate has not a visible friend in the Empire. "The majority still want the Kaiser, or at least a monarchy," one heard the frequent assertion; "we are not ripe for a republic."

If I were forced to answer definitely myself I should say that most educated Germans want nothing more to do with the Kaiser and his family. Their reply to a query on this point is most apt to be an energetic, "*Ausgeschlossen!*" On the question of no monarchy at all they are by no means so decided. Naturally there is still a monarchical class left; there still is even in France. "A vote would probably give a small majority for the monarchy to-day," said a young psychologist. "I have no politics myself; a psychologist must keep his mind clear of those squabbles, as an engineer must his gears of sand, but at least the Hohenzollerns gave us peace and quiet, and while there were some unpleasant things about their system, they now seem slight in comparison with what the war has brought us.... The German people are really democratic (*sic!*), but they are also monarchical; they want a paternal government, such as they have been used to during all the living generations. But we shall probably remain a republic now."

Said the peasant innkeeper already introduced: "The monarchy is probably the best system for us; it fits our mentality and training. But now that we have changed there is no use in changing back again. There is not enough difference between the two schemes of government. So we shall probably stay what we are. The great trouble with this king and prince business"—he lived in Saxe-Weimar, where every seventh man used to wear a crown—"was that it was so *übertrieben*, so overdone, with us. They demanded such swarms of *Beamters*, of employees, courtiers, uniforms. And all their petty little nobles! We peasants don't mind supporting a few such decorations, but.... Now the Kaiser gets eighty thousand marks a year instead of twenty-four million, and I doubt if he is suffering from hunger—which is less than can be said for many of the people he left behind."

Possibly the most frequently expressed opinion in the length and breadth of Germany was the frank, "It does not much matter what kind of a government we have so long as we can get wise and honest men at the top." That, after all, is the final answer to the whole problem that has been teasing the world for centuries. "Remember," smiled a Dutchman, "that this democracy you are shouting about is no new American discovery. We tried a republic centuries ago, and we still have it, though now under a hereditary president called a king—or just now a queen—and we find that works best of all." "We are like birds just let out of a lifetime cage," protested a Socialist. "Give us time to try our wings. We shall fly much better two years from now. There was a strong republican feeling in Germany long before the war, but the Kaiser and his crowd ruthlessly strangled it." "How fair, how revolutionary, how socialistic is the 'new' Germany," raged the Independent Socialists, "is shown by the acquittal of the assassins of Liebknecht and Luxembourg contrasted with the death-sentence of Leviné, who was no more a 'traitor against the constituted authorities' than was Hoffmann, who drove him out, or those who upset the monarchy and established the 'republic.'"

But we must be careful not to let partizan rage, sour grapes, obscure the problem. There has certainly been a considerable change of feeling in Germany; whether a sufficient, a final change remains to be seen. The Germans, whatever their faults, are a foresighted and a deliberate people. They are scanning the horizon with unprejudiced eyes in quest of a well-tested theory of government that will fit their problem. Though they seem for the instant to be inclined to the left, they are really balancing on the ridge between republicanism and monarchy, perhaps a more responsible monarchy than the one they have just cast off, and it will probably not take much to tip them definitely to either side. In the offing, too, Bolshevism is always hovering; not so close, perhaps, as the Germans themselves fear, or are willing to have the world believe, but distinctly menacing, for all that. In things political at least the German is no idealist. Of the rival systems of government he has an eye chiefly to the material advantages. Which one will bring him the most *Kultur*, in the shape of all those things ranging from subsidized opera to municipal baths with which the Kaiser régime upholstered his slavery? Above all, which will give him the earliest and surest opportunity to get back to work and to capitalize undisturbed his world-famed diligence? Those are his chief questions. I never heard in all Germany the hint of a realization that a republic may be the best form of government because it gives every citizen more or less of a chance to climb to the topmost rung of the ladder. But I did now and then see encouraging signs that the masses are beginning to realize that a people is responsible for the actions of its government just as a business man is responsible for his clerk's errors— and that is already a long step forward for Germany.

X
SENTENCED TO AMPUTATION

The terms of the Peace Treaty having broken upon Berlin without arousing any of the excited scenes I had expected, I decided to go away from there. General apathy might be ruling in the provinces also, but at least I would be "on my own" if anything happened, and not where I could dart under the protecting wing of the Ally-housing Adlon at the first signs of storm. I laid a plan that promised to kill two birds with one stone. I would jump to the far eastern border of the Empire, to a section which Paris had just decreed should be handed over to the Poles, and I would walk from there into a section which the Poles had already taken. In other words, I would examine side by side an amputated member and one which the consultation of international doctors about the operating-table on which Germany lay had marked for amputation.

Luckily I took the wrong train on the teeming Friedrichsstrasse Bahnhof platform next morning, or I should have been sent back before reaching my goal. I learned just in time to drop off there that travelers into Polish territory must have their passports viséed in Frankfurt-am-Oder. There was a considerable gathering of nervous petitioners about the door of the haughty German officer who represented the Empire in this matter, at one of the huge barracks on the outskirts of town. But the delay was not correspondingly long, thanks not only to the efficient system of his office, but to the fact that many of the applicants remained only long enough to hear him dismiss them with an uncompromising "No!" All men of military age—and in the Germany of 1919 that seemed to mean every male between puberty and senility—were being refused permission to enter the amputated province, whether they were of Polish or German origin. My own case was different. The officer scowled a bit as the passport I laid before him revealed my nationality, but he stamped it quickly, as if in haste to be done with an unpleasant duty. Whether or not this official right of exit from the Empire included permission to return was a question which he curtly dismissed as no affair of his. Evidently I was burning my bridges behind me.

Frankfurt-am-Oder pulsated with soldiers, confirming the impression that reigned in khaki-clad circles at Coblenz that the German army had turned its face toward the east. Food seemed somewhat less scarce than in the capital. A moderately edible dinner cost me only eight marks. In the market-place, however, the stalls and bins were pathetically near to emptiness. A new annoyance—one that was destined to pursue me during all the rest of my travels in Germany—here first became personal. It was the scarcity of matches. In the days to come that mere hour's search for a single box of uncertain, smoke-barraging *Streichhölzer* grew to be a pleasant memory. Not far from the city was one of those many camps of Russian prisoners, rationed now by American doughboys, some of whose inmates had nearly five years of German residence to their discredit. If the testimony of many constant observers was trustworthy, they dreaded nothing so much as the day when they must turn their backs on American plenitude and regain their own famished, disrupted land. True, they were still farmed out to labor for their enemies. But they seldom strained themselves with toil, and in exchange were they not growing efficient in baseball and enhancing their Tataric beauty with the silk hats and red neckties furnished by an all-providing Red Cross?

The station platform of Frankfurt, strewn pellmell with Polish refugees and their disheveled possessions, recalled the halcyon days of Ellis Island. A "mixed" train of leisurely temperament wandered away at last toward the trunk line to the east which I had fortunately not taken that morning. Evidently one must get off the principal arteries of travel to hear one's fellow-passengers express themselves frankly and freely. At any rate, there was far more open discussion of the question of the hour during that jolting thirty miles than I had ever heard in a day on sophisticated express trains.

"The idea," began an old man of sixty or more, apropos of nothing but the thought that had evidently been running through his head at sight of the fertile acres about us, "of expecting us to surrender this, one of the richest sections of the Fatherland, and to those improvident Poles of all people! They are an intelligent race—I have never been one of those who denied them intelligence. But they can never govern themselves; history has proved that over and over again. In my twenty-three years' residence in Upper Silesia I have seen how the laborers' houses have improved, how they have thrived and reached a far higher plane of culture under German rule. A Polish government would only bring them down to their natural depths again. They will never treat the working-man as fairly, as generously as we have.

"But," he continued, suddenly, with increased heat, "we will *not* see the Fatherland torn to pieces by a band of wolfish, envious enemies. We will fight for our rights! We *cannot* abandon our faithful fellow-countrymen, our genuine German brethren, to be driven from their homes or misruled by these wretched Poles. It would be unworthy of our German blood! There will be a *Bürgerkrieg*—a peasants' war, with every man fighting for his own sacred possessions, before we will allow German territory to be taken from us. I will sacrifice my entire family rather than allow the Fatherland to be dismembered."

Our fellow-passengers listened to this tirade of testy old age with the curious apathy of hunger or indifference which seemed to have settled upon the nation. Now and then one or two of them nodded approval of the sentiments expressed; occasionally they threw in a few words of like tenor. But on the whole there was little evidence of an enthusiasm for rescuing their "genuine German brethren" that promised to go the length of serious personal sacrifice.

All Germany was in bloom, chiefly with the white of early fruit-trees, giving the landscape a maidenly gaiety that contrasted strangely with the funereal gloom within the car. Gangs of women were toiling with shovels along the railway embankment. The sandy flatlands, supporting little but scrubby spruce forests, gave way at length to a rich black soil that heralded the broad fertile granary which Germany had been called upon to surrender. Barefoot women and children, interspersed with only a small percentage of men, stood erect from their labors and gazed oxlike after the rumbling train. Here and there great fields of colza, yellow as the saffron robe of a Buddhist priest, stretched away toward the horizon. The plant furnished, according to one of my fellow-passengers, a very tolerable *Ersatz* oil. Fruit-trees in their white spring garments, their trunks carefully whitewashed as a protection against insects, lined every highway. Other trees had been trimmed down to mere trunks, like those of Brittany and La Vendée in France, as if they, too, had been called upon to sacrifice all but life itself to the struggle that had ended so disastrously.

In the helter-skelter of finding seats in the express that picked us up at the junction I had lost sight of the belligerent old man. A husband and wife who had formed part of his audience, however, found place in the same compartment as I. For a long time I attempted to draw them into conversation by acting as suspiciously as possible. I took copious notes, snapped my kodak at everything of interest on the station platforms, and finally took to reading an English newspaper. All in vain. They stared at me with that frankness of the continental European, but they would not be moved to words, not even at sight of the genuine cigar I ostentatiously extracted from my knapsack. At length I gave up the attempt and turned to them with some casual remark, bringing in a reference to my nationality at the first opportunity.

"Ah," boasted the woman, "I *told* my husband that you looked like an Englishman, or something. But he insisted you were a Dane."

"I wonder if the old fellow got a seat, and some one else to listen to him—with his *Bürgerkrieg*," mused the husband, a moment later. "We Germans have little to boast of, in governing ourselves. Germany should be divided up between Belgium, France, and England, or be given an English king." Apparently he was quite serious, though he may have been indulging in that crude sarcasm to which the German sometimes abandons himself and which he thinks nicely veiled. "We are not ripe for a republic. What we are evidently trying to do is to make ourselves a super-republic in one jump. The Socialists were against the Kaiser because he put on too much pomp, but we Germans need that kind of a ruler, some one who will be stern but kind to us, like a father. The Kaiser himself was not to blame. At least half, if not a majority, of the people want him back—or at least another one like him."

"We surely will have our Kaiser back again, sooner or later," cried the woman, in a tone like that of a religious fanatic.

Just then, however, the pair reached their station and there was no opportunity to get her to elaborate her text. They shook hands heartily, wished me a *"Glückliche Reise,"* and disappeared into the night.

Sunset and dusk had been followed by an almost full moon that made the evening only a fainter replica of the perfect cloudless day. Toward nine, however, the sky became overcast and the darkness impenetrable. This was soon the case inside as well as out, for during an unusually protracted stop at a small station a guard marched the length of the train, putting out all its lights. It seemed we were approaching the "danger zone." I had been laboring under the delusion that the armistice which Germany had concluded with her enemies was in force on all fronts. Not at all. The Poles, it seemed, were intrenched from six hundred to three thousand yards away all along this section of the line. They had been there since January, soon after the province of Posen had revolted against German rule. Almost every night they fired upon the trains, now and then even with artillery. Sometimes the line was impassable. German troops, of course, were facing them. Trench raids were of almost nightly occurrence; some of them had developed into real battles.

Now and again as we hurled on through the night there were sounds of distant firing. It was only at Nakel, however, that we seemed in any personal danger. There the Poles were barely six hundred yards away, and between the time we halted at the station and got under way again at least a hundred shots were fired, most of them the rat-a-tat of machine-guns and all of them so close at hand that we unconsciously ducked our heads. The train apparently escaped unscathed, however, and two stations farther on the guard lighted it up again, with the announcement that danger was over. We rumbled on into Bromberg, where I descended toward midnight. Soldiers held the station gate and subjected every traveler—or, more exactly, his papers—to a careful scrutiny before permitting him to pass. My own credentials they accepted more readily than those of many of their fellow-countrymen, some of whom were herded into a place of detention. As I stepped out through the gate, another soldier thrust into my hand an *Ausweis* permitting me to remain on the streets after dark, for Bromberg was officially in a state of siege.

When I entered the nearest hotel I found that unofficially in the same condition. A drunken army officer, who was the exact picture of what Allied cartoonists would have us believe all his class, was prancing about the hotel office with drawn sword, roaring angrily and threatening to spit on his needle-pointed saber every one in the room. The possible victims were two half-grown hotel clerks, ridiculous in their professional evening dress, and a thin, mottled-faced private soldier, who cowered speechless in different corners. I was inside before I noticed the disturbance, and pride would not permit me to retreat. I took station near a convenient stool and studied the exact degree of uncertainty of the bully's legs, with a view to future defense. But for some reason he took no notice of me and at length lurched out again into the street, cursing as he went.

I owe it to the goddess of truth to state that this was the one and only case I ever personally saw of a German officer living up to the popular Allied conception of his caste. On the contrary, I found the great majority of them quiet, courteous and gentlemanly to a high degree, with by no means so large a sprinkling of the "roughneck" variety as was to be found among our own officers in Europe. Which does not mean that they were not often haughty beyond reason, nor that they may not sometimes have concealed brutal instincts beneath their polished exteriors. But while we are on the subject, let me read into the record the testimony of their own fellow-countrymen, particularly that of many a man who served under them.

"Our active officers," would be the composite answer of all those I questioned on the subject, "were excellent. They still had something *adel* about them—something of the genuine nobility of the old knights from which the caste sprang. Their first and foremost thought was the fatherly care of their men—rendered with a more or less haughty aloofness, to be sure—that was necessary to discipline—but a genuine solicitude for the welfare of their soldiers. Above all"—and here, perhaps, is the chief point of divergence between them and our own officers of the same class—"they were rarely or never self-seeking. Our reserve officers, on the other hand, were by no means of the same high character. One so often felt the *Kaufmann*—the soul of a merchant underneath. Many of them were just plain rascals, who stole the presents that came addressed to their soldiers and looted for their own personal benefit. Then there were many who, though honest and well-meaning enough, had not the preparation required for so important an office. They were teachers, or scholars, or young students, who did not realize that a quiet voice is more commanding than a noisy one. The great drawback of our military system, of our national life, in fact, under the monarchy, was the impenetrable wall that separated us into the compartments of caste. Old *Feldwebels* who had served in the army for twenty years were refused positions which they could have filled to excellent advantage, in war-time, because they were not considered in the "officer class"; and there were set over them men half their own age, school-boy officers, in some cases, who were barely eighteen, and who naturally could not have the training and experience which are required of a lieutenant. Sixty per cent. of our active officers were slain, and many others were not able to return to the line. Only 30 per cent. of our reserve officers were killed, with the result that before the war ended a man was lucky to have a superior whom he could honor and unquestioningly obey."

It was in Bromberg that I came into personal contact with more of the class in question than I had in any other city of the Empire. Not only were soldiers more numerous here, but I purposely "butted in" upon a half-dozen military offices, ostensibly to make sure that my papers were in order, really to feel out the sentiment on the peace terms and measure the sternness of martial law. But though I deliberately emphasized my nationality, not once did an officer show any resentment at my presence. In fact, most of them saw me to the door at the end of the interview, and bowed me out with all the ceremony of their exacting social code. If the verdict that had just been issued in Paris had burst like a shell among them, they showed no evidence of panic. The official day's work went deliberately on, and the only comment on the peace terms I succeeded in arousing was a quiet, uncompromising "Quite unacceptable, of course."

The city itself was as astonishingly placid in the midst of what an outsider would have supposed to be exciting times. Being not only in a state of siege, but having just heard that it was soon to transfer its allegiance to another race, one was justified in expecting a town as large as Trenton or San Antonio to show at least some ripples on its surface. I looked for them in vain. It was Sunday, just the day for popular demonstrations in Germany, yet not only was there no sign whatever of rejoicing among the Polish population, but nothing even suggesting the uprising of protest among the German residents which had been so loudly prophesied. The place resembled some New England factory town on the same day of the week. Groups of Polish-looking young men, somewhat uncomfortable and stiff in their Sunday best, lounged on the street-corners, ogling the plump Polish girls on their way to church. Strollers seemed interested only in keeping to the shaded side of the street, youths and children only in their games. Tramways rumbled slowly along as usual—and, before I forget it, their female conductors wore breeches; such shops as were habitually open on Sunday seemed to be doing their customary amount of business. The whole town was as staid, heavy, and unenthusiastic as the German character.

In the face of a wide divergence of opinion among its own inhabitants it was hard for a stranger to decide which of the two races predominated in Bromberg. The Germans asserted that only 40 per cent. of the population were Poles, and that many of them preferred to see things remain as they were. The Poles defied any one to find more than twenty Germans among every hundred inhabitants, or to point out a single member of their race who sincerely wished to keep his allegiance to the Fatherland. Street and shop signs were nearly all in German, but that may have been due to legal requirement. The rank and file of the populace had a Polish look, yet they seemed to speak German by choice. Moreover, there is but scant difference of appearance between Teutons and Poles, particularly when they have lived their entire lives together in the same environment. On the wall of a church I dropped into during morning service there were five columns of names, forty-five each, of the men who had "Patriotically sacrificed their lives for a grateful Fatherland." At least one half of them ended in "ski," and in one column alone I counted thirty unquestionably Polish names. But then, it was a Catholic church, so there you are again. Perhaps the most unbiased testimony of all was the fact that the little children playing in the park virtually all spoke Polish.

I drifted into conversation with an intelligent young mechanic taking his Sunday ease in a *Bierhalle*. He turned out to be a Pole. As soon as he was convinced of my identity he shed his mask of commonplace remarks and fell to talking frankly and sincerely. I do not speak Polish, hence the rulers of Bromberg might have been startled to hear the statements that were poured into my ear in their own tongue. Yet my companion discussed their shortcomings and the war they had waged, quite openly, with far less circumspection than a similar criticism of the powers that be would have required in France or the United States at the same date.

"You don't hear much Polish on the streets, do you?" he began. "But if I could take you into the homes you would find that the street-door is the dividing line between the two tongues. In the family circle we all stick to the old language, and the memory of the ancient nation that is just being resurrected has never been obscured. We are not exactly *forbidden* to speak Polish in public, but if we do we are quite likely to be thumped on the head, or kicked in the back, or called "dirty Polacks." Besides, it is never to our advantage to admit that we are Poles. You never know, when you meet a man, whether he is one or not. I feel sure the waiter there is one, for instance, yet you see he carefully pretends to understand nothing but German. We are treated with unfair discrimination from the cradle to the grave. When I first went to public school I could not speak German, and there was hardly a day that a gang of little *Deutschen* did not beat me to tears. I used to go home regularly with lumps as big as walnuts on my head. Even the teacher whipped us for speaking Polish. When it came time to go to work we could only get the hardest and most poorly paid jobs. The railways, the government offices, all the better trades were closed to us. If we applied for work at a German factory, the first thing they asked was whether we were Catholics and Poles. In the courts a "ski" on the end of a name means a double sentence. Our taxes were figured far more strictly than those of the Germans. In the army we are given the dirtiest jobs and most of the punishments. At the front we were thrown into the most dangerous positions.

"The Germans could have won the Poles over if they had done away with these unfair differences and treated us as equals. They are an efficient people and some of their ways are better than our ways, but they cannot get rid of their arrogance and their selfishness. They are short-sighted. I spent four years at the front, yet I never once fired at the enemy, but into the air or into the ground. The majority of Poles did the same thing. You can imagine the ammunition that was wasted. There is not much work at home, yet you will not find one Pole in a hundred of military age in the German volunteer army. You see many of them in uniform on the streets here—all those redheaded young fellows are Poles—but that is because they are still illegally held under the old conscription act. Shortsightedness again, for if trouble ever starts, the garrison will eat itself up without any one outside bothering with it. No Pole of military age can get into the province of Posen, not even if he was born there. In Berlin there are thousands of young Poles wandering around in uniform, half starved, with nothing to do, yet who are not allowed to come home.

"No, there has been very little mixture of the two races. Intermarriage is rare. I know only one case of it among my own acquaintants. It is not the German government that is opposed to it—on the contrary—but the Church, and Polish sentiment. The Catholics are against the old order of things and want a republic; it is the Protestants who want the Kaiser restored"—here one detected a religious bias that perhaps somewhat obscured the truth. "The old-German party wants to fight to the end. If they had their say Poland would never get the territory that has been awarded her. Sign? Of course they will sign. They are merely stalling, in the hope of having the blow softened. Nor will the government that accepts the treaty be overthrown. The Social Democrats are strong, very strong; they will sign and still live. The Poles? With very few exceptions they are eager to join the new empire. Paderewski has become a national hero. Especially are the peasants strong for the change. For one thing, it will fatten their pocketbooks. The Germans pumped them dry of everything. They had to deliver so many eggs per hen, buying them if the fowls did not lay enough. Or the guilty hen had to be turned over for slaughter. It usually went into the officers' messes. Each farmer was allowed only one rooster. The same exactions ruled among all the flocks and herds. Thousands of girls were sent into the pine forests to gather pitch for turpentine. No, I do not believe they were mistreated against their will, except perhaps in a few individual cases, no more than would happen anywhere under similar circumstances. Nor do I think the Germans wantonly destroyed trees by 'ringing' them. What they did, probably, was tap them too carelessly and too deep.

"All this talk about Bolshevism overspreading Germany is nonsense. The Bolshevists are poor, simple fellows who have nothing to lose and perhaps something to gain, many of them Chinese laborers brought to Russia in the time of the Czar, fatalists who think nothing of throwing their lives away—or of taking those of others. The other day the Bolshevists decreed in one of the cities they have captured that the bourgeois should move out into the outskirts and the proletariat take all the fine houses. Then they named a 'poor day' during which any one who had no shoes could go into all the houses and take a pair wherever he found two pairs. Can you imagine the orderly, plodding Germans subscribing to any such doctrine as that? I certainly cannot, for I have lived all my life among them and I know how they worship *Ordnung* and *Gemütlichkeit*.

"Yes, we have several Polish newspapers published here in Bromberg. But even if you could read them it would not be worth your while, for they do not mean what they say. They are doctored and padded and censored by the German authorities until the only reason we read them is for the local gossip of our friends and acquaintances. If it were not Sunday I would take you to meet the editor of one of them, and you would find that he speaks quite differently from what he writes in his paper, once he is sure he is not talking to a German spy."

The mechanic told me all this without once showing the slightest evidence of prejudice or bitterness against the oppressors of his race. He treated the matter with that academic aloofness, that absence of personal feeling, which I had so often been astounded to see the Germans themselves display toward the woes that had come upon them. Perhaps a lifelong grievance grows numb with years, perhaps it is less painful when swaddled in calm detachment, perhaps, the temperamental Polish character takes on a phlegmatic coating in a German environment. At any rate, all those groups of youths that lounged on the street-corners, ogling the girls as they passed on their way homeward from church, had a get-along-with-as-little-trouble-as-possible-seeing-we-can't-avoid-it manner toward the still somewhat arrogant Germans that made Bromberg outwardly a picture of peace and contentment.

The half-dozen Teuton residents with whom I talked seemed rather apathetic toward the sudden change in their fortunes. The shopkeepers, with one exception, announced their intention of continuing business in Bromberg, even if it became necessary to adopt Polish citizenship. The exception was of the impression that they would be driven out, and was not yet making any plans for the future. A station guard, on the other hand, denounced the decision of Paris with a genuine Prussian wrath. "Every railway employee is armed," he asserted, "and *die Polacken* will not get anything that belongs to the Fatherland without a struggle. It is absurd," he vociferated, "to expect that we will surrender a genuine German city like Bromberg to a lot of improvident wastrels. Let them keep the part about Posen and south of it; there the Poles are in the majority. But here"—as usual, it seemed, the section to which they were entitled was somewhere else.

A lawyer whom I found sunning himself on a park bench before the fantastic bronze fountain discussed the problem more quietly, but with no less heat.

"You Americans," he perorated, "the whole Allied group, do not understand the problem in its full significance. We look upon the Poles very much as you do upon your negroes. They have much the same shiftlessness, much the same tendency to revert to the semi-savagery out of which we Germans have lifted them. Now just imagine, for the moment, that you had been starved to submission in a war with, say, Mexico, Japan, and England. Suppose a so-called 'peace conference' made up entirely of your enemies, and sitting, say, in Canada, decreed that Mississippi, Florida, Alabama—that half a dozen of your most fertile Southern states must be turned over to the negroes, to form part of a new negro nation. It is possible that your people in the North, whom the problem did not directly touch, might consent to the arrangement. But do you for a moment think that your hot-blooded Southerners, the white men who would have to live in that negro nation or escape with what they could carry with them, would accept the decision without springing to arms even though it was signed by a dozen Northerners? That is exactly our case here, and whether or not this alleged Peace Treaty is accepted by the government in Berlin, the Germans of the East will not see themselves despoiled without a struggle."

That evening I attended an excellent performance of Südermann's *Die Ehre* in the subsidized municipal theater. Tickets were even cheaper than in Coblenz, none of them as high as four marks, even with war tax, poor tax, and "wardrobe." The house was crowded with the serious-minded of all classes, Poles as well as Germans; the actors were of higher histrionic ability than the average American town of the size of Bromberg sees once a year. Yet equally splendid performances were offered here at these slight prices all the year round. As I strolled hotelward with that pleasant sensation of satisfaction that comes from an evening of genuine entertainment, I could not but wonder whether this, and those other undeniable advantages of German *Kultur*, whatever sins might justly be charged against it, would be kept up after the Poles had taken Bromberg into their own keeping.

As to the walking trip through these eastern provinces which I had planned, fate was once more against me. I might, to be sure, have set out on foot toward the region already amputated from the Empire, but in the course of an hour I should have had the privilege of walking back again. The German-Polish front was just six kilometers from Bromberg, and a wandering stranger would have had exactly the same chance of crossing its succession of trenches as of entering Germany from France a year before. The one and only way of reaching the province of Posen was by train from the village of Kreuz, back along the railway by which I had come.

The place had all the appearance of an international frontier, a frontier hastily erected and not yet in efficient running order. Arrangements for examining travelers and baggage consisted only of an improvised fence along the station platform, strewn pellmell with a heterogeneous throng bound in both directions, and their multifarious coffers and bundles. The soldiers who patrolled the line of demarkation with fixed bayonets were callow, thin-faced youths, or men past middle age who had plainly reached the stage of uselessness as combat troops. All wore on their collars the silver oak-leaves of the recently formed "frontier guard." Their manner toward the harassed travelers was either brutal or cringingly friendly. The Germans in civilian garb who examined passports and baggage were cantankerous and gruff, as if they resented the existence of a frontier where the Fatherland had never admitted that a frontier existed. They vented their wrath especially against men of military age who wished to enter Polish territory—and their interpretation of their duties in that respect was by no means charitable. Among others, a wretched little dwarf past fifty, whom a glance sufficed to recognize as useless from a military point of view, even had his papers not been stamped with the official *Untauglich*, was wantonly turned back. Many a family was left only the choice of abandoning the attempt to reach its home or of leaving its adult male members behind.

The churls allowed me to pass readily enough, but rescinded their action a moment later. Once beyond the barrier, I had paused to photograph the pandemonium that reigned about it. A lieutenant bellowed and a group of soldiers and officials quickly swarmed about me. Did I not know that photography was forbidden at the front? I protested that the station scenes of Kreuz could scarcely be called military information. What of that? I knew that it was within the zone of the armies, did I not? Rules were rules; it was not the privilege of every Tom, Dick, and Harry to interpret them to his own liking. A lean, hawk-faced civilian, who seemed to be in command, ordered me to open my kodak and confiscated the film it contained. If I set great store by the pictures on it, he would have it developed by the military authorities and let me have those that proved harmless, upon my return. I thanked him for his leniency and strolled toward the compartment I had chosen. Before I had reached it he called me back.

"Let me see your papers again," he demanded, in a far gruffer tone.

He glanced casually at them, thrust them into a pocket of his coat, and snapped angrily: "Get your baggage off the train! I am not going to let you through."

It was plain that he was acting from personal rather than official motives. Probably he considered my failure to raise my hat and to smile the sycophant smile with which my fellow-passengers addressed him as an affront to his high Prussian caste. Fortunately he was not alone in command. A more even-tempered official without his dyspeptic leanness beckoned him aside and whispered in his ear. Perhaps he called his attention to the importance of my credentials from Wilhelmstrasse. At any rate, he surrendered my papers after some argument, with an angry shrug of the shoulders, and his less hungry-looking companion brought them back to me.

"It has all been arranged," he smirked. "You may take the train."

This was still manned by a German crew. For every car that left their territory, however, the Poles required that one of the same class and condition be delivered to them in exchange. Several long freight-trains, loaded from end to end with potatoes, rumbled past us on the parallel track. Two hundred thousand tons of tubers were sent to Germany each month in exchange for coal. It was at that date the only commercial intercourse between the two countries, and explained why potatoes were the one foodstuff of comparative abundance even in Berlin. At Biala the station guards were Polish, but there was little indeed to distinguish them from those of Kreuz and Bromberg. Their uniforms, their rifles, every detail of their equipment, were German, except that some of them wore the square and rather clumsy-looking Polish cap or had decorated their round, red-banded fatigue bonnets with the silver double-eagle of the resurrected empire. Many were without even this insignia of their new allegiance, and only the absence of oak-leaves on their collars showed that they were no longer soldiers of the Fatherland.

We halted at Wronki for two hours, which made our departure three hours later, for clocks and watches were turned ahead to correspond with Polish time. Frontier formalities were even more leisurely and disorganized than they had been in Kreuz. The Poles seemed to have something of the amiable but headless temperament of the French. Their officers, too, in their impressive new uniforms with broad red or yellow bands, and their rattling sabers, bore a certain resemblance to children on Christmas morning that did not help to expedite matters under their jurisdiction. They were a bit less "snappy" than the more experienced Germans, somewhat inclined to strut and to flirt, and there were suggestions in their manner that they might not have been horrified at the offer of a tip. When at length my turn had come they found my credentials unsatisfactory. Why had they not been viséed by the Polish consul in Berlin, as well as by the Germans at Frankfurt? I had never dreamed that Berlin boasted a Polish consul. Indeed! Who, then, did I suppose handled the interests of their nation there? However, it was all right. As an American and a fellow-Ally they would let me pass. But I must promise to report at a certain office in Posen within twenty-four hours of my arrival.

Barefoot boys were selling huge slabs of bread and generous lengths of sausage through the car windows. All things are relative, and to the travelers from Germany these "ticket-free" viands of doubtful origin seemed a kingly repast. With every mile forward now it was easier to understand why the loss of the province of Posen had been so serious a blow to the hungry Empire. Here were no arid, sandy stretches, but an endless expanse of rich black loam, capable of feeding many times its rather sparse population. If it had been "pumped dry" by the former oppressors, it was already well on the road to recovery. Wheat, corn, and potatoes covered the flat plains to the horizons on either hand. Cattle and sheep were by no means rare; pigs, goats, ducks, and chickens flocked about every village and farm-house, evidently living in democratic equality with the human inhabitants. There were other suggestions that we were approaching the easy-going East. Men in high Russian boots sauntered behind their draft animals with the leisureliness of those who know the world was not built in a day, nor yet in a year. Churches of Oriental aspect, with steep roofs that were still not Gothic, broke the sameness of the prevailing German architecture. There was something softly un-Occidental in the atmosphere of the great city into which we rumbled at sunset, a city which huge new sign-boards on the station platform stridently announced was no longer Posen, but "Poznan."

XI
AN AMPUTATED MEMBER

(Posen under the Poles)

The same spirit that had led the Poles to impress so forcibly upon the traveler the fact that the city in which he had just arrived was now called Poznan (pronounced Poznánya) had manifested itself in a thousand other changes. In so far as time had permitted, every official signboard had already been rendered into Polish and the detested German ones cast into outer darkness. Only those familiar with the Slavic tongue of the new rulers could have guessed what all those glitteringly new enameled placards that adorned the still Boche-featured station were commanding them to do or not to do. Every street in town had been baptized into the new faith and gaily boasted that fact on every corner. For a time the names had been announced in both languages, as in Metz; but a month or so before my arrival the radicals had prevailed and the older placards had been abolished. True, in most cases the new ones were merely translations of the old. But what did it help the German resident who had neglected to learn Polish to know that the "Alte Markt" was still the "Old Market" so long as he could not recognize it under the new designation of "Stary Rynek"? Imagine, if you can, the sensation of waking up some morning to find that Main Street has become Ulica Glòwna, or to discover that the street-car you had always taken no longer runs to Forest Park but to Ogrott Lass.

Nothing but the few things that defied quick change, such as post-boxes or names deeply cut into stone façades, had escaped the all-embracing renovation. Indeed, many of these had been deliberately defaced. The cast-iron "Haltestelle der Strassenbahn" high up on the trolley-supports had been daubed with red paint, though they were still recognizable to motormen and would-be passengers. Many business houses had followed the official lead, and private signs were more apt than not to have the German words that had once called attention to the excellence of the wares within crudely effaced or changed to the new tongue. Sometimes it was not merely the language that had been altered, but the whole tenor of the proprietor's allegiance. A popular underground beer-hall in the heart of town was no longer the "Bismarck Tunnel," but the "Tunel Wilsona." German trucks thundering by on their iron tires bore the white eagle of Poland instead of the black Prussian bird of prey. German newspapers were still published, but as the streets they mentioned were nowhere to be found in all Poznan, their advertisements and much of their news were rather pointless. It gave me a curiously helpless feeling to find myself for the first time in years unable to guess a word of the language about me. Fortunately all Poznan still spoke German. Only once during my stay there did I find myself hampered by my ignorance of Polish—

when a theater-ticket office proved to be in charge of a pair recently arrived from Warsaw. On more than one occasion my advances were received coldly, sometimes with scowls. But a reply was always forthcoming, and whenever I announced myself an American, who spoke the less welcome of the two tongues by necessity rather than by choice, apology and friendly overtures immediately followed.

Having effaced the lingual reminders of their late oppressors, the Poznanians had proceeded to pay their respects to the bronze heroes they had left behind. The Germans, as is their custom, had littered the public squares with statues of their chief sword-brandishers, in gigantic size—tender reminders to the conquered people of the blessings that had been forced upon them. The downfall of these had been sudden and unceremonious. Some had descended so hastily that the allegorical figures at their feet had suffered the fate so often overtaking faithful henchmen of the fallen mighty. The stone image of an old woman representing "Sorrow" looked doubly sorrowful with broken nose, legs, and fingers. Kaiser Friedrich, Doctor Bismarck with his panacea of "blood and iron," the world-famed Wilhelm, had all left behind them imposing pedestals, like university chairs awaiting exponents of newer and more lasting doctrines. Here and there a statue had remained, because it was Polish, but these were few and small and tucked away into the more obscure corners.

Next to its change of tongue the most striking feature of the new Poznan was its military aspect. The streets swarmed with soldiers even during the day; in the evening the chief gathering-places became pulsating seas of field gray. For it was still the garb of their former servitude that clothed the vast majority of these warriors of the reborn nation. The silver double-eagle on his service-faded cap was all that was needed to turn a wearer of the German uniform into a soldier of Poland. Many still wore their "*Gott mit uns*" belt-buckles and their Prussian buttons. A scattering minority, officers for the most part, were conspicuous in the full new Polish uniform—double-breasted, with a forest-green tinge. The high, square cap, distinctive only of the province of Poznan, was more widely in evidence; the less cumbersome headgear of military visitors from Warsaw or Galizia now and then broke the red-banded monotony. But the only universal sign of new fealty was the silver double-eagle. This gleamed everywhere. Men in civilian garb wore it on their hats or in their coat lapels; women adorned their bodices with it; boys and girls proudly displayed it in some conspicuous position. It fluttered on a thousand banners; it bedecked every Polish shop-front; it stared from the covers of newly appeared books, pamphlets, music-sheets in the popular tongue; the very church spires had replaced their crosses with it. One could buy the resurrected insignia, of any size or material, in almost any shop—

providing one could produce "legitimation papers" or other proof that it would not be used to disguise a German as a Pole.

An over-abundance of swords tended to give the new army a comic-opera aspect, but this detail was offset by the genuine military bearing of all but a few of the multitude in uniform. The great majority, of course, had had German training. Now, however, they put the "pep" of a new game into the old forms of soldierly etiquette. Their two-finger salute was rendered with the precision of ambitious recruits and at the same time with the exactitude of "old-timers." They sprang unfailingly to attention at sight of a superior officer and stood like automatons until he turned away. Yet there seemed to be an un-German comradeship between the rank and file and the commissioned personnel, a democracy of endeavor, a feeling that they were all embarked together on the same big new adventure. There were, to be sure, some officers and a few men whose sidewalk manners suggested that they had learned Prussian ways a bit too thoroughly, but they were lost in a mass that had something of the easy-going temperament of the East or the South.

All classes of the Polish population were represented in the new army from the bulking countryman who ran after me to say that the photograph I had just taken of him would not be a success because he had not been looking at the lens during the operation to the major who granted me special permission to use my kodak in spite of military rules. This officer had been late in reaching his office, and I passed the time in his anteroom in conversation with his sergeant-major. When he entered at last the entire office force sprang to its feet with what in an older army would have been an exaggeration of discipline. The sergeant-major, his middle finger glued to the seams of his trousers, explained my presence and request. The major asked several questions in Polish, which the sergeant repeated to me in German, relaying my replies back to the major in his native tongue. When the latter had nodded his approval and disappeared, and the office force had relaxed into mere human beings, I expressed my surprise that an officer of such high rank knew no German.

"Knows no German!" cried the sergeant-major, bursting into laughter. "The major was for nine years a captain in the German army. He is a graduate of the War College in Berlin and was a member of Hindenburg's staff. But he never lets a word of the accursed tongue pass his lips if he can possibly avoid it."

The new Polish government had established a conscription act as drastic as if it had been taken bodily from the old German statute-books. All males between the ages of seventeen and forty-five were liable to service. Those between eighteen and thirty had already been called to the colors, though thus far German residents had been tacitly exempted. Every afternoon of my stay in Poznan a hundred or two of recruits, flower-bedecked and carrying each his carton of travel rations, marched in column of squads from the railway station to what had once been the Kaiser's barracks, singing as they went some rousing Polish song of the olden days. At least half of them wore more or less complete German uniforms. Some were so under-sized that a rifle in their hands would have resembled a machine-gun. But with few exceptions their military bearing testified to previous training under the exacting drill-sergeants of their former rulers. Watching this new addition each day to the hordes in uniform that already crowded the city, one could not but wonder whether the new Poland was not giving refuge, perhaps unconsciously, to the discredited spirit of militarism that had so recently been expelled from its German Fatherland.

The "revolution," or "*Putsch*," as the Poles call it, that brought about all this new state of affairs had been brief and to the point. Paderewski, relying, perhaps, on Germany's promise to help re-establish the ancient Polish Kingdom, had come to Posen for the Christmas holidays. The hotel he occupied had been decorated with the flags of the Allies. It is scarcely surprising that the Germans proceeded to tear them down in spite of the armistice that had recently been concluded. According to several observers, they might even have "got away with" this had they not persisted in their Prussian aggressiveness. On December 27th a Polish youth paused to ask another for a light from his cigarette. Matches had long been precious things in Posen. A German officer pounced upon the pair and demanded to know what conspiracy they were hatching together. The Polish youths quite properly knocked him down. Their companions joined in the fracas. The Polish turnvereins had long had everything prepared for just such an eventuality. Word swept like prairie fire through the city. French and Italian prisoners of war sprang to such arms as they could lay hands on and added their assistance. The soldiers of the garrison, being chiefly Poles or of Polish sympathies, walked out almost in a body and joined the revolt. It raged for twenty-four hours. In the words of the sergeant-major already introduced: "It was a busy day from four in the morning until the following dawn. At least sixty ribs were broken—mostly German ones." There have been bloodier revolutions, however, for the number killed is set at ten. The Polish leaders were soon masters of the situation. In three days they had established order. Their search for arms was thorough and included Polish as well as German houses. The government they had already established in secret soon tautened the reins that had been struck from the hands of the Germans, and by New Year's Day Poznan had already settled down to peace and to a contentment it had not known in more than a century.

As far, at least, as outward appearances go, there was nothing particularly oppressive about the new rule. Civilians were not permitted on the streets after midnight, but those with any legitimate excuse for night-hawking were granted special passes. The Poles showed a tendency to meet half-way their next-door neighbor and late oppressor. With the exception of a few "*Polen-fresser*," German residents were not driven out, as in Metz and Strassburg. Boche merchants continued to do business at the old stand. Newspapers published in Germany were refused admittance, but that was a fair retaliation for similar action by the new authorities of the late Empire. Even the detested statues were not overthrown until March, when the Germans declined to give the Poles port facilities at Danzig. The language of the schools, as well as of government offices, was changed to Polish; but as soon as Berlin consented to a reciprocal arrangement, German was restored to the curriculum, though it was taught only a few hours a week, as a foreign tongue. In short, the conditions of Bromberg had been nicely reversed in Poznan. It must, to be sure, have been rather a tough life for the town braggart who had always espoused the German cause; but there was apparently nothing to be feared by those who know how to hold their tongues and confine their attention to their own affairs—and the German is a past-master at lying low when it is to his interest to do so. His native tongue was almost never heard on the streets, such arrogance as existed was confined now to the Poles, and the just-let-us-alone-and-we'll-be-good rôle had been assumed by the Teutons.

There were suggestions, however, that the Poles were not yet adepts at governing, nor likely soon to establish a modern Utopia. Already they had succeeded in encumbering themselves with fully as much red-tape as the French. A musician as national leader and rallying-point seemed to be in keeping with the Polish temperament. There was a lack of practical directness in their methods, a tendency toward the erratic, at the expense of orderly progress. One of their foremost business men turned high official, to whom I applied for a signature and the imprint of a government stamp, received me with a protest that he was "too busy to breathe"—and spent two hours reciting Polish poetry to me and demonstrating how he had succeeded in photographing every secret document that had reached Posen during the war without being once suspected by the Germans. "I am not experienced in this business of government," he apologized, when I succeeded at last in taking my leave, "but I am ready to sacrifice myself and all I have to the new Poland."

The statement rang true in his case, but there were others whose repetition of it would have raised grave suspicions that they were putting the cart before the horse. The rush for government jobs under the new régime had in it something of the attitude of the faithful henchmen toward the periodical return to power of their beloved Tammany. There were tender reminiscences of the A. E. F. in the flocks of incompetent pretty girls who encumbered government offices, dipping their charming noses into everything except that which concerned them, as there was in the tendency on the part of both sexes to consider government transportation synonymous with opportunity for "joy-riding." It will be strange if the Polish servant-girls and factory hands who come to us in the future bring with them the accept-anything spirit of the past, at least after the period of orientation to their new environment is over. They are "feeling their oats" at home now and will be apt to set their worth and their rights to full equality correspondingly higher.

The Poles, evidently, are not by nature a frolicsome people, but they seemed to have thrown away the "lid" in Poznan and given free play to all the joy within them. Pianos were more in evidence than they had been during all the twenty months I had spent in war-torn Europe. Children appeared to have taken on a new gaiety. Night life was almost Parisian, except in the more reprehensible features of the "City of Light." It may have been due only to a temporary difference of mood in the two races, but Polish Poznan struck me as a far more *livable* place than German Berlin. Evidently the people of the provinces were not letting this new attractiveness of the restored city escape them; the newspapers bristled with offers of reward for any one giving information of apartments or houses for rent. Underneath their merriness, however, the religious current of the race still ran strong and swift. The churches discharged multitudes daily at the end of morning mass; no male, be he coachman, policeman, soldier, or newsboy, ever passed the crucifix at the end of the principal bridge without reverently raising his hat. There are Protestant Poles, but they apparently do not live in Poznan. Now and again, too, there were episodes quite the opposite of gay to give the city pause in the midst of its revelry—the drunken sots in uniform, for instance, who canvassed the shops demanding alms and prophesying the firing-squad for those who declined to contribute. Were they not perhaps the outposts of Bolshevism? But all this was immersed in the general gaiety, tinged with a mild Orientalism that showed itself not only in the architecture, but in such leisurely customs as closing shops and offices from one to three, in defiance of nearly a century and a half of the sterner German influence.

It is quite possible that the increased liveliness of the Poznanians was as much due to the fact that they had plenty to eat as to their release from Teutonic bondage. The two things had come together. Being perhaps the richest agricultural district of the late Empire, the province of Posen was quick to recover its alimentary footing, once its frontiers had been closed against the all-devouring German. With the exception of potatoes, of which the supply was well in excess of local needs, the exportation of foodstuffs toward the hungry West had absolutely ceased. The result was more than noticeable in Poznan; it was conspicuous, all but overpowering, particularly to those arriving from famished Germany. Street after street was lined with a constant tantalization to the new-comer from the West, arousing his resentment at the appetite that was so easily satisfied after its constant vociferations in days gone by—and still to come. Butcher shops displayed an abundance of everything from frankfurters to sides of beef. Cheese, butter, eggs by the bushel, candy, sugar, sweetmeats were heaped high behind glass fronts that would have been slight protection for them in Berlin. In what were now known as "*restauracya*" one might order a breakfast of eggs, bacon, milk, butter, and all the other things the mere mention of which would have turned a German *Wirt* livid with rage, without so much as exciting a ripple on the waiter's brow. At the rathskeller of Poznan's artistic old city hall a "steak and everything," such a steak as not even a war-profiteer could command anywhere in Germany, cost a mere seven marks, including the inevitable mug of beer and the "10 per cent. for service" that was exacted here also by the *Kellners'* union. With the low rate of exchange—for Poznan was still using German money—the price was considerably less than it would have been in New York at the same date. Far from being short of fats, the Poles were overgenerous with their grease and gravies. Bacon could be had in any quantity at six marks a pound; eggs at thirty pfennigs each. Bread, brown but excellent, was unlimited. Food-tickets, unknown in hotels and restaurants, were theoretically required for a few of the principal articles in the shops, but there was little difficulty in purchasing without them, at least with the payment of a slight "premium." On market-days the immense square allotted to them was densely crowded from corner to corner by curiously garbed female hawkers and countrymen offering every conceivable product of their farms and gardens. Poznan still consumed a few things that do not appear on the American bill of fare, such as doves, gull eggs, and various species of weeds and grasses; but the fact remains that the well-to-do could get anything their appetites craved, and the poor were immensely better off than in any city of Germany. There was only one shortage that irked the popular soul. Expression of it rang incessantly in my ears—"Please tell America to send us tobacco!" The queues before tobacconists' shops were as long and as persistent as in Germany. Ragged men of the street eagerly parted with a precious fifty-pfennig "shin-plaster" for a miserable "cigarette" filled for only half its length with an unsuccessful imitation of tobacco. The principal café, having husbanded its supply of the genuine article, placed a thousand of them on sale each evening at eight, "as a special favor to our clients." By that hour entrance was quite impossible, and though only two were allowed each purchaser, there was nothing but the empty box left five minutes later.

Unselfishness is not one of mankind's chief virtues, particularly in that chaos of conflicting interests known to the world as central Europe. In view of all they had won in so short a time, and amid the German shrieks of protest, it was disconcerting to find that the Poles were far from satisfied with what had been granted them by the Peace Conference. From high government officials to the man in the street they deluged me with their complaints, often naïvely implying that I had personally had some hand in framing the terms of the proposed treaty, or at least the power to have them altered before it was too late. They were dissatisfied with the western frontier that had been set for them, especially in West Prussia; they were particularly disgruntled because they had not been given Danzig outright. A nation of thirty million people should have a harbor of its own. Danzig was essentially Polish in its sympathies, in spite of the deliberate Germanization that had been practised upon it. Strangely enough they accused America of having blocked their aspirations in that particular. They blamed Wilson personally for having shut them out of Danzig, as well as for the annoying delay in drawing up the treaty. The Germans had "got at him" through the Jews. The latter had far too much power in the American government, as well as in American finances. The impression was wide-spread in Poznan that Mrs. Wilson is Jewish. The Germans and the Jews had always stuck together. Poland had always been far too lenient with the Jews. She had let them in too easily; had granted them citizenship too readily. As they spoke either Yiddish, an offshoot of German, or Russian, they had always lined up with the enemies of Poland. Half the German spies, every one of the Russian spies with whom Polish territory had been flooded during the war, had been Jews. The Poles in America had gathered money for the alleviation of suffering in their home-land, and had given it to Jews, Germans, and Poles, irrespective of race. The Jews in America had collected similar funds and had expended them only among the Jews. From whatever point of view one approached him, the resident of Poznan had nothing good to say of the Chosen People.

The story of Posen's existence under German rule, now happily ended, was largely a repetition of what had already been told me in Bromberg. In some ways this region had been even more harshly treated, if my informants were trustworthy. Polish skilled workmen "clear down to button-makers" had been driven out of the province. Great numbers had been more or less forcibly compelled to migrate into Germany. There were at least four hundred thousand Poles in the mines and factories of Westphalia. Saxony was half Polish; the district between Hamburg and Bremen was almost entirely Slavish in population. The *Ansiedler*—the German settlers whom the government had brought to Posen—had acquired all the best land. On the other hand, German Catholics were not allowed to establish themselves in the province of Posen, lest they join their coreligionists against the Protestant oppressors. Perhaps the thing that rankled most was the banishment of the Polish language from the schools. One could scarcely speak it with one's children at home, for fear of their using it before the teacher. Many of the youngsters had never more than half learned it. In twenty years more no one would have dared speak Polish in public. Men had been given three, and even four, months in prison for privately teaching their children Polish history. The schools were hopelessly Prussianized; the German teachers received a special premium of one thousand marks or more a year over the regular salaries. All railway jobs went to Germans, except those of section men at two marks a day. There had been Polish newspapers and theaters, but they had never been allowed any freedom of thought or action.

"The trouble with the German, or at least the Prussian," one new official put in, "is that it is his nature to get things by force. He was born that way. Why, the Prussians stole even their name; it was originally Barrusen, as the little corner of Russia was called where the robbers first banded together. They marauded their way westward and southward, treading first little people and then little nations under their iron heels. The very word the German uses for "get" or "obtain" tells his history. It is *kriegen*, to win by war—*krieg*. You seldom hear him use the gentler *bekommen*. Everything he possesses he has *gekriegt*. Then he is such a hypocrite! In 1916, when we Poles first began to suffer seriously from hunger, some German officers came with baskets of fruit and sandwiches, gathered a group of Polish urchins, filled their hands with the food, and had themselves photographed with them, to show the world how generous and kind-hearted they were. But they did not tell the world that the moment the photographs had been taken the food was snatched away from the hungry children again, some of the officers boxing their ears, and sent back to the German barracks. How do you think the Poles who have been crippled for life fighting for the 'Fatherland' feel as they hobble about our streets? What would you say to serving five years in the German army only to be interned as a dangerous enemy alien at the end of it, as is the case with thousands of our sons who were not able to get across the frontier in time? No, the Germans in Poznan are not oppressed as our people were under their rule. We are altogether *too* soft-hearted with them."

The German residents themselves, as was to be expected, took a different view of the situation. When the Polish authorities had decorated my passport with permission to return to Berlin, I took no chances of being held up by the cantankerous dyspeptic at Kreuz and applied for a new visé by the German *Volksrat* of Posen. It occupied a modest little dwelling-house on the wide, curving avenue no longer recognizable under its former title of "Kaiser Wilhelm Ring." Barely had I established my identity when the gloomy Germans took me to their bosom. Had I been fully informed of *their* side of the situation? Would I not do them the kindness to return at eleven, when they would see to it that men of high standing were there to give me the real facts of the case? My impressions of Posen would be wholly false if I left it after having consorted only with Poles.

As a matter of fact I had already "consorted" with no small number of German residents, chiefly of the small-merchant class. Those I had found somewhat mixed in their minds. A few still prophesied a "peasants' war" in the territory allotted to Poland; a number of them shivered with apprehension of a "general Bolshevist uprising." But fully as many pooh-poohed both those cheerful bogies. One thing only was certain—that without exception they were doing business as usual and would continue to do so as long as the Poles permitted it. The feeling for the "Fatherland" did not seem strong enough among the overwhelming majority of them to stand the strain of personal sacrifice.

When I returned at eleven the *Volksrat* had been convoked in unofficial special session. A half-dozen of the men who had formerly held high places in the Municipal Council rose ostentatiously to their feet as I was ushered into the chief sanctum, and did not sit down again until I had been comfortably seated. The chief spokesman had long been something corresponding to chairman of the Board of Aldermen. His close-cropped head glistened in the sunshine that entered through the window at his elbow, and his little ferret-like eyes alternately sought to bore their way into my mental processes and to light up with a winsome naïveté which he did not really possess. Most of the words I set down here are his, though some of them were now and then thrown in by his subservient but approving companions.

"With us Germans," he began, "it has become a case of '*Vogel friss oder starb*'—eat crow or die. We are forced, for the time at least, to accept what the Poles see fit to allow us. The German residents of Posen are not exactly oppressed, but our lives are hemmed in by a thousand petty annoyances, some of them highly discouraging. Take, for instance, this matter of the street names. Granted that the Poles had the right to put them up in their own language. It was certainly a sign of fanaticism to tear down the German names. More than a fourth of the residents of Posen cannot read the new street placards. There is not a Polish map of the city in existence. When the province of Posen came back to us the Polish street names were allowed to remain until 1879—for more than a hundred years. It is a sign of childishness, of retarded mentality, to daub with red paint all the German signs they cannot remove! It isn't much more than that to have forbidden the use of our tongue in governmental affairs. We Germans used both languages officially clear up to 1876. We even had the old Prussian laws translated into Polish. It is only during the last ten years that nothing but German was permitted in the public schools; and there have always been plenty of Polish private schools. I am still technically a member of the Municipal Council, but I cannot understand a word of the proceedings, because they are in Polish. Our lawyers cannot practise unless they use that language, although the judges, who pretend not to know German, speak it as readily as you or I. Yet these same lawyers cannot get back into Germany. At least give us time to learn Polish before abolishing German! Many a man born here cannot speak it. There are German children of eighteen or twenty, who have never been outside the province, who are now learning Polish—that is, to write and speak it correctly.

"Oh yes, to be sure, we can most of us get permission in three or four weeks to leave the province, but only by abandoning most of our possessions and taking an oath never to return. No wonder so many Germans become Poles overnight. You can hardly expect otherwise, when they have lived here all their lives and have all their property and friends and interests here. No, military service is not required of Germans, even if they were born here; but many of our youths have voluntarily become Polish soldiers, for the same reason that their parents have suddenly turned Poles. Naturally, there is fighting along the boundary of the province. The Poles *want* to fight, so they can have an excuse to keep their men under arms, and what can Germany do but protect herself? Poland is planning to become an aggressive, militaristic nation, as was falsely charged against the Fatherland by her enemies.

"The complaints of the Poles at our rule were ridiculous. We paid German teachers a premium because they had harder work in teaching German to Polish children and in seeing that they did not speak the language that was unwisely used at home. Railroad jobs, except common labor, were given to Germans because they were more efficient and trustworthy. Besides, does not Germany own the railroads? They complain that the best land was taken by German settlers; but the Poles were only too glad to sell to our *Ansiedler*—at high prices. Now they are attacking us with a fanaticism of the Middle Ages. Eighteen hundred German teachers, men who have been educating the Poles for twenty or twenty-five years, have suddenly been discharged and ordered to vacate government property within four weeks—yet they are not allowed to go back to Germany. The Pole is still part barbarian; he is more heartless than his cousin the Russian.

"Seventy per cent. of the taxes in the province of Posen are paid by Germans. Yet no German who was not born here can vote, though Poles who were not can. I know a village where there are seventy Germans and five Poles—and the five Poles run things to suit themselves. Husbands, wives, and sons often have different rights of suffrage. The family of Baron X has lived here for a hundred and fifty years. The baron himself happens to have been born in Berlin, because his mother went there to see a doctor. So *he* cannot vote, though his Polish coachman, who has not been here ten years, has all the rights of citizenship. The result is that government affairs are getting into a hopeless muddle. An ignorant fellow by the name of Korfanti—a Polish 'German-eater'—has now the chief voice in the Municipal Council. The Poles boycott German merchants. They deluge the city with placards and appeals not to buy of Germans. For a long time they refused to trade even a miserable little Polish theater for our splendid big *Stadttheater*. When the director of that finally got permission to take over the wholly inadequate little playhouse for next season he had to advertise in order to find out how many Germans intend to stay in Posen—as you have seen in our German paper. What can the Poles do with our magnificent *Stadttheater*? *They* have no classics to give in it, nor people of sufficient culture to make up an audience. We are still allowed to give German opera, because they know they cannot run that themselves, and a few of the more educated Poles like it. But our splendid spoken classics seem to be doomed.

"Then there is their ridiculous hatred of the Jews. The race may have its faults, but the five or six thousand Jews of Posen province play a most important business and financial rôle. They have always understood the advantages of German *Kultur* far better than the Poles. There is a Jewish *Volksrat* here that tries to keep independent of both the other elements of the population; but the great majority of the Jews stand with the Germans. They have no use for this new Zionism—except for the other fellow—unless you take seriously the aspirations of a few impractical young idealists"—a statement, by the way, which I heard from Jews of all classes in various parts of Germany.

"We Germans lifted the Poles out of their semi-savagery. We brought them *Kultur*. Do not be deceived by what you see in Posen. It is a magnificent city, is it not?—finer, perhaps, than you Americans found Coblenz? Yet everything that gives it magnificence was built by the Germans—the well-paved streets, the big, wide boulevards, the splendid parks, all the government buildings and the best of the private ones, the street-cars, the electric lights, even the higher state of civilization you find among the masses. There is not a Pole in the province of Posen who cannot read and write. Do not make the mistake of thinking all these things are Polish because the Poles have stolen them. Before you leave, go and compare Posen with the Polish cities *outside* Germany. That will tell the story. In non-German Poland you will be struck by the appalling lack of schools, roads, doctors, hospitals, education, culture, by the sad condition of the workmen and the peasants— all those things that are included in the German word *Kultur*. In Galizia, where Austria virtually allowed the Poles to run themselves, the houses are only six feet high, and you could walk all day without finding a man who can read and write, or who can even speak German. Their cities are sunk in a degradation of the Middle Ages. Posen will fall into the same state, if the present Municipal Council continues in power. There are already frontier troubles between German and Russian Poland, and quarrels between the different sections that confirm what we Germans have always known—that the Poles cannot govern themselves. Warsaw does not wish to keep up our splendid system of workmen and old-age insurance because there is none in

Russian Poland. Galizia complains that farm land is several times higher in price in the province of Posen, without admitting that it is German railroads and German settlers that have made it so. That advantage will soon disappear. The Poles will make a mess of the whole province and will have it sunk into the degradation in which we found it by the time a real ruling nation takes charge of it again."

Just how much truth there was mixed in with the considerable amount of patent nonsense in the ex-chairman's declamation only a long stay in Poznan, or time itself, would show. The fact that the Poles allowed many of these statements, particularly the protests against the sudden change of language, to be published in the local German newspaper speaks at least for their spirit of tolerance. Though the new government was visibly making mistakes, and had not yet settled down to the orderliness that should come from experience, no one but a prejudiced critic could have discovered immediate evidence that it was making any such complete "mess" of matters as the German *Volksrat* testified. Even if it had been, at least the mass of the population showed itself happy and contented with the change, and contentment, after all, may in time result in more genuine and lasting progress than that which comes from the forcible feeding of German *Kultur*.

I dropped in at the Teatro Apollo one evening, chiefly to find out how it feels to see a play without understanding a word of it. An immense barnlike building, that looked as if it had once been a skating-rink or a dancing-pavilion, was crowded to suffocation with Poles of every class and variety, from servant-girls in their curious leg-of-mutton sleeves to colonels in the latest cut of Polish uniform. The actors—if they could have been dignified with that title—had recently been imported from Warsaw, and the alleged play they perpetrated could scarcely have been equaled by our silliest rough-and-tumble "comedians." The herd-like roar with which their inane sallies were unfailingly greeted testified that the audience found them entertaining. But it may be that Poznan was in a particularly simple-minded mood during its first months of relief from a century of bitter oppression. I hope so, for I should regret to find that the startling contrast between this Polish audience and the German one at the artistic *Stadttheater* the following evening fairly represented the difference between the two races. I believe I am not prejudiced by the fact that the *Volksrat* presented me with a free ticket when I say that the latter performance was one of which any manager might have been justly proud. The audience, too, resembled the other about as a gathering of college professors resembles a collection of factory hands. There was a well-bred solemnity about it that could not, in this case, have been due merely to hunger, for there was no munching whatever between the acts, none even under cover of the darkened house, except here and there of candy, a luxury so long since forgotten in Berlin that the happy possessor would never have dreamed of giving his attention at the same time to the merely esthetic appeal of the theater. There may have been Poles in the house, but at least the new army was conspicuous by its absence. Not a uniform was to be seen, with the exception of three scattered through the "peanut gallery." Two crown boxes, destined only for Hohenzollern royalty or its representatives, sat empty, with something of the solemn demeanor of the vacant chair at the head of the table the day after the funeral. Who would occupy them when the Poles had taken over the playhouse? What, moreover, would they do toward maintaining the high standards of the stage before us? For the most indefatigable enemy of the Germans must have admitted that here was something that could ill be spared. If only they had been contented with bringing the masses these genuine benefits, without militarism, with more open competition, without so much appeal to the doctrine of force— but it has ever been Germany's contention that only by force can the mass of mankind be lifted to higher levels; that only an army can protect the self-appointed missionaries of a loftier civilization.

Armed with what those who read Polish assured me was permission to do so, I set out on foot one morning to the eastward. Beyond the last group of guards wearing the silver double-eagle on their threadbare German uniforms, I fell in with three barefooted Polish peasant women. They were barely thirty, yet all three were already well-nigh toothless, and their hardy forms and faces were plainly marked with the signs that testify to grueling labor and the constant bearing of children. The German they spoke was far superior to the dialects of many regions of purely Teutonic population. Their demeanor was cheerful, yet behind it one caught frequent glimpses of that background of patient, unquestioning acceptance of life as it is which distinguishes the country people of Europe.

The most energetic of the trio showed a willingness to enter into conversation; the others confined themselves to an occasional nod of approval, as if the exertion of keeping pace with us left them no strength to expend in mere words. It was plain from the beginning that they were not enthusiastic on the subject then uppermost in the city behind us. They greeted my first reference to it with expressions that might have been called indifferent, had they not been tinged with evidence of a mild resentment.

"What does it matter to us people of the fields," retorted the less taciturn of the group, "whether Poles or Germans sit in the comfort of government offices, so long as they let us alone? Things were all right as they were, before the war came. Why trouble us with all these changes? Now they are breaking our backs with new burdens, as if we had not had enough of them for five years. First they take our men and leave us to do their work. I have not a male relative left, except my husband, and he is so sickly that he is no longer a man. He is paid twelve marks for eight hours' work; fifteen for ten. But what help is that when he cannot work ten hours, or even eight? They offered him the iron cross. He told them he would rather have something to feed his family with at home. They asked him if he was not already getting forty marks a month for the support of his family. How could I feed four children, even after the other two had died, with forty marks a month? For three winters I had nothing but dried potatoes and salt. I could not have bread for myself because the flour for the children took all the tickets. Now the war is over, yet they are still taking away what we have left. The same soldiers come and drive off our horses—for the silver eagle on their caps has not changed their natures. Pay for them? *Ach*, what is eight hundred marks for a horse that is worth six thousand? And how can we cultivate our fields without them? Who started the war? *Ach*, they are all arguing. What does it matter, so long as they stop it? Will the Germans sign? They should, and have done with it. If they don't, all the men over fifty, including the Germans and even the Jews"— there was a sneer in this last word, even in the country—"will be at it again. We have had enough of it. Yet if the soldiers come and tell my husband to go he must go, sick though he is."

The basket each of the trio carried contained the midday lunch of her husband in the fields. I turned aside to the grassy slope on which two of the couples assembled. The men insisted that I share their meal with them. It was more nourishing than a ten-mark repast in a Berlin restaurant, but the absence of bread was significant. When I gave the men each a pinch of tobacco crumbs they announced themselves delighted at the exchange, and mumbled halting words about the well-known generosity of Americans. As I turned my kodak upon them they greeted it with a laughing "Oh, là là!" There was no need to ask where they had picked up that expression. It oriented their war experiences as definitely as it will distinguish for years to come the Americans, in whatever garb one finds them, who were members of the A. E. F. in France.

The men were less indifferent to the recent change of government than their wives, but even they could not have been called enthusiastic. What struck one most was the wider outlook on life the Germans had been forced to give them in spite of themselves. Had they been left to till their farms, these plodding peasants would probably still have swallowed whole the specious propaganda of their erstwhile rulers. Now, after four years of military service that had carried them through all central Europe, they had developed the habit of forming their own opinions on all questions; they took any unverified statement, from whatever source, with more than a grain of salt. It would be a mistake nowadays to think of the European peasant as the prejudiced conservative, the plaything of deliberate misinformation, which he was five years ago. In the light of his new experiences he is in many cases doing more individual thinking than the average city resident.

Yet, I must admit, the conclusions of this well-traveled pair did not boil down into anything very different from the consensus of opinion, even though they reached them by their own peculiar trains of thought. Germany, they were convinced, had the full guilt of the war; not the Kaiser particularly—they call him "Wilhelm" in Posen province now, and even there one detects now and again a tendency toward the old idolatry he seems personally to have enjoyed throughout the whole Empire—but the military crowd, "and the capitalists." They disclaimed any hatred of the Germans, "until they wanted to rule the earth" and sought to make the peasants the instruments of their ambition. They, too, charged Wilson personally with delaying the conclusion of peace—on the fate of Danzig they seemed to be supremely indifferent.

"It's all politics, anyway," concluded one of them. "They are all playing politics. If the Germans don't sign they will be divided up as Poland was a hundred and forty years ago. But this new government in Posen is no better than the old. What we need is something entirely new—a government of the peasants and of the working-classes."

The women had from the beginning tried to lead their husbands away from "arguing politics," chiefly with ludicrously heavy attempts at coquetry, and at length they succeeded. I regained the highway. On either hand lay slightly rolling fields of fertile black soil, well cultivated as far as the eye could see, with only a scattering of trees. Miles away an abandoned Zeppelin hangar bulked into the sky. There were more women laborers than men; several gangs of them were working with picks and shovels; another group was slowly but patiently loading bricks. Horses were to be seen here and there, but oxen were in the majority. Farm-houses showed a rough comfort and a tolerable cleanliness, villages a passable neatness that may or may not have been due to German influence. Certainly the architecture, the farming methods, the communal customs, were little different from those of Prussia or the Rhineland.

The dinner served me in the chief tavern of a village of some two thousand inhabitants was nothing to complain of, either in variety or price. A general-shop keeper stated that "with the exception of a few semi-luxuries, such as cocoa and toilet soap," his grocery department could still meet the decreased demands made upon it. In the clothing lines everything was scarce or wholly lacking. Worst of all, there was nothing fit to drink or smoke. The strong spirits that had once been his chief trade had become so weak no one but boys would drink them. If only America would send concentrated alcohol they could doctor the stock of liquor they had on hand so that no one would know the difference. Then if they could only get some American tobacco! Life was not what it used to be, without a real cigarette from one month's end to the other. The German rule, on the whole, had not been so bad as many of the Allies seemed to believe. They got along, though it was rather pleasant to be relieved of the arrogant fellows, or see them crawl into their shells. No German resident in the village had given any sign of intending to move away. The communal school was still teaching the German language— two or three hours a week now. No one had noticed any other change of any importance. The French prisoners confined in the province during the war had been brutally treated. There was no doubt about that; he had seen it himself. But on the whole the German authorities had not been much harder on the Polish population than upon their own people, in Prussia and elsewhere. It was all part of the war, and every one in the Empire had to bear his share of the burdens. Happily, it was over now, if only the new Polish government did not grow ambitious for military conquests also, with the millions of soldiers, some of them patriotic to the point of self-sacrifice, under its command.

My hope of walking out of Posen province suffered the same fate as my plan of tramping into it from Germany. In the end I was forced to return to Poznan and make my exit by train over the same route by which I had entered. In the third-class compartment I occupied there were five German residents who had renounced forever their right to return, for the privilege of leaving now with the more portable of their possessions. Two of them had been born in the amputated province; the others had lived there most of their lives. All spoke Polish as readily as German. One masterly, yet scholarly youth, who had served through the war as a lieutenant, was a school-teacher by profession, as was the uncle who accompanied him. They had taught six and twenty-six years, respectively, but had been dispossessed of their positions and of their government dwellings by the new rulers. Up to the time we reached the frontier all five of my companions laid careful emphasis on the statement that they were going to seek re-establishment in their civilian professions in what was left of the Fatherland.

At Wronki the Polish authorities were far more inquisitive than they had been toward travelers from the other direction. One by one each compartment group was herded together, bag and baggage, and strained through the sieve of a careful search-and-questioning bureau. The soldier who examined my knapsack glared at the half-dozen precious American cigars I had left as if nothing but the presence of his superiors could have prevented him from confiscating them. Only sufficient food for the day's journey was allowed to pass. In some cases this rule was interpreted rather liberally, but no one got through with more than ten or twelve pounds to the person. The amount that was confiscated easily sufficed to feed the garrison of Wronki for the twenty-four hours before the next westbound train was due. An old woman, riding fourth class, who resembled one of India's famine victims, was despoiled of almost the entire contents of her trunk-sized chest—several sacks of flour, a dozen huge loaves of bread, and a generous supply of sausage. The fact that she spoke only Polish did not seem to impress the searchers in her favor, who silenced her wails at last by bundling her bodily back into the coach and tossing her empty coffer after her.

When at last we were under way again the Germans in my compartment took to comparing notes. One, a doctor, was bewailing the "plain theft" of a surgical appliance of rubber which the Poles had confiscated in spite of what seemed to be complete proof that it was his private property and not part of the German army supplies. A foxy-faced country youth, who had carefully changed from shoes to high boots just before the arrival at Wronki, changed back again now with the announcement that there were some four thousand marks concealed between the boot soles. The younger schoolmaster threw off the disguise with which he had covered his real thoughts and announced, vociferously:

"You drive me out to work for my livelihood! I will work for my Fatherland at the same time. I will go to Bromberg this very evening and join the army again. We shall see whether the Poles can keep Posen."

The two other young men asserted that they, too, had left with exactly that intention. An indignation meeting against the Poles raged for an hour or more.

"I could have remained and kept my position," went on the schoolmaster, "if I had wanted to turn Polack. Both my parents were Polish; I spoke it before I did German; but I shall always remain a true son of the Fatherland, no matter what happens to it."

A few hundred yards from Kreuz station our train halted for more than an hour and gave us the pleasure of watching the Berlin express go on without us. Though it would have been a matter of twenty seconds to have sprinted across the delta between the two lines, armed boy soldiers prevented any one from leaving his compartment. To all appearances it was a case of "pure meanness" on the part of the German authorities. Our wrath at being forced to wait a half-day for a dawdling local train was soon appeased, however, by the announcement that we were the last travelers who would be allowed to enter Germany from the province of Posen "until the war was over." The frontier had been closed by orders from Berlin. It is a long way round from Poland to Holland, and amid the turmoil of gloomy men, disheveled women, and squalling children who had been turned back with their goal so near I found cause to be personally thankful, particularly as I succeeded in eluding during all the afternoon the glassy eye of the cantankerous dyspeptic, who buffeted his way now and then through the throng.

Some things are still cheap in Germany. A twelve-word telegram from Kreuz to Berlin cost me nine cents—and it was delivered in telegraphic haste. The hungry passengers from farther east with whom I shared a compartment that evening eyed me greedily as I supped on the supplies I had brought from Posen. One man wearing several diamonds leaned toward me as I was cutting my coffee-brown loaf and sighed, reminiscently, "What beautiful white bread!" When I offered to share it with him, however, he refused vigorously, as if his pride would not permit him to accept what his appetite was so loudly demanding. Unable to find a place in the section to which my third-class ticket entitled me, I was riding second-class. The train-guard on his rounds confiscated my ticket and ignored my offer to pay the difference, with a stern, "It is unlawful to ride in a higher class." On the Friedrichstrasse platform, however, instead of conducting me to his superiors, he sidled up to me in the darkness and murmured, "If you have a five-mark note with you it will be all right." Germany is changing indeed if her very railway employees are taking on these Latin characteristics.

XII
ON THE ROAD IN BAVARIA

An excellent express raced all day southward across a Germany lush-green with May. Cattle were scarcer in the fields, horses so rare a sight as to be almost conspicuous, but the fields themselves seemed as intensively, as thoroughly cultivated as my memory pictured them fifteen and ten years before. Within the train there was no crowding; the wide aisles and corridors were free from soldiers and their packs, for though there were a hundred or more in uniform scattered between the engine and the last car, a furlong behind, seats were still to be had. The question naturally arose, Are the Germans so short of rolling-stock, after complying with the terms of the armistice, as they pretend? A traveler racing across the Empire in this roomy, almost luxurious *Schnellzug* might easily have concluded that their whining on that score was mere camouflage. There were even curtains at the wide windows, though of rather shoddy stuff, and the window-straps of paper were so nicely disguised as to be almost indistinguishable from real leather. He who took pains, however, to dip a bit more deeply into the question found that even this great trunk line was carrying barely a third of its peace-time traffic. The red figures, indicating expresses, on the huge porcelain time-tables decorating station walls were nearly all pasted over with slips of paper, while the black ones of *Personenzüge*, the stop-everywhere-a-long-time trains, were more than half canceled. The branch lines had contributed even more to the Allies. Nor did our aristocratic Berlin-München express entirely escape overburdening. At Nürnberg came with sunset such hordes of passengers of all grades that every available foot of the train was as densely packed as a fourth-class coach on market-day. The throng it disgorged at Munich was sufficient to have peopled a town of very respectable size.

I had made the sudden leap to the southern end of the Empire as a starting-point of a tramp across it instead of reversing the process in the hope that here at last I should find "something doing," some remnants of excitement. Munich had just been snatched from the hands of the Sparticists—or the Bolshevists; the distinction between the two dreaded groups is not very clear in the German mind. Leviné, the half-mad Russian Jew who was reputed the organizing spirit of the revolt, was still dodging from one hiding-place to another somewhere in the vicinity. To read the breathless cables to the foreign press was to fancy Munich under a constant hail of shrapnel and machine-gun bullets. Ours was the second passenger-train that had ventured into the city in weeks. All Bavaria was blazing with huge posters, often blood-red in color, headed by the dread word "STANDRECHT" in letters to be seen a hundred yards away, proclaiming martial law and threatening sudden and dire fate to any one who strayed from the straight and narrow path of absolute submission to the "government-faithful" troops that were still pouring in from the north. Surely here, if anywhere, was a chance for a wandering American to get into trouble.

Like so many dreadful things, however, martial law and beleaguered cities prove more terrible at a distance than on the spot. True, a group of soldiers in full fighting equipment held the station exit; but their only act of belligerency toward the invading throng was to hand each of us a red slip granting permission to walk the streets until two in the morning. A bedraggled hotel directly across the way spared me that necessity. The information its registry-pad required of guests was more exacting than its interior aspect, but neither here nor at the station exit was there any demand for proof of identity.

Toward midnight, as I was falling asleep, a score of erratically spaced shots and the brief rat-a-tat of a machine-gun sounded somewhere not far away. Their direction was too uncertain, however, to make it worth while to accept the permission granted by the red slip. In the morning the city was thronged with the business-bent quite as if disorders had never dodged in and out of its wide streets. The main hotels, however, had been partly taken over by the staffs of the newly arrived troops, and pulsated with field gray. At the doors very young men in iron hats leaned their fixed bayonets in the crook of an elbow while they examined the *Ausweis* with which each civilian was supposed to prove his identity. I entered several of them in the vain hope that the flash of my American passport would "start something." The youths in uniform handed it back each time without so much as a flicker of curiosity on their rather dull faces. Inside, another boy volunteer ran his hands hastily over me in quest of concealed weapons; but not even the most obviously harmless Bavarian escaped that attention.

The staff evidently had no secrets from the world at large. At any rate, I wandered into a dozen hotel rooms that had been turned into offices and idled about undisturbed while majors gave captains their orders for the day and lieutenants explained to sergeants the latest commands from higher up. What had become of that stern discipline and the far-famed secrecy of the German army? The soldiers of democratic America were automatons in the presence of their officers compared with these free-and-easy youths in gray; over in Posen the Poles were manyfold more exacting. Had I been a spy, there were several opportunities to have pocketed papers strewn about tables and improvised desks. When at last an officer looked up at me inquiringly I explained my presence by asking for written permission to take photographs within the beleaguered city, and it was granted at once without question.

Berlin had been sinister of aspect; Munich was bland, a softer, gentler, less *verboten* land. Its citizens were not merely courteous; they were aggressively good-natured, their cheerfulness bubbled over on all who came in contact with them. It was almost as easy to distinguish a native from the stiff Prussians who had descended upon them as if the two groups had worn distinctive uniforms. Yet Munich had by no means escaped war-time privations. Long lines of hollow-eyed women flowed sluggishly in and out of under-stocked food-shops; still longer ones, chiefly though not entirely male, crept forward to the door of the rare tobacconists prepared to receive them, and emerged clutching two half-length cigarettes each, their faces beaming as if they had suddenly come into an unexpected inheritance. They were good-natured in spite of what must have been the saddest cut of all from the Bavarian point of view—the weakness and high cost of their beloved beer. In those vast underground *Bierhallen* for which Munich had been far-famed for centuries, where customers of both sexes and any age that can toddle pick out a stone mug and serve themselves, the price per liter had risen to the breathless height of thirty-four pfennigs. As if this calamity were not of itself enough to disrupt the serenity of the Bavarian temperament, the foaming beverage had sunk to a mere shadow of its former robust strength.

In the "cellar" of the beautiful *Rathaus* a buxom barmaid reminded me that Tuesday and Friday were meatless days in Germany. The fish she served instead brought me the added information that Munich is far from the sea. My fellow-sufferers constituted a truly democratic gathering. The still almost portly mayor chuckled with his cronies at a table barely visible through the smoke-screened forest of massive pillars. Collarless laborers clinked their mugs, quite unawed by the presence of city councilors or "big merchants." A leather-skinned old peasant sat down opposite me and opened conversation at once, with no suggestion of that aloofness of the north. From the rucksack that had slipped from his shoulders he took a half-loaf of dull-brown peasant bread and a square of boiled smoked pork, ordering nothing but a half-bottle of wine. Beer, he explained, had fallen too low in its estate to be worthy of his patronage, at least city beer. In his village, three hours away, he could still endure it. *Ach*, how the famous beer of Munich had deteriorated! How far away those happy days seemed! And to think of paying three marks for a half-bottle of wine! Why, in the good old days.... And this dinner of mine—a plate of fish bones, some stewed grass, city bread, and city beer—worthless stuff—potatoes, to be sure, but not enough to keep a man's legs under him for half the afternoon—and a bill of more than *eight marks*! I restrained my impulse to tell him of that prize dinner in Berlin.

He had not always been a peasant. Twenty years before he had started a factory—roof tiles and bricks. But in 1915 he had gone back to the farm. At least a *Bauer* got something to eat. The peace terms? What else could Germany do but sign? If the shoe had been on the other foot the war lords in Berlin would have demanded as much or more. If they hadn't wanted war in the first place! Wilhelm and all his crowd should have quit two or three years ago while the quitting was good. What did it all matter, anyway, so long as order returned and the peasants could work without being pestered with all this military service, and the taxes, not to mention the "hamsterers," the pests! American, was I? He had noticed I was not a Bavarian. (So had I, straining my ears to catch the meaning of his atrocious dialect.) He had taken me for a man from the north, a Hamburger perhaps. American? They say that is a rich country. He had read somewhere that even the peasants sometimes had automobiles! How about the beer? Deteriorating there, too, eh? *Ach*, this war! Going to abolish beer! What an insane idea! What will people live on? They can't afford wine, and *Schnapps* is not good for a man in the long run, and too strong for the women and children. Well, he must be getting back to his beet-field. Glad to have met an American. He had often heard of them. Good day and a happy journey.

Troops were still pouring into Munich. That afternoon what before the war would have looked to Americans like a large army marched in column of fours along the bank of the swift, pale-blue Isar and swung in through the heart of town. There were infantry, machine-gun, and light-artillery sections, both horse- and motor-drawn, and from end to end they were decorated with flowers, which clung even to the horses' bridles and peered from the mouths of the cannon. All the aspect of a conquering army was there, an army that had retaken one of its own cities after decades of occupation by the enemy. Greetings showered upon the columns, a trifle stiff and irresponsive with pride, after the manner of popular heroes; but it was chiefly voiceless greetings, the waving of hands and handkerchiefs, in striking contrast to similar scenes among the French.

The Boy Scouts of a year or two ago filled a large portion, possibly a majority, of the ranks. The older men scattered among them bore plainly imprinted on their faces the information that they had remained chiefly for lack of ambition or opportunity to re-enter civil life. Their bronzed features were like frames for those of the eager, life-tasting youths they surrounded, not so much in color as in their disillusioned, nothing-new-to-us expressions. All wore on their collars the gold or silver oak-leaves of volunteers for "home and border protection"; an insignia belonging to generals only before the flight of the Kaiser. Rumor had it, however, that there were many still held under the old conscription laws, particularly those of Polish blood. The same inarticulate voices whispered that, despite the opinion of Allied staffs, Germany still had a million men under arms; on the books they were carried as discharged; in reality they were sustained by the government as "out-of-works" and housed in barracks near enough to arsenals or munition dumps to equip themselves in a twinkling. What percentage of truth the assertion possessed could only have been determined by long and deliberate study, for though Munich, like many another city and even the country districts, seemed to swarm with soldiers, many of them were so only in outward appearance. Discharged men were permitted to use their uniforms until they were worn out; the mere removal of the shoulder-straps made one a civilian—unlike the soldiers resident in the occupied region, where civilian garb of field gray was furnished with the discharged papers—and boys of all ages, in many cases large enough to have the appearance of real soldiers, were as apt to wear the uniform and the red-banded cap without visor as anything else.

The Sparticist uprising in Munich, now crushed, evidently made less trouble on the spot, as usual, than in foreign newspapers. All classes of the population—except perhaps that to which the turn of events had brought the wisdom of silence—admitted that it had been a nuisance, but it had left none of them ashen with fear or gaunt with suffering. Indeed, business seemed to have gone on as usual during all but the two or three days of retaking the city. Banks and the larger merchants had been more or less heavily levied upon; lawyers and a few other classes whom the new doctrine ranked as "parasitic" had found it wise to leave their offices closed; but in the main all agreed that the population at large was never troubled in their homes and seldom on the street. The mistreatment of women, with rumors of which foreign newspapers reeked, was asserted to have been rare, and their "nationalization," which the cables seem to have announced, had not, so far, at least, been contemplated. All in all, the Bavarian capital suffered far less than Winnipeg under a similar uprising of like date.

The moving spirit had come from Russia, as already mentioned, with a few local theorists or self-seekers of higher social standing as its chief auxiliaries. The rank and file of the movement were escaped Russian prisoners and Munich's own out-of-works, together with such disorderly elements as always hover about any upheaval promising loot or unearned gain. But the city's chief scare seemed to have been its recapture by government troops under orders from Berlin. Then for some fifty hours the center of town was no proper place for those to dally who had neglected their insurance premiums. A hundred more or less of fashionable shop-fronts bore witness to the ease with which a machine-gunner can make a plate-glass look like a transparent sieve without once cracking it; rival sharpshooters had all but rounded off the corners of a few of the principal buildings. The meek, plaster-faced Protestant church had been the worst sufferer, as so often happens to the innocent bystander. The most fire-eating Münchener admitted that barter and business had lagged in the heart of town during that brief period.

But Munich's red days had already faded to a memory. Even the assassination of hostages, among them some of the city's most pompous citizens, by the fleeing Sparticists was now mentioned in much the same impersonal tone with which the Swiss might refer to the death of William Tell or an Englishman regret the loss of Kitchener. The blue-and-white flag of Bavaria fluttered again from the staffs that had been briefly usurped by the red banner of revolt; the dark-blue uniform of the once half-autonomous kingdom again asserted its sway over local matters in the new *Volksreich Bayern*. At the Deutsches Theater a large audience placidly sipping its beer set on little shelves before each seat alternately roared and sniffled at the bare-kneed mountaineers in feathered hats and the buxom *Mädels* who bounced through a home-made but well-done "custom picture" in the local dialect. It was evident that life in Munich was not likely to afford any more excitement than had the apathetic north. The atmosphere of the place only helped to confirm the ever-hardening conviction that the German, north or south, east or west, had little real sympathy for revolutions compared with the privilege of pursuing his calling steadily and undisturbed. It was high time to take to the road while a faint hope still remained that something might lay in wait for me along the way to put a bit of ginger into a journey that had thus far lamentably failed to fulfil its promise.

I breakfasted next morning with the German staff. At least I was the only civilian in the palm-decked dining-room where a score of high ranking wearers of the iron cross munched their black bread and purple *Ersatz* marmalade with punctilious formality. Away from their men, they seemed to cling as tenaciously to the rules of their caste as if disaster had never descended upon it. Each officer who entered the room paused to click his heels twice resoundingly and bow low to his seated fellows, none of whom gave him the slightest attention. It was as truly German a gesture as the salute with which every wearer of the horizon blue enters a public eating-place is French.

Nine o'clock had already sounded when I swung over my back the rucksack containing my German possessions and struck out toward the north. Now, if ever, was the time for the iron hand of the enemy to fall upon me. Perhaps my mere attempt to leave the city on foot would bring me an adventure. Vain hope! Neither civilians nor the endless procession of soldiers gave me any more attention than they did the peasants returning to their rich acres. Two sadly uneventful hours out of town a new promise appeared in the offing. A soldier under a trench helmet, armed with a glistening fixed bayonet, was patrolling a crossroad. He stepped forward as he caught sight of me, grasped his piece in an alert attitude, stared a moment in my direction, and—turning his back, leaned against a tree and lighted a cigarette. Evidently I should have to fly the Stars and Stripes at my masthead if I hoped to attract attention. Not far beyond stood weather-blackened barracks sufficient to have housed a regiment. I paused to photograph a company that was falling in. I marched out in front of the jostling throng and took a "close-up" of the lieutenant who was dressing it. He smiled faintly and stepped to the end of the line to run his eye along it. I refrained from carrying out an impulse to slap him on the back and shout: "Heh, old top! I am an American, just out of the army! What are you going to do about it?" and plodded on down the broad highway. How could a city be called beleaguered and a country under martial law if strangers could wander in and out of them at will, photographing as they went?

Fifteen kilometers from the capital I stopped at a crossroads *Gasthaus*, quite prepared to hear my suggestion of food answered with a sneer. Two or three youthful ex-soldiers still in uniform sat at one of the bare wooden tables, sipping the inevitable half-liter mugs of beer. I ordered one myself, not merely because I was thirsty, but because that is the invariable introduction to any request in a Bavarian inn. As the ponderous but neat matron set the foaming glass before me with the never-lacking "May it taste well!" I opened preliminaries on the food question, speaking gently, lest so presumptive a request from a total stranger awaken the wrath of the discharged soldiers. Mine hostess had no such misgivings. In a voice as loud and penetrating as my own had been inarticulate she bade me explain my desires in detail. I huskily whispered eggs, fried eggs, a plebeian dish, perhaps, in the land of my birth, but certainly a greater height of luxury in Germany than I had yet attained. I quail still at the audacity of that request, which I proffered with an elbow on the alert to protect my skull from the reply by physical force I more than half expected. Instead she made not a sound, after the manner of Bavarian innkeepesses when taking orders, and faded heavily but noiselessly away in the direction of the kitchen.

A few minutes later I beheld two *Spiegeleier* descending upon me, not merely real eggs, but of that year's vintage. One of them alone might have been an astonishment; a whole pair of them trotting side by side as if the Kaiser had never dreamed how fetching the letters Rex Mundis would look after his name was all but too much for me. I caught myself clinging to the bench under me as one might to the seat of an airplane about to buck, or whatever it is ships of the air do when they feel skittish. A whole plateful of boiled potatoes bore the regal couple attendance, and a generous slab of almost edible bread, quite unlike a city helping both in size and quality, brought up the rear. When I reached for a fifty-mark note and asked for the reckoning the hostess went through a laborious process in mental arithmetic and announced that, including the two half-liters of beer, I was indebted to the extent of one mk. twenty-seven! In the slang of our school-days, "You could have knocked me over with a feather," particularly as four hours earlier, back in a modest Munich hotel, I had been mulcted twelve marks for an *Ersatz* breakfast of "coffee, bread, marmalade," and four very thin slices of ham.

Twenty kilometers out of the city the flat landscape became slightly rolling. Immense fields of mustard planted in narrow rows splashed it here and there with brilliant saffron patches. Now and then an *Ersatz* bicycle rattled by, its rider, like the constant thin procession of pedestrians, decorated with the inevitable rucksack, more or less full. The women always seemed the more heavily laden, but no one had the appearance of being burdened, so natural a part of the custom of rural Germany is the knapsack of Swiss origin. Each passer-by looked at me a bit sourly, as if his inner thoughts were not wholly agreeable, and gave no sign or sound of greeting, proof in itself that I was still in the vicinity of a large city. But their very expressions gave evidence that I was not being taken for a tramp, as would have been the case in many another land. Germany is perhaps the easiest country in the world in which to make a walking trip, for the habit of wandering the highways and footpaths, rucksack on back, is all but universal. Yet this very fact makes it also in a way the least satisfactory, so little attention does the wanderer attract, and there are consequently fewer openings for conversation.

Many fine work-horses were still to be seen in spite of the drain of war, but oxen were in the majority. At least half the laborers in the fields still wore the red-banded army cap, often with the Bavarian *cocarde* still upon it. One could not but wonder just what were the inner reflections of the one-armed or one-legged men to be seen here and there struggling along behind their plows, back in their native hills again, maimed for life in a quarrel in which they really had neither part nor interest. Whatever they thought, they were outwardly as cheerful as their more fortunate fellows.

I had intended to let my fellow-pedestrians break the ice first, out of curiosity to know how far from the city they would begin to do so. But the continued silence grew a bit oppressive, and in mid-afternoon I fell into step with a curiously mated couple who had quenched their thirst in the same *Gasthaus* as I a few minutes before. The woman was a more than buxom *Frau* of some forty summers, intelligent, educated, and of decided personality. She was bareheaded, her full-moon face sunburnt to a rich brown, her massive, muscular form visibly in perspiration, an empty rucksack on her back. Her husband, at least sixty, scrawny, sallow-faced under the cap of a forest-ranger, hobbled in her wake, leading two rather work-broken horses. He was what one might call a faint individual, one of those insignificant characters that fade quickly from the memory, a creature of scanty mentality, and a veritable cesspool of ignorance, prejudice, and superstition thrown into relief by the virility of his forceful spouse.

The man had set out that morning from Munich to deliver the horses to a purchaser a hundred miles away in the Bavarian hills. Poor as they were, the animals had been sold for seven thousand marks. A first-class horse was worth six to ten thousand nowadays, he asserted. Times had indeed changed.

A few years ago only an insane man would have paid as many hundred. It was a hot day for the middle of May, a quick change from the long, unusual cold spell. The crops would suffer. He didn't mind walking, if only beer were not so expensive when one got thirsty. Having exhausted his scant mental reservoir with these and a few as commonplace remarks, he fell into the rear conversationally as well as physically, and abandoned the field to his sharp-witted spouse.

She, having more than her share of all too solid flesh to carry, had left the afternoon before and passed the night at a wayside inn. It was not that she was fond of such excursions nor that she could not trust her husband away from home. While he was delivering the horses she would go "hamstering," buying up a ruck-sackful of food among the peasants of that region, if any could be coaxed out of them, and they would return by train. Fortunately, fourth-class was still cheap. Before the war she had never dreamed of going anything but second. I broke my usual rule of the road and mentioned my scribbling proclivities. A moment later we were deeply engrossed in a discussion of German novelists and dramatists. The placid, bourgeois-looking *Frau* had read everything of importance her literary fellow-countrymen had produced; she was by no means ignorant of the best things in that line in the outside world. Thrown into the crucible of her forceful mentality, the characters of fiction had emerged as far more living beings than the men and women who passed us now and then on the road— immensely more so, it was evident, though she did not say so, than the husband who plodded behind us, frankly admitting by his very attitude that we had entered waters hopelessly beyond his depth. Of all the restrictions the war had brought, none had struck her quite so directly as the decrease in quality and number of the plays at Munich's municipal theater. Luckily they were now improving. But she always had to go alone. *He*—with a toss of her head to the rear—didn't care for anything but the movies. He laughed himself sick over those. As to opera, her greatest pleasure in life, he hadn't the faintest conception of what it was all about. He liked American ragtime (she pronounced it "rhakteam"), however. Still, America had opera also, *nicht wahr?* Had not many of Germany's best singers gone to my country? There was Slézak, for instance, and Schumann-Heink and Farrar....

I might have questioned her notion of the nationality of some of the names she mentioned, but what did it matter?

Obviously it was a waste of breath to ask whether she was pleased with the change of events that had given Germany universal suffrage for both sexes. She had voted, of course, at the first opportunity, dragging *him* along with her; he had so little interest in those matters. Her political opinions were no less decided than her artistic. Ludwig? She had often seen him. He was rather a harmless individual, but his position had not been harmless. It was a relief to be rid of him and all his clan. He would have made a much better stable-boy than king. He had wanted war just as much as had the Kaiser, whose robber-knight blood had shown up in him. But the Kaiser had not personally been so guilty as some others, Ludendorff, for instance ... and so on. The Crown Prince! A clown, a disgrace to Germany. Nobody had ever loved the Crown Prince—except the women of a certain class.

Bavaria would be much better off separated from the Empire. She was of the opinion that the majority of Bavarians preferred it. At least they did in her circle, though the strict Catholics—she glanced half-way over her shoulder—perhaps did not. Republican, Sparticist, or Bolshevik—it didn't matter which, so long as they could get good, efficient rulers. So far they had been deplorably weak—no real leaders. The recent uprising in Munich had been something of a nuisance, to be sure. They were rather glad the government troops had come. But the soldiers were mostly Prussians, and once a Prussian gets in you can never pry him out again.

We had reached the village of Hohenkammer, thirty-five kilometers out, which I had chosen as my first stopping-place. My companion of an hour shook hands with what I flattered myself was a gesture of regret that our conversation had been so brief, fell back into step with her movie-and-ragtime-minded husband, and the pair disappeared around the inn that bulged into a sharp turn of the highway.

I entered the invitingly cool and homelike *Gasthaus* prepared to be coldly turned away. Innkeepers had often been exacting in their demands for credentials during my earlier journeys in Germany. With the first mug of beer, however, the portly landlady gave me permission—one can scarcely use a stronger expression than that for the casual way in which guests are accepted in Bavarian public-houses—to spend the night, and that without so much as referring to registration or proofs of identity. Then, after expressing her placid astonishment that I wanted to see it before bedtime, she sent a muscular, barefoot, but well-scrubbed kitchen-maid to show me into room No. 1 above. It was plainly furnished with two small wooden bedsteads and the prime necessities, looked out on the broad highway and a patch of rolling fields beyond, and was as specklessly clean as are most Bavarian inns.

Rumor had it that any stranger stopping overnight in a German village courted trouble if he neglected to report his presence to the Bürgermeister, as he is expected to do to the police in the cities. I had been omitting the latter formality on the strength of my Wilhelmstrasse pass. These literal countrymen, however, might not see the matter in the same light. Moreover, being probably the only stranger spending the night in Hohenkammer, my presence was certain to be common knowledge an hour after my arrival. I decided to forestall pertinent inquiries by taking the lead in making them.

The building a few yards down the highway bearing the placard "Wohnung des Bürgermeisters" was a simple, one-story, whitewashed cottage, possibly the least imposing dwelling in town. These village rulers, being chosen by popular vote within the community, are apt to be its least pompous citizens, both because the latter do not care to accept an unpaid office and because the "plain people" hold the voting majority. The woman who tried in vain to silence a howling child and a barking dog before she came to the door in answer to my knock was just a shade better than the servant class. The husband she summoned at my request was a peasant slightly above the general level.

He took his time in coming and greeted me coldly, a trifle sharply. One felt the German official in his attitude, with its scorn for the mere petitioner, the law's underling, the subject class. Had I reported my arrival in town in the regulation manner, he would have kept that attitude. I should have been treated as something between a mild criminal and an unimportant citizen whom the law had required to submit himself to the Bürgermeister's good pleasure. Instead, I assumed the upper caste myself. I drew forth a visiting-card and handed it to him with a regal gesture, at the same time addressing him in my most haughty, university-circles German. He glanced at my unapologetic countenance, stared at the card, then back into my stern face, his official manner oozing slowly but steadily away, like the rotundity of a lightly punctured tire. By the time I began to speak again he had shrunk to his natural place in society, that of a simple, hard-working peasant whom chance had given an official standing.

The assertion that I was a traveling correspondent meant little more to him than did the card which he was still turning over and over in his stubby fingers like some child's puzzle. The Germans are not accustomed to the go-and-hunt method of gathering information to satisfy popular curiosity concerning the ways of foreign lands. I must find a better excuse for coming to Hohenkammer or I should leave him as puzzled as the card had. A brilliant idea struck me. On the strength of the "Hoover crowd" letter in my pocket, I informed him that I was walking through Germany to study food conditions, wording the statement in a way that caused him to assume that I had been officially sent on such a mission. He fell into the trap at once. From the rather neutral, unofficial, yet unresponsive attitude to which my unexpected introduction had reduced him he changed quickly to a bland, eager manner that showed genuine interest. Here was an American studying food conditions; Germany was anxiously awaiting food from America; it was up to him, as the ruler of Hohenkammer, to put his best foot forward and give me all the information I desired.

Here in the country, he began, people had never actually suffered for want of food. They had lived better than he had during his four years at the front.

Fats were the only substance of which there was any serious want. Milk was also needed, but they could get along. They did not suffer much for lack of meat; there were tickets for it here in the country also, but they were issued only after the meat each family got by slaughtering its own animals had been reckoned out. Some families got no food-tickets whatever, unless it was for bread. They were what Germans call *Selbstversorger* ("self-providers")—that is, the great majority of the peasants and all the village residents except the shopkeepers who cultivated no land, the priest, the schoolmaster, and so on. No, they had not received any American bacon or any other *Lebensmittel*; every one took that to be a joke, something the Allies were dangling before their eyes to keep them good-natured. He had never actually believed before I turned up on this official mission for studying the food situation that America actually meant to send food. Yes, he had been on the western front the entire war, fifty-two months in the trenches, and never once wounded. His first Americans he had seen at St.-Mihiel; as soldiers they seemed to be pretty good, but of course I must not forget that the German army was far different in 1918 from what it was in 1914. He very much doubted whether Americans could have driven them back in those days. More likely it would have been the opposite.

As I turned to go he took his leave with a mixture of deference and friendliness. He had not asked to see the papers bearing out all these statements I had been making, but there was a hint in the depth of his eyes that he felt it his duty to do so, if only he could venture to make such a demand of so highly placed a personage. I went far enough away to make sure he would not have the courage to demand them—which would have been his first act had I approached him as a mere traveler—then turned back, drawing the documents from a pocket as if I had just thought of them. He glanced at them in a most apologetic manner, protesting the while that of course he had never for an instant doubted my word, and returned them with a deferential bow.

All in all, this plan of posing as an official scout of the "Amerikanische Lebensmittel Kommission" had been a brilliant idea, marked with a success that moved me to use the same innocent ruse a score of times when any other means of gathering information might have been frustrated. One must have a reasonable excuse for traveling on foot in Germany. To pretend to be doing so for lack of funds would be absurd, since fourth-class fare costs an infinitesimal sum, much less than the least amount of food one could live on for the same distance. The only weakness in my simple little trick was the frequent question as to why the Americans who had sent me out on my important mission had not furnished me a bicycle. The German roads were so good; one could cover so much more ground on a *Fahrrad*.... Driven into that corner, there was no other defense but to mumble something about how much more closely the foot traveler can get in touch with the plain people, or to take advantage of some fork in the conversation to change the subject.

When I returned to the inn, the "guest-room" was crowded. Stocky, sun-browned countrymen of all ages, rather slow of wit, chatting of the simple topics of the farm in their misshapen Bavarian dialect, were crowded around the half-dozen plain wooden tables that held their immense beer-mugs, while the air was opaque with the smoke from their long-stemmed porcelain pipes. The entrance of a total stranger was evidently an event to the circle. The rare guests who spent the night in Hohenkammer were nearly always teamsters or peddlers who traveled the same route so constantly that their faces were as familiar as those of the village residents. As each table in turn caught sight of me, the conversation died down like a motor that had slowly been shut off, until the most absolute silence reigned. How long it might have lasted would be hard to guess. It had already grown decidedly oppressive when I turned to my nearest neighbor and broke the ice with some commonplace remark. He answered with extreme brevity and an evidence of something between bashfulness and a deference tinged with suspicion. Several times I broke the silence which followed each reply before these reached the dignity of full sentences. It was like starting a motor on a cold morning. Bit by bit, however, we got under way; others joined in, and in something less than a half-hour we were buzzing along full speed ahead, the entire roomful adding their voices to the steady hum of conversation which my appearance had interrupted.

Thus far I had not mentioned my nationality at the inn, being in doubt whether the result would be to increase our conversational speed or bring it to a grating and sudden halt. When I did, it was ludicrously like the shifting of gears. The talk slowed down for a minute or more, while the information I had vouchsafed passed from table to table in half-audible whispers, then sped ahead more noisily, if less swiftly, than before. On the whole, curiosity was chiefly in evidence. There was perhaps a bit of wonder and certainly some incredulity in the simple, gaping faces, but quite as surely no signs of enmity or resentment. Before long the table at which I sat was doubly crowded and questions as to America and her ways were pouring down upon me in a flood which it was quite beyond the power of a single voice to stem. Friendly questions they certainly were, without even a suggestion of the sarcasm one sometimes caught a hint of in more haughty German circles. Yet in the gathering were at least a score of men who had been more or less injured for life in a struggle which they themselves admitted the nation I represented had turned against them. I have been so long absent from my native land that I cannot quite picture to myself what would happen to the man who thus walked in upon a gathering of American farmers, boldly announcing himself a German just out of the army, but something tells me he would not have passed so perfectly agreeable an evening as I did in the village inn of Hohenkammer.

With my third mug of beer the landlord himself sat down beside me. Not, of course—prohibition forbid!—that I had ordered a third pint of beer in addition to the two that the plump matron had served me with a very satisfying supper. In fact, I had not once mentioned the subject of beverages. Merely to take one's seat at any inn table in Bavaria is equivalent to shouting, *"Glas Bier?"* No questions were asked, but mine host—so far more often mine hostess—is as certain to set a foaming mug before the new arrival as he—or she—is to abhor the habit of drinking water; and woe betide the man who drains what he hopes is his last mug without rising instantly to his feet, for some sharp-eyed member of the innkeeper's family circle is sure to thrust another dripping beaker under his chin before he can catch his breath to protest. On the other hand, no one is forced to gage his thirst by that of his neighbors, as in many a less placid land. The treating habit is slightly developed in rural Bavaria. On very special occasions some one may "set 'em up" for the friend beside him, or even for three or four of his cronies, but it is the almost invariable rule that each client call for his own reckoning at the end of the evening.

The innkeeper had returned at late dusk from tilling his fields several miles away. Like his fellows throughout Bavaria, he was a peasant except by night and on holidays. During the working-day the burden, if it could be called one, of his urban establishment fell upon his wife and children. It was natural, therefore, that the topic with which he wedged his way into the conversation should have been that of husbandry. Seeds, he asserted, were still fairly good, fortunately, though in a few species the war had left them sadly inferior. But the harvest would be poor this year. The coldest spring in as far back as he could remember had lasted much later than ever before. Then, instead of the rain they should have had, scarcely a drop had fallen and things were already beginning to shrivel. As if they had not troubles enough as it was! With beer gone up to sixteen pfennigs a pint instead of the ten of the good old days before the war! And such beer! Hardly 3 per cent. alcohol in it now instead of 11! The old peasants had stopped drinking it entirely—the very men who had been his best customers. They distilled a home-made *Schnapps* now, and stayed at home to drink it. Naturally such weak stuff as this—he held up his half-empty mug with an expression of disgust on his face—could not satisfy the old-fashioned Bavarian taste. Before the war he had served an average of a thousand beers a day. Now he drew barely two hundred. And as fast as business fell off taxes increased. He would give a good deal to know where they were going to end. Especially now, with these ridiculous terms the Allies were asking Germany to sign. How could they sign? It would scarcely leave them their shirt and trousers. And they, the peasants and country people, would have to pay for it, they and the factory hands; not the bigwigs in Berlin and Essen who were so ready to accept England's challenge. No, it would not pay Bavaria to assert her independence. They did not love the northern German, but when all was said and done it would be better to stick with him.

Suddenly the brain-racking dialect in which the *Wirt* and his cronies had been sharing their views on this and other subjects halted and died down to utter silence, with that same curious similarity to a shut-off motor that my entrance had caused. I looked about me, wondering what I had done to bring on this new stillness. Every man in the room had removed his hat and all but two their porcelain pipes. Except for the latter, who puffed faintly and noiselessly now and then, the whole assembly sat perfectly motionless. For a moment or more I was puzzled; then a light suddenly broke upon me. The bell of the village church was tolling the end of evening vespers.

Hohenkammer, like the majority of Bavarian towns, was a strictly Catholic community. The women, from the barefoot kitchen servant to the highest lady of the village, had slipped quietly off to church while their husbands gathered in the *Gasthaus*, and the latter were now showing their respect for the ceremony they had attended by proxy. They sat erect, without a bowed head among them, but in the motionless silence of "living statues," except that toward the end, as if in protest that their good crony, the village priest, should take undue advantage of his position and prolong their pose beyond reason with his persistent tolling, several squirmed in their seats, and two, possibly the free-thinkers of the community, hawked and spat noisily and what seemed a bit ostentatiously. As the ringing ceased, each clumsily crossed himself rather hastily, slapped his hat back upon his head, and the buzz of conversation rapidly rose again to its previous volume.

XIII
INNS AND BYWAYS

A brilliant, almost tropical sun, staring in upon me through flimsy white cotton curtains, awoke me soon after five. Country people the world over have small patience with late risers, and make no provision for guests who may have contracted that bad habit. My companions of the night before had long since scattered to their fields when I descended to the *Gastzimmer*, veritably gleaming with the sand-and-water polish it had just received. The calmly busy landlady solicitously inquired how I had slept, and while I forced down my "breakfast" of *Ersatz* coffee and dull-brown peasant bread she laid before me the inn register, a small, flat ledger plainly bearing the marks of its profession in the form of beer and grease stains on its cover and first pages. I had been mistaken in supposing that Bavaria's change to a republic had dispensed with that once important formality. In fact, I recall but one public lodging on my German journey where my personal history was not called for before my departure. But there was nothing to have hindered me from assuming a fictitious identity. When I had scrawled across the page under the hieroglyphics of previous guests the half-dozen items required by the police, the hostess laid the book away without so much as looking at the new entry. My bill for supper, lodging, "breakfast," and four pints of beer was five marks and seventy-two pfennigs, and the order-loving *Frau* insisted on scooping out of her satchel the last tiny copper to make the exact change before she wished me good day and a pleasant journey.

The single village street, which was also the main highway, was thronged with small boys slowly going to school when I stepped out into the flooding sunshine soon after seven. One of the most striking sights in Germany is the flocks of children everywhere, in spite of the wastage of more than four years of war and food scarcity. Certainly none of these plump little "square-heads" showed any evidence of having suffered from hunger; compared with the pale, anemic urchins of large cities they were indeed pictures of health. They resembled the latter as ripe tomatoes resemble gnarled and half-grown green apples. At least half of them wore some portion of army uniform, cut down from the war-time garb of their elders, no doubt, the round, red-banded cap covered nearly every head, and many carried their books and coarse lunches in the hairy cowhide knapsacks of the trenches, usually with a cracked slate and the soiled rag with which they wiped their exercises off it swinging from a strap at the rear. They showed as much curiosity at the sight of a stranger in town as their fathers had the night before, but when I stealthily opened my kodak and strolled slowly toward them they stampeded in a body and disappeared pellmell within the schoolhouse door.

The sun was already high in the cloudless sky. It would have been hard to imagine more perfect weather. The landscape, too, was entrancing; gently rolling fields deep-green with spring alternating with almost black patches of evergreen forests, through which the broad, light-gray highroad wound and undulated as soothingly as an immense ocean-liner on a slowly pulsating sea. Every few miles a small town rose above the horizon, now astride the highway, now gazing down upon it from a sloping hillside. Wonderfully clean towns they were, speckless from their scrubbed floors to their whitewashed church steeples, all framed in velvety green meadows or the fertile fields in which their inhabitants of both sexes plodded diligently but never hurriedly through the labors of the day. It was difficult to imagine how these simple, gentle-spoken folk could have won a world-wide reputation as the most savage and brutal warriors in modern history.

Toward noon appeared the first of Bavaria's great hop-fields, the plants that would climb house-high by August now barely visible. In many of them the hop-frames were still being set up—vast networks of poles taller than the telegraph lines along the way, crisscrossed with more slender crosspieces from which hung thousands of thin strings ready for the climbing vines. The war had affected even this bucolic industry. Twine, complained a peasant with whom I paused to chat, had more than quadrupled in price, and one was lucky at that not to find the stuff made of paper when the time came to use it. In many a field the erection of the frames had not yet begun, and the poles still stood in clusters strikingly resembling Indian wigwams, where they had been stacked after the harvest of the September before.

At Pfaffenhofen, still posing as a "food controller," I dropped in on a general merchant. The ruse served as an opening to extended conversation here even better than it had in the smaller town behind. The *Kaufmann* was almost too eager to impress me, and through me America, with the necessity of replenishing his shrunken stock. He reiterated that fats, soap, rice, soup materials, milk, cocoa and sugar were most lacking, and in the order named. Then there was tobacco, more scarce than any of these, except perhaps fats. If only America would send them tobacco! In other lines? Well, all sorts of clothing materials were needed, of course they had been hoping ever since the armistice that America would send them cotton. People were wearing all manner of *Ersatz* cloth. He took from his show-window what looked like a very coarse cotton shirt, but which had a brittle feel, and spread it out before me. It was made of nettles. Sometimes the lengthwise threads were cotton and the cross threads nettle, which made a bit more durable stuff, but he could not say much even for that. As to the nettle shirt before me, he sold it for fourteen marks because he refused to accept profit on such stuff. But what good was such a shirt to the peasants? They wore it a few days, washed it once and—*kaput*, finished, it crumpled together like burnt paper. Many children could no longer go to school; their clothes had been patched out of existence. During the war there had been few marriages in the rural districts because, the boys being away at war, a fair division of the inheritances could not be made even when the girls found matches. Now many wanted to marry, but most of them found it impossible because they could not get any bed-linen or many of the other things that are necessary to establish a household. No, he did not think there had been any great increase in irregularities between the sexes because of war conditions, at least not in such well-to-do farming communities as the one about Pfaffenhofen. He had heard, however, that in the large cities....

The Bavarians are not merely great lovers of flowers; they have no hesitancy in showing that fondness, as is so often the case with less simple people. The house window, be it only that of the humblest little crossroads inn, which was not gay with blossoms of a half-dozen species was a curiosity. About every house, in every yard were great bushes of lilac, hydrangea, and several other flowering shrubs; add to this the fact that all fruit-trees were just then in full bloom and it will be less difficult to picture the veritable flower-garden through which I was tramping. Nor were the inhabitants satisfied to let inanimate nature alone decorate herself with spring. The sourest-looking old peasant was almost sure to have a cluster of flowers tucked into a shirt buttonhole or the lapel of his well-worn jacket; girls and women decked themselves out no more universally than did the males of all ages, from the tottering urchin not yet old enough to go to school to the doddering grandfather leaning his gnarled hands on his home-made cane in the shade of the projecting house eaves. Men and boys wore them most often in the bands of their curious slouch-hats, beside the turkey feather or the shaving-brush with which the Bavarian headgear is frequently embellished the year round.

In each village a new May-pole towered above everything else, often visible when the hamlet itself was quite out of sight. On the first day of the month that of the year before had been cut down and the tallest pine-tree available, trimmed of its branches except for a little tuft at the top, had been set up before the chief *Gasthaus*, amid celebrations that included the emptying of many kegs of beer. Its upper half encircled with wreaths, streamers, and winding, flower-woven lianas, and decorated with a dozen flags, it suggested at a distance the totem-pole of some childlike tropical tribe rather than the plaything of a plodding and laborious people of western Europe.

I set my pace in a way to bring me into the larger towns at noon and to some quaint and quiet village at nightfall. In the latter, one was surer to find homelike accommodations and simpler, more naïve people with whom to chat through the evening. The cities, even of only a few thousand inhabitants, too nearly resembled Berlin or Munich to prove of continued interest. The constant traveler, too, comes to abhor the world-wide sameness of city hotels. Moreover, the larger the town the scantier was the food in the Germany of 1919. The guest who sat down to an excellently cooked dinner of a thick peasant soup, a man's size portion of beef, veal, or pork, potatoes in unlimited quantity, bread that was almost white and made of real wheat, and a few other vegetables thrown in, all for a cost of two marks, might easily have imagined that all this talk of food shortage was mere pretense. Surely this last month before the beginning of harvest, in the last year of the war, with the question of signing or not signing the peace terms throbbing through all Germany, was the time of all times to find a certain answer to the query of the outside world as to the truth of the German's cry of starvation. But the answer one found in the smaller villages of Bavaria would have been far from the true one of the nation at large.

Now and then my plans went wrong. Conditions differed, even in two towns of almost identical appearance. Thus at Ingolstadt, which was large enough to have been gaunt with hunger, there was every evidence of plenty. Here I had expected trouble also of another sort. The town was heavily garrisoned, as it had been even before the war. Soldiers swarmed everywhere; at the inn where my tramping appetite was so amply satisfied they surrounded me on every side. I was fully prepared to be halted at any moment, perhaps to be placed under arrest. Instead, the more openly I watched military maneuvers, the more boldly I put questions to the youths in uniform, the less I was suspected. In Reichertshofen the night before, where I had sat some time in silence, reading, in a smoke-clouded beer-hall crowded with laborers from the local mills, far more questioning glances had been cast in my direction.

On the other hand the hamlet I chose for the night sometimes proved a bit too small. One must strike a careful average or slip from the high ridge of plenitude. Denkendorf, an afternoon's tramp north of the garrison city, was so tiny that the waddling old landlady gasped at my placid assumption that of course she could serve me supper. Beer, to be sure, she could furnish me as long as the evening lasted; das beste Zimmer—the very best room in the house—and it was almost imposing in its speckless solemnity—I could have all to myself, if I cared to pay as high as a whole mark for the night! But food.... She mumbled and shook her head, waddled like a matronly old duck back and forth between the "guest-room" and the kitchen, with its massive smoked beams and medieval appliances, she brought me more beer, she pooh-poohed my suggestion that the chickens and geese that flocked all through the hamlet might offer a solution to the problem, and at length disappeared making some inarticulate noise that left me in doubt whether she had caught an idea or had decided to abandon me to my hungry fate.

The short night had fallen and I had fully reconciled myself to retiring supperless when the kitchen door let in a feeble shaft of light which silhouetted my cask-shaped hostess approaching with something in her hands. No doubt she was foisting another mug of beer upon me! My mistake. With a complacent grunt she placed on the no longer visible table two well-filled plates and turned to light a strawlike wick protruding from a flat bottle of grease. By its slight rays I made out a heaping portion of boiled potatoes and an enormous *Pfannkuchen*—the German cross between an omelet and a pancake. It must have been a robust appetite indeed that did not succumb before this substitute for the food which Denkendorf, in the opinion of the landlady, so entirely lacked.

Meanwhile I had made a new acquaintance. A young soldier in the uniform of a sergeant had for some time been my only companion in the "guest-room." His face suggested intelligence and an agreeable personality. For a long time we both sipped our beer in silence at opposite tables. I broke the ice at last, well aware that he would not have done so had we sat there all night. As in the older sections of our own country, so in the Old World it is not the custom to speak unnecessarily to strangers.

He answered my casual remark with a smile, however, rose, and, carrying his mug of beer with him, sat down on the opposite side of my table. I took pains to bring out my nationality at the first opportunity.

"American?" he cried, with the nearest imitation I had yet heard in Germany of the indignant surprise I had always expected that information to evoke, "and what are you doing here?"

There was something more than mere curiosity in his voice, though his tone could not quite have been called angry. It was more nearly the German official guttural. I smiled placidly as I answered, throwing in a hint, as usual, about the food commission. He was instantly mollified. He did not even suggest seeing my papers, though he announced himself the traveling police force of that region, covering some ten small towns. Within five minutes we were as deep in conversation as if we had discovered ourselves to be friends of long standing. He was of a naturally sociable disposition, like all Bavarians, and his sociability was distinctly enhanced when I shared with him my last nibble of chocolate and "split" with him one of my rare American cigars. He had not had a smoke in a week, not even an *Ersatz* one; and it was at least a year since he had tasted chocolate. In return for my appalling sacrifice he insisted on presenting me with the two eggs he had been able to "hamster" during that day's round of duty. When I handed them to the caisson-built landlady with instructions to serve us one each in the morning, my relations with the police-soldier were established on a friendly basis for life.

Before bedtime we had reached the point where he turned his revolver over to me, that I might satisfy my curiosity as to its inner workings. In return I spread all but one of my official and pseudo-official papers out before him in the flickering light of the grease wick, not because he had made any formal request to see them, but that I might keep him amused, as one holds the interest of a baby by flashing something gaudy before it or holding a ticking watch to its ear. Not, let it be plainly understood, that my new friend was of low intellectual level. Far from it. A Nürnberger of twenty-five who had seen all the war, on several fronts, he was judicious and "keen," quite equal to his new position as country gendarme. But there is something naïve, babylike in the Bavarian character even after it has been tempered and remolded by wide and varied experience.

The next morning he insisted on rising early to accompany me a few miles on my journey. He expressed his astonishment that I carried no weapon, and though he laughed at the notion that I was in any danger without one, he did not propose that anything should befall me on his "beat." As we advanced, our conversation grew more serious. He was not quite ready to admit that Germany had started the war, but he was forceful in his assertion that the capitalists and the "Old German" party had wanted it. The working-class, he insisted, would never have gone into the war if those higher up had not made them think Germany had been treacherously attacked, that England and France had determined to annihilate her. He was still not wholly convinced that those were not the facts, but he was enraged at what he insisted were the crimes of the capitalists. It goes without saying that he was a Socialist, his leanings being toward the conservative side of that widely spread party. He told several tales of fraternization with French soldiers of similar opinions during his years in the trenches. The republican idea, he asserted, had been much in evidence among the working-classes long before the war, but it had never dared openly show its head. For German rulers, from Kaiser and princes down to his own army officers, he had the bitterest scorn. Their first and foremost interest in life he summed up under the head of "women." Some of his personal-knowledge anecdotes of the "high and mighty" were not fit to print. His opinions of German womanhood, or at least girlhood, were astonishingly low for a youth of so naïve and optimistic a character. On the other hand he lapsed every little while into childlike boasting of Germany's military prowess, quite innocently, as one might point to the fertility or the sunshine of one's native land. The Germans had first used gas; they had been the first to invent gas-masks; they had air-raided the capitals of their enemies, sunk them at sea long before the slow-witted Allies had ever thought of any such weapons or contrivances.

Some ten miles from our eating-place we drifted into the street-lanes of a huddled little village, older than the German Empire, in quest of the *Gasthaus*. Three hours of tramping are sufficient to recall the refreshing qualities of Bavarian beer. However reprehensible it may have been before the war, with its dreadful eleven percentage of alcohol, it was certainly a harmless beverage in 1919, superior in attack on a roadside thirst even to nature's noblest substitute, water. If the reader will promise not to use the evidence against me, I will confess that I emptied as many as eight pint mugs of beer during a single day of my German tramp, and was as much intoxicated at the end of it as I should have been with as many quarts of milk. Nor would the natural conclusion that I am impervious to strong drink be just; the exact opposite is the bitter truth. The adult Bavarian who does not daily double, if not treble, my best performance is either an oddity or a complete financial failure, yet I have never seen one affected by his constant libations even to the point of increased gaiety.

The justly criticized features of our saloons are quite unknown in the Bavarian *Gasthäuser*. In the first place, they are patronized by both sexes and all classes, with the consequent improvement in character. On Sunday evening, after his sermon, the village priest or pastor, the latter accompanied by his wife, drops in for a pint before retiring to his well-earned rest. Rowdyism, foul language, obscenity either of word or act are as rare as in the family circle. Never having been branded society's black sheep, the Bavarian beer-hall is quite as respected and self-respecting a member of the community as any other business house. It is the village club for both sexes, with an atmosphere quite as ladylike as, if somewhat less effeminate, than, a sewing-circle; and it is certainly a boon to the thirsty traveler tramping the sun-flooded highways. All of which is not a plea for beer-drinking by those who do not care for the dreadful stuff, but merely a warning that personally I propose to continue the wicked habit as long—whenever, at least, I am tramping the roads of Bavaria.

These village inns are all of the same type. A quaint and placid building with the mellowed atmosphere that comes with respectable old age, usually of two stories, always with an exceedingly steep roof from which peer a few dormer-windows, like wondering urchins perched in some place of vantage, is pierced through the center by a long, low, cool passageway that leads to the family garden or back yard. Just inside the street entrance this hallway is flanked by two doors, on one of which, in old Gothic letters, is the word "Gastzimmer" (guest-room). Thus the new-comer is spared the embarrassment of bursting in upon the intimacies of the family circle that would result from his entering the opposite door. The world has few public places as homelike as the cool and cozy room to which the placarded door gives admittance. Unpainted wooden tables, polished gleaming white with sand and water, fill the room without any suggestion of crowding. At one side sits a porcelain stove, square-faced and high, its surface broken into small square plaques, the whole shining intensely with its blue, blue-gray, or greenish tint. Beyond this, in a corner, a tall, old-time clock with weights tick-tacks with the dignified, placid serenity of quiet old age. Three or four pairs of antlers protrude from the walls; several small mirrors, and a number of framed pictures, most of them painful to the artistic sense that has reached the first stage of development, break the soothingly tinted surfaces between them. In the corner behind the door is a small glass-faced cupboard in which hang the long, hand-decorated porcelain pipes of the local smoking-club, each with the name of its owner stenciled upon it. Far to the rear sits a middle-aged phonograph with the contrite yet defiant air of a recent comer who realizes himself rather out of place and not over-popular in the conservative old society upon which he has forced himself. Deep window embrasures, gay with flowers in dull-red pots, hung with snowy little lace curtains, are backed by even more immaculate glass, in small squares. This bulges outwardly in a way to admit a maximum of light, yet is quite impenetrable from the outside, from where it merely throws back into the face of the would-be observer his own reflection. In the afternoon a powerfully built young woman, barefoot or shod only in low slippers, is almost certain to be found ironing at one of the tables. At the others sit a guest or two, their heavy glass or stone mugs before them. No fowls, dogs, or other domestic nuisances are permitted to enter, though the placid, Bavarian family cat is almost sure to look each new-comer over with a more or less disapproving air from her place of vantage toward the rear. It would take sharp eyes indeed to detect a fleck of dust, a beer stain, or the tiniest cobweb anywhere in the room.

Over the door is a sign, as time-mellowed as an ancient painting, announcing the price of a liter of beer—risen to thirty-two or thirty-four pfennigs in these sad war-times—though seldom mentioning the beverage by name. That information is not needed in a community where other drinks are as strangers in a strange land. About the spigots at the rear hovers a woman who might resent being called old and fat, yet who would find it difficult to convince a critical observer that she could lay any claim to being either young or slender. As often as a guest enters to take his seat at a table, with a mumbled "*Scoot*" she waddles forward with a dripping half-liter mug of beer, bringing another the instant her apparently dull but really eagle eye catches sight of one emptied. At her waist hangs from a strap over the opposite shoulder a huge satchel-purse of ancient design from which she scoops up a pudgy handful of copper and pewter coins whenever a guest indicates that he is ready to pay his reckoning, and dismisses him with another "*Scoot*" as he opens the door. From a score to a hundred times an hour, depending on the time of day, the size of the village, and the popularity of that particular establishment, a bell tinkles and she waddles to a little trap-door near the spigots to fill the receptacle that is handed in by some neighbor, usually an urchin or a disheveled little girl barely tall enough to peer in at the waist-high opening, and thrusts it out again as she drops another handful of copper coins into her capacious wallet.

They are always named in huge letters on the street façade, these Bavarian *Gasthäuser*. *"Zum Rothen Hahn"* ("To the Red Rooster"), *"Zum Grauen Ross"* ("To the Gray Steed"), "To the Golden Star," "To the Black Bear," "To the Golden Angel," "To the Blue Grapes," "To the White Swan," "To the Post," and so on through all the colors of the animal, vegetable, and heavenly kingdom. Whether in reference to the good old days when Bavaria's beer was more elevating in its strength, or merely an evidence of the mixture of the poetic and the religious in the native character, one of the favorite names is "To the Ladder of Heaven."

In the evening the interior scene changes somewhat. The laundress has become a serving-maid, the man of the house has returned from his fields and joins his waddling spouse in carrying foaming mugs from spigots to trap-door or to tables, crowded now with muscular, sun-browned peasants languid from the labors of the day. Then is the time that a rare traveling guest may ask to be shown to one of the clean and simple little chambers above. The wise man will always seek one of these inns of the olden days in which to spend the night, even in cities large enough to boast more presumptuous quarters. The establishment announcing itself as a "Hotel" is certain to be several times more expensive, often less clean and comfortable, superior only in outward show, and always far less homelike than the modest *Gasthaus*.

It may have been imagination, but I fancied I saw a considerable variation in types in different villages. In some almost every inhabitant seemed broad-shouldered and brawny; in others the under-sized prevailed. This particular hamlet in which the police-soldier and I took our farewell glass appeared to be the gathering-place of dwarfs. At any rate, a majority of those I caught sight of could have walked under my outstretched arm. It may be that the war had carried off the full-grown, or they may have been away tilling the fields. The head of the inn family, aged sixty or more, was as exact a copy of the gnomes whom Rip van Winkle found playing ninepins as the most experienced stage manager could have chosen and costumed. Hunched back, hooked nose, short legs, long, tasseled, woolen knit cap, whimsical smile and all, he was the exact picture of those play-people of our childhood fairy-books. Indeed, he went them one better, for the long vest that covered his unnatural expanse of chest gleamed with a score of buttons fashioned from silver coins of centuries ago, of the size of half-dollars. He sold me an extra one, at the instigation of my companion, for the appalling price of two marks! It proved to date back to the days when Spain held chief sway over the continent of Europe. His wife was his companion even in appearance and suggested some medieval gargoyle as she paddled in upon us, clutching a froth-topped stone mug in either dwarfish hand. She had the fairy-tale kindness of heart, too, for when my companion suggested that his thirst was no greater than his hunger she duck-footed noiselessly away and returned with a generous wedge of her own bread. It was distinctly brown and would not have struck the casual American observer as a delicacy, but the Nürnberger fell upon it with a smacking of the lips and a joyful: "*Na! Das ist Bauernbrod*—genuine peasant's bread. You don't get *that* in the cities, *na!*"

He took his final leave at the top of the rise beyond the village, deploring the fact that he could not continue with me to Berlin and imploring me to come again some other year when we could tramp the Bavarian hills together. When I turned and looked back, nearly a half-mile beyond, he stood in the selfsame spot, and he snatched off his red-banded fatigue cap and waved it half gaily, half sadly after me.

Miles ahead, over a mountainous ridge shaded by a cool and murmuring evergreen forest, I descended through the fields toward Beilngries, a reddish patch on the landscape ahead. A glass-clear brook that was almost a river hurried away across the meadow. I shed my clothes and plunged into it. A thin man was wandering along its grassy bank like a poet hunting inspiration or a victim of misfortune seeking solace for his tortured spirit. I overtook him soon after I had dressed. His garb was not that of a Bavarian villager; his manner and his speech suggested a Prussian, or at least a man from the north. I expected him to show more curiosity at sight of a wandering stranger than had the simple countrymen of the region. When I accosted him he asked if the water was cold and lapsed into silence. I made a casual reference to my walk from Munich. In any other country the mere recital of that distance on foot would have aroused astonishment. He said he had himself been fond of walking in his younger days. I implied in a conversational footnote that I was bound for Berlin. He assured me the trip would take me through some pleasant scenery. I emphasized my accent until a man of his class must have recognized that I was a foreigner. He remarked that these days were sad days for Germany. I worked carefully up to the announcement, in the most dramatic manner I could command, that I was an American recently discharged from the army. He hoped I would carry home a pleasant impression of German landscapes, even if I did not find the country what it had once been in other respects. As we parted at the edge of the town he deplored the scarcity and high price of food, shook hands limply, and wished me a successful journey. In other words, there was no means of arousing his interest, to say nothing of surprise or resentment, that the citizen of a country with which his own was still at war should be wandering freely with kodak and note-book through his Fatherland. His attitude was that of the vast majority of Germans I met on my journey, and to this day I have not ceased to wonder why their attitude should have been so indifferent. Had the whole country been starved out of the aggressive, suspicious manner of the Kaiser days, or was there truth in the assertion that they had always considered strangers honored guests and treated them as such? More likely the form of government under which they had so long lived had left the individual German the impression that personally it was no affair of his, that it was up to the officials who had appointed themselves over him to attend to such matters, while the government itself had grown so weak and disjointed that it took no cognizance of wandering strangers.

Whatever else may be said of them, the Germans certainly are a hard-working, diligent people, even in the midst of calamities. Boys of barely fourteen followed the plow from dawn to dark of these long northern summer days. Laborers toiled steadily at road-mending, at keeping in repair the material things the Kaiser régime had left them, as ambitiously as if the thought had never occurred to them that all this labor might in the end prove of advantage only to their enemies. Except that the letters "P. G." or "P. W." were not painted on their garments, there was nothing to distinguish these gangs of workmen in fields and along the roads from the prisoners of war one had grown so accustomed to see at similar tasks in France. They wore the same patched and discolored field gray, the same weather-faded fatigue caps. How those red-banded caps had permeated into the utmost corners of the land!

Between Beilngries and Bershing, two attractive towns with more than their share of food and comfort in the Germany of armistice days, I left the highway for the towpath of the once famous Ludwig Canal that parallels it. To all appearances this had long since been abandoned as a means of transportation. Nowhere in the many miles I followed it did I come upon a canal-boat, though its many locks were still in working order and the lock-tenders' dwellings still inhabited. The disappearance of canal-boats may have been merely temporary, as was that of automobiles, of which I remember seeing only three during all my tramp in Germany, except those in the military service.

For a long time I trod the carpet-like towpath without meeting or overtaking any fellow-traveler. It was as if I had discovered some unknown and perfect route of my own. The mirror surface of the canal beside me pictured my movements far more perfectly than any cinema film, reproducing every slightest tint and color. Now and again I halted to stretch out on the grassy slope at the edge of the water, in the all-bathing sunshine. Snow-white cherry-trees were slowly, regretfully shedding their blossoms, flecking the ground and here and there the edge of the canal with their cast-off petals. Bright-pink apple-trees, just coming into full bloom, were humming with myriad bees. A few birds sang gaily, yet a bit drowsily, falling wholly silent now and then, as if awed by nature's loveliness. A weather-browned woman, her head covered with a clean white kerchief with strands of apple-blossom pink in it, knelt at the edge of the waterway a bit farther on, cutting the long grass with a little curved sickle, her every motion, too, caught by the mirroring canal.

Along the highway below tramped others of her species, bearing to town on their backs the green fodder similarly gathered, in long cone-shaped baskets or wrapped in a large cloth. One had heaped her basket high with bright-yellow mustard, splashing the whitish roadway as with a splotch of paint. Vehicles there were none, except the little handcarts drawn by barefoot women or children, and now and then a man sometimes similarly unshod. Oxen reddish against green meadows or whitish against the red soil were standing idle, knee-deep in grass or slowly plowing the gently rolling fields. Farther off, clumps of cattle ranging from dark brown to faint yellow speckled the rounded hillocks. Fields white with daisies, yellow with buttercups, lilac with some other species of small flower, vied with one another in beautifying the more distant landscape. Still farther off, the world was mottled with clumps of forest, in which mingled the black evergreen of perennial foliage with the light green of new leaves. An owl or some member of his family hooted contentedly from the nearest woods. Modest little houses, with sharp, very-old-red roofs and whitewashed walls dulled by years of weather, stood in clusters of varying size on the sun-flooded hillsides. Nothing in the velvety, gentle scene, so different from the surly landscape of factory districts, suggested war, except now and again the red-banded caps of the men. The more wonder came upon me that these slow, simple country people with their never-failing greetings and their entire lack of warlike manner could have formed a part of the most militaristic nation in history.

XIV
"FOOD WEASELS"

For some days past every person I met along the way, young or old, had bidden me good day with the all-embracing *"Scoot"*. I had taken this at first to be an abbreviation of *"Es ist gut,"* until an innkeeper had explained it as a shortening of the medieval *"Grüss Gott"* ("May God's greeting go with you"). In mid-afternoon of this Saturday the custom suddenly ceased, as did the solitude of the towpath. A group of men and women, bearing rucksacks, baskets, valises, and all manner of receptacles, appeared from under the flowery foliage ahead and marched past me at a more aggressive pace than that of the country people. Their garb, their manner, somewhat sour and unfriendly, particularly the absence of any form of greeting, distinguished them from the villagers of the region. More and more groups appeared, some numbering a full dozen, following one another so closely as to form an almost continual procession. Some marched on the farther bank of the canal, as if our own had become too crowded with traffic for comfort, all hurrying by me into the south, with set, perspiring faces. I took them to be residents of the larger towns beyond, returning from the end of a railway spur ahead with purchases from the Saturday-morning market at Nürnberg. It was some time before I discovered that quite the opposite was the case.

They were "hamsterers," city people setting out to scour the country for food. "Hamster" is a German word for an animal of the weasel family, which squirms in and out through every possible opening in quest of nourishment. During the war it came to be the popular designation of those who seek to augment their scanty ticket-limited rations by canvassing among the peasants, until the term in all its forms, as noun, verb, adjective, has become a universally recognized bit of the language. Women with time to spare, children free from school, go "hamstering" any day of the week. But Saturday afternoon and Sunday, when the masses are relieved of their labors, is the time of a general exodus from every city in Germany. There is not a peasant in the land, I have been assured, who has not been regularly "hamstered" during the past two years. In their feverish quest the famished human weasels cross and crisscross their lines through all the Empire. "Hamsterers" hurrying north or east in the hope of discovering unfished waters pass "hamsterers" racing south or west bound on the same chiefly vain errand. Another difficulty adds to their misfortunes, however, and limits the majority to their own section of the country. It is not the cost of transportation, except in the case of those at the lowest financial ebb, for fourth-class fare is more than cheap and includes all the baggage the traveler can lug with him. But any journey of more than twenty-five kilometers requires the permission of the local authorities. Without their *Ausweis* the railways will not sell tickets to stations beyond that distance. Hence the custom is to ride as far into the country as possible, make a wide circle on foot, or sometimes on a bicycle, during the Sunday following, "hamstering" as one goes, and fetch up at the station again in time for the last train to the city. In consequence the regions within the attainable distance around large cities are so thoroughly "fished out" that the peasants receive new callers with sullen silence.

I had been conscious of a sourness in the greetings of the country people all that Saturday, quite distinct from their cheery friendliness of the days before. Now it was explained. They had taken me for a "hamsterer" with a knapsack full of the food their region could so ill spare. Not that any of them, probably, was suffering from hunger. But man is a selfish creature. He resents another's acquisition of anything which may ever by any chance be of use to him. Particularly "*der Deutsche Bauer* (the German peasant)," as a "hamsterer" with whom I fell in later put it, "is never an idealist. He believes in looking out for himself first and foremost"—which characteristic, by the way, is not confined to his class in Germany, nor indeed to any land. "War, patriotism, Fatherland have no place in his heart when they clash with the interests of his purse," my informant went on. "Hence he has taken full advantage of the misery of others, using the keen competition to boost his prices far beyond all reason."

Many a labor-weary workman of the cities, with a half-dozen mouths to fill, many a tired, emaciated woman, tramps the byways of Germany all Sunday long, halting at a score or two of farm-houses, dragging aching legs homeward late at night, with only three or four eggs, a few potatoes, and now and then a half-pound of butter to show for the exertion. Sometimes other food-seekers have completely annihilated the peasant's stock. Sometimes he has only enough for his own needs. Often his prices are so high that the "hamsterer" cannot reach them—the *Bauer* knows by years of experience now that if he bides his time some one to whom price is a minor detail will appear, perhaps the agents of the rich man's hotels and restaurants of Berlin and the larger cities. Frequently he is of a miserly disposition, and hoards his produce against an imagined day of complete famine, or in the hope that the unreasonable prices will become even more unreasonable. There are laws against "hamstering," as there are against selling foodstuffs at more than the established price. Now and again the weary urban dweller who has tramped the country-side all day sees himself held up by a gendarme and despoiled of all his meager gleanings. But the peasant, for some reason, is seldom molested in his profiteering.

The northern Bavarian complains that the people of Saxony outbid him among his own villages; the Saxon accuses the iron-fisted Prussian of descending upon his fields and carrying off the food so badly needed at home. For those with influence have little difficulty in reaching beyond the legal twenty-five kilometer limit. The result is that foodstuffs on which the government has set a maximum price often never reach the market, but are gathered on the spot at prices several times higher than the law sanctions.

"You see that farm over there?" asked a food-canvasser with whom I walked an hour or more one Sunday. "I stopped there and tried to buy butter. 'We haven't an ounce of butter to our names,' said the woman. 'Ah,' said I, just to see if I could not catch her in a lie, 'but I pay as high as twenty marks a pound.' 'In that case,' said the *Unverschämte*, 'I can let you have any amount you want up to thirty pounds.' I could not really pay that price, of course, being a poor man, working hard for nine marks a day. But when I told her I would report her to the police she laughed in my face and slammed the door."

It was easy to understand now why so many of those I had interviewed in my official capacity at Coblenz had expressed the opinion that sooner or later the poor of the cities would descend upon the peasants in bands and rob them of all their hoardings. The countrymen themselves showed that fear of this now and then gnawed at their souls, not so much by their speech as by their circumspect actions. The sight of these swarms of "hamsterers" descended from the north like locusts from the desert gave the prophecy new meaning. It would have been so easy for a few groups of them to join together and wreak the vengeance of their class on the "hard-hearted" peasants. Had they been of a less orderly, lifelong-disciplined race they might have thus run amuck months before. Instead, they plodded on through all the hardships circumstances had woven for them, with that all-suffering, uncomplaining sort of fatalism with which the war seems to have inoculated the German soul.

Thus far the question of lodging had always been simple. I had only to pick out a village ahead on the map and put up at its chief *Gasthaus*. But Saturday night and the "hamsterers" gave the situation a new twist. With a leisurely twenty miles behind me I turned aside to the pleasing little hamlet of Mühlhausen, quite certain I had reached the end of that day's journey. But the *Gastzimmer* of the chief inn presented an astonishing afternoon sight. Its every table was densely surrounded by dust-streaked men, women, and older children, their rucksacks and straw coffers strewn about the floor. Instead of the serene, leisurely-diligent matron whom I expected to greet my entrance with a welcoming "*Scoot*" I found a sharp-tongued, harassed female vainly striving to silence the constant refrain of, "*Hier! Glas Bier, bitte!*" Far from having a mug set before me almost at the instant I took my seat, I was forced to remain standing, and it was several minutes before I could catch her attention long enough to request "*das beste Zimmer*." "Room!" she snapped, in a tone I had never dreamed a Bavarian landlady could muster; "overfilled hours ago!" Incredible! I had scarcely seen a fellow-guest for the night during all my tramp from Munich. Well, I would enjoy one of those good *Gasthaus* suppers and find lodging in another public-house at my leisure. Again I had reckoned without my hostess. When I succeeded in once more catching the attention of the distracted matron, she flung at me over a shoulder: "Not a bite! 'Hamsterers' have eaten every crumb in town."

It was only too true. The other inn of Mühlhausen had been as thoroughly raided. Moreover, its beds also were already "overfilled." The seemingly impossible had come to pass—my chosen village not only would not shelter me for the night; it would not even assuage my gnawing hunger before driving me forth into the wide, inhospitable world beyond. Truly war has its infernal details!

As always happens in such cases, the next town was at least twice as far away as the average distance between its neighbors. Fortunately an isolated little "beer-arbor" a few miles farther on had laid in a Saturday stock. The *Wirt* not only served me bread, but a generous cut of some mysterious species of sausage, without so much as batting an eyelid at my presumptuous request. Weary, dusty "hamsterers" of both sexes and all ages were enjoying his Spartan hospitality also, their scanty fare contrasting suggestively with the great slabs of home-smoked cold ham, the hard-boiled eggs, *Bauernbrod* and butter with which a group of plump, taciturn peasant youths and girls gorged themselves at another mug-decorated table with the surreptitious demeanor of yeggmen enjoying their ill-gotten winnings. The stragglers of the human weasel army punctuated the highway for a few kilometers farther. Some were war victims, stumping past on crippled legs; some were so gaunt-featured and thin that one wondered how they had succeeded in entering the race at all. The last one of the day was a woman past middle age, mountainous of form, her broad expanse of ruddy face streaked with dust and perspiration, who sat weightily on a roadside boulder, munching the remnants of a black-bread-and-smoked-pork lunch and gazing despairingly into the highway vista down which her more nimble-legged competitors had long since vanished.

In the end I was glad Mühlhausen had repulsed me, for I had a most delightful walk from sunset into dusk in forest-flanked solitude along the Ludwig Canal, with a swim in reflected moonshine to top it off. Darkness had completely fallen on the long summer day when I reached Neumarkt with thirty miles behind me. Under ordinary circumstances I should have had a large choice of lodgings; the place was important enough to call itself a city and its broad main street was lined by a continuous procession of peak-gabled *Gasthäuser*. But it, too, was flooded with "hamsterers." They packed every beer-dispensing "guest-room"; they crowded every public lodging, awaiting the dawn of Sunday to charge forth in all directions upon the surrounding country-side. I made the circuit of its cobble-paved center four times, suffering a score of scornful rebuffs before I found a man who admitted vaguely that he might be able to shelter me for the night.

He was another of those curious fairy-tale dwarfs one finds tucked away in the corners of Bavaria, and his eyrie befitted his personal appearance. It was a disjointed little den filled with the medieval paraphernalia—and incidentally with much of the unsavoriness—that had collected there during its several centuries of existence. One stooped to enter the beer-hall, and rubbed one's eyes for the astonishment of being suddenly carried back to the Middle Ages—as well as from the acrid clouds of smoke that suddenly assailed them; one all but crawled on hands and knees to reach the stoop-shouldered, dark cubbyholes miscalled sleeping-chambers above. Indeed, the establishment did not presume to pose as a *Gasthaus*; it contented itself with the more modest title of *Gastwirtschaft*.

But there were more than mere physical difficulties in gaining admittance to the so-called lodgings under the eaves. The dwarfish *Wirt* had first to be satisfied that I was a paying guest. When I asked to be shown at once to my quarters, he gasped, protestingly, *"Aber trinken Sie kein Glas Bier?"* I would indeed, and with it I would eat a substantial supper, if he could furnish one. That he could, and did. How he had gathered so many of the foodstuffs which most Germans strive for in vain, including such delicacies as eggs, veal, and butter, is no business of mine. My chief interest just then was to welcome the heaping plates which his gnomish urchins brought me from the cavernous hole of a kitchen out of which peered now and then the witchlike face of his wife-cook. The same impish little brats pattered about in their bare feet among the guests, serving them beer as often as a mug was emptied and listening with grinning faces to the sometimes obscene anecdotes with which a few of them assailed the rafters. Most of the clients that evening were of the respectable class, being "hamstering" men and wives forced to put up with whatever circumstances required of them, but they were in striking contrast to the disreputable *habitués* of what was evidently Neumarkt's least gentlemanly establishment.

In all the wine-soaked uproar of the evening there was but a single reference to what one fancied would have been any German's chief interest in those particular days. A maudlin braggart made a casual, parenthetical boast of what he "would do to the cursed Allies if he ever caught them again." The habitual guests applauded drunkenly, the transient ones preserved the same enduring silence they had displayed all the evening, the braggart lurched on along some wholly irrelevant theme, and the misshapen host continued serving his beer and pocketing pewter coins and "shin-plasters" with a mumble and a grimace that said as plainly as words, "Vell, vhat do I care vhat happens to the country if I can still do a paying pusiness?" But then, he was of the race that has often been accused of having no patriotism for anything beyond its own purse, whatever country it inhabits.

When we had paid rather reasonable bills for the forbidden fruits that had been set before us, the *Wirt* lighted what seemed to be a straw stuffed with grease and conducted me and three "hamstering" workmen from Nürnberg up a low, twisting passageway to a garret crowded with four nests on legs which he dignified with the name of beds. I will spare the tender-hearted reader any detailed description of our chamber, beyond remarking that we paid eighty pfennigs each for our accommodations, and were vastly overcharged at that. It was the only "hardship" of my German journey. My companions compared notes for a half-hour or more, on the misfortunes and possibilities of their war-time avocation, each taking care not to give the others any inkling of what corner of the landscape he hoped most successfully to "hamster" on the morrow, and by midnight the overpopulated rendezvous of Neumarkt had sunk into its brief "pre-hamstering" slumber.

Being ahead of my schedule, and moreover the day being Sunday, I did not loaf away until nine next morning. The main highway had swung westward toward Nürnberg. The more modest country road I followed due north led over a gently rolling region through many clumps of forest. Scattered groups of peasants returning from church passed me in almost continual procession during the noon hour. The older women stalked uncomfortably along in tight-fitting black gowns that resembled the styles to be seen in paintings of a century ago, holding their outer skirts knee-high and showing curiously decorated petticoats. On their heads they wore closely fitting kerchiefs of silky appearance, jet black in color, though on week-days they were coiffed with white cotton. Some ostentated light-colored aprons and pale-blue embroidered cloths knotted at the back of the neck and held in place by a breastpin in the form of a crucifix or other religious design. In one hand they gripped a prayer-book and in the other an amber or black rosary. The boys and girls, almost without exception, carried their heavy hob-nailed shoes in their hands and slapped along joyfully in their bare feet. In every village was an open-air bowling-alley, sometimes half hidden behind a crude lattice-work and always closely connected with the beer-dispensary, in which the younger men joined in their weekly sport as soon as church was over. Somewhere within sight of them hovered the grown girls, big blond German *Mädchen* with their often pretty faces and their plowman's arms, hands, ankles, and feet, dressed in their gay, light-colored Sunday best.

Huge lilac-bushes in fullest bloom sweetened the constant breeze with their perfume. The glassy surface of the canal still glistened in the near distance to the left; a cool, clear stream meandered in and out along the slight valley to the right. Countrymen trundled past on bicycles that still boasted good rubber tires, in contrast with the jolting substitutes to which most city riders had been reduced. A few of the returning "hamsterers" were similarly mounted, though the majority trudged mournfully on foot, carrying bags and knapsacks half filled with vegetables, chiefly potatoes, with live geese, ducks, or chickens. One youth pedaled past with a lamb gazing out of the rucksack on his back with the wondering eyes of a country boy taking his first journey. When I overtook him on the next long rise the rider displayed his woolly treasure proudly, at the same time complaining that he had been forced to pay "a whole seven marks" for it. As I turned aside for a dip in the inviting stream, the Munich-Berlin airplane express *bourdonned* by overhead, perhaps a thousand meters above, setting a bee-line through the glorious summer sky and contrasting strangely with the medieval life underfoot about me.

At Gnadenberg, beside the artistic ruins of a once famous cloister with a hillside forest vista, an inn supplied me a generous dinner, with luscious young roast pork as the chief ingredient. The traveler in Germany during the armistice was far more impressed by such a repast than by mere ruins of the Middle Ages. The innkeeper and his wife had little in common with their competitors of the region. They were a youthful couple from Hamburg, who had adopted this almost unprecedented means of assuring themselves the livelihood which the war had denied them at home. Amid the distressing Bavarian dialect with which my ears had been assailed since my arrival in Munich their grammatical German speech was like a flash of light in a dark corner.

By four I had already attained the parlor suite of the principal *Gasthaus* of Altdorf, my three huge windows looking out upon the broad main street of a truly picturesque town. Ancient peaked gables cut the horizon with their saw edge on every hand. The entire façade of the aged church that boomed the quarter-hours across the way was shaded by a mighty tree that looked like a giant green haystack. A dozen other clocks, in towers or scattered about the inn, loudly questioned the veracity of the church-bells and of one another at as frequent intervals. Time may be of less importance to the Bavarian than to some less tranquil people, but he believes in marking it thoroughly. His every room boasts a clock or two, his villages resemble a *horlogerie* in the throes of anarchy, with every timepiece loudly expounding its own personal opinion, until the entire twenty-four hours becomes a constant uproar of conflicting theories, like the hubbub of some Bolshevik assembly. Most of them are not contented with single statements, but insist on repeating their quarter-hourly misinformation. The preoccupied guest or the uneasy sleeper refrains with difficulty from shouting at some insistent timepiece or church-bell: "Yes, you said that a moment ago. For Heaven's sake, don't be so redundant!" But his protest would be sure to be drowned out by the clangor of some other clock vociferously correcting the statements of its competitors. It is always a quarter to, or after, something or other according to the clocks of Bavaria. The wise man scorns them all and takes his time from the sun or his appetite.

Over my beer I fell into conversation with an old merchant from Nürnberg and his sister-in-law. The pair were the most nearly resentful toward America of any persons I met in Germany, yet not so much so but that we passed a most agreeable evening together. The man clung doggedly to a theory that seemed to be moribund in Germany that America's only real reason for entering the war was to protect her investments in the Allied cause. The woman had been a hack writer on sundry subjects for a half-century, and a frequent contributor to German-language papers in America. As is frequently the case with her sex, she was far more bitter and decidedly less open-minded toward her country's enemies than the men. Her chief complaint, however, was that America's entrance into the war had cut her off from her most lucrative field, and her principal anxiety the question as to how soon she would again be able to exchange manuscripts for American drafts. She grew almost vociferous in demanding, not of me, but of her companion, why American writers were permitted to roam at large in Germany while the two countries were still at war, particularly why the Allies did not allow the same privileges to German writers. I was as much in the dark on that subject as she. Her companion, however, assured her that it was because Germany had always been more frank and open-minded than her enemies; that the more freedom allowed enemy correspondents the sooner would the world come to realize that Germany's cause had been the more just. She admitted all this, adding that nowhere were justice and enlightenment so fully developed as in her beloved Fatherland, but she rather spoiled the assertion by her constant amazement that I dared go about the country unarmed. In all the torrent of words she poured forth one outburst still stands out in my memory:

"Fortunately," she cried, "Roosevelt is dead. He would have made it even harder for poor Germany than Wilson has. Why should that man have joined our enemies, too, after we had treated him like a king? His daughter accepted a nice wedding-present from our Kaiser, and then he turned against us!"

One sensed the curious working of the typical German mind in that remark. The Kaiser had given a friendly gift, he had received a man with honor, hence anything the Kaiser chose to do thereafter should have met with that man's unqualified approval. It was a most natural conclusion, from the German point of view. Did not the Kaiser and his clan rise to the height from which they fell partly by the judicious distribution of "honors" to those who might otherwise have successfully opposed them, by the lavishing of badges and medals, of honorariums and preferences, of iron crosses and costly baubles?

A young man at an adjacent table took exception to some accusation against America by the cantankerous old merchant, and joined in the conversation. From that moment forth I was not once called upon to defend my country's actions; our new companion did so far more effectively than I could possibly have done. He was professor of philosophy in the ancient University of Altdorf, and his power of viewing a question from both sides, with absolute impartiality, without the faintest glow of personal feeling, attained the realms of the supernatural. During the entire war he had been an officer at the front, having returned to his academic duties within a month after the signing of the armistice. As women are frequently more rabid than men in their hatred of a warring enemy, so are the men who have taken the least active part in the conflict commonly the more furious. One can often recognize almost at a glance the real soldier—not the parader in uniform at the rear, but him who has seen actual warfare; he is wiser and less fanatical, he is more apt to realize that his enemy, too, had something to fight for, that every war in history has had some right on both sides.

When we exchanged names I found that the professor was more familiar than I with a tale I once wrote of a journey around the world, republished in his own tongue. The discovery led us into discussions that lasted late into the evening. In the morning he conducted me through the venerable seat of learning to which he was attached. It had suffered much from the war, not merely financially, but in the loss of fully two-thirds of its faculty and students. Three-fourths of them had returned now, but they had not brought with them the pre-war atmosphere. He detected an impatience with academic pursuits, a superficiality that had never before been known in German universities. Particularly the youths who had served as officers during the war submitted themselves with great difficulty to the discipline of the class-room. The chief "sight" of the institution was an underground cell in which the afterward famous Wallenstein was once confined. In his youth the general attended the university for a year, the last one of the sixteenth century. His studies, however, had been almost entirely confined to the attractions of the *Gasthäuser* and the charms of the fair maidens of the surrounding villages. The attempt one day to enliven academic proceedings with an alcoholic exhilaration, of which he was not even the legal possessor financially, brought him to the sobering depths of the iron-barred cellar and eventually to expulsion. But alas for diligence and sobriety! While the self-denying grinds of his day have sunk centuries deep into oblivion, the name of Wallenstein is emblazoned in letters a meter high across the façade of the steep-gabled dwelling in which he recuperated during the useless daylight hours from his nightly lucubrations.

The professor pointed out to me a byway leading due northward over the green hills. Now it strode joyfully across broad meadows and ripening wheat-fields about which scampered wild rabbits as I advanced; now it climbed deliberately up into the cathedral depths of evergreen forests that stretched away for hours in any direction. Bucolic little hamlets welcomed me as often as thirst suggested the attractiveness of dropping the rucksack from my shoulders to the bench of a refreshing country inn. I had struck a Protestant streak, wedged in between two broad Catholic regions. It may have been but a trick of the imagination, but the local dialect seemed to have grown more German with the change. Certainly the beer was different, pale yellow in contrast with the mahogany brown of the far heavier brew to the south. Whether or not it was due to mere chance or to a difference in taste, the two types of the beverage seemed to go with their respective form of Christianity through all Bavaria. But, alas! none of it was the beer of yesteryear. On the walls of one tiny *Gastzimmer* hung large framed portraits, dauby in composition, of four youthful soldiers. The shuffling old woman who served me caught my questioning glance at the largest of them.

"My youngest," she explained, in her toothless mumble. "He has been missing since October, 1914. Never a word. He, over there, was slaughtered at Verdun. My oldest, he with the cap of an *Unteroffizier*, is a prisoner in France. They will never let him come back, it is said. The other, in the smallest picture, is working in the fields out yonder, but he has a stiff arm and he cannot do much. Pictures cost so now, too; we had to get a smaller one each year. My man was in it also. He still suffers from the malady of the trenches. He spends more than half his days in bed. War is *schrecklich*— frightful," she concluded, but she said it in the dull, dispassionate tone in which she might have deplored the lack of rain or the loss of a part of her herd. Indeed, there seemed to be more feeling in her voice as she added: "And they took all our horses. We have only an ox left now, and the cows."

Descending into a valley beyond, I met a score of school-boys, of about fifteen, each with a knapsack on his back, climbing slowly upward into the forest. They crowded closely around a middle-aged man, similarly burdened, who was talking as he walked and to whom the boys gave such fixed attention that they did not so much as glance at me. His topic, as I caught from the few words I heard, was Roman history, on which he was discoursing as deliberately as if the group had been seated in their stuffy class-room in the village below. Yet it was mid-morning of a Monday. This German custom of excursion-lessons might be adopted to advantage in our own land; were it not that our fondness for co-education would tend to distract scholarly attention.

Toward noon the byways descended from the hills, became a highway, and turned eastward along a broad river valley. Hersbruck, at the turning-point, was surrounded on two sides by railways, with all their attendant grime and clatter, but the town itself was as peak-gabled and cobble-paved, as Middle-

Aged in appearance, as if modern science had never invaded it. The population left over after the all-important brewing and serving of beer had been accomplished seemed to busy itself with supplying the peasants of the neighboring regions. I declined the valley road and climbed again into the hills to the north. Their first flanks, on the edge of the town, were strewn with impressive villas, obviously new and strikingly out of keeping with the modest old town below. They reminded one of the flashy, rouge-lacquered daughters of our simple immigrants. A youth in blouse and field-gray trousers, who was setting me on my way, smiled faintly and quizzically when I called attention to them.

"Rich men?" I queried.

"Yes, indeed," he answered, with something curiously like a growl in his voice.

"What do they do?" I went on, chiefly to make conversation.

"Nothing," he replied, in a tone that suggested the subject was distasteful.

"Then how did they get rich?" I persisted.

"Wise men," he mumbled, with a meaning side glance.

"All built since the war?" I hazarded, after a moment, gazing again along the snowy hillside.

He nodded silently, with something faintly like a wink, at the same time glancing cautiously upward, as if he feared the ostentatious villas would vent their influential wrath upon him for giving their questionable pedigree to a stranger.

Farther on, along a soft-footed country road that undulated over a landscape blooming with fruit-trees and immense lilac-bushes, I came upon a youthful shepherd hobbling after his grazing sheep on a crude wooden leg that seemed to have been fashioned with an ax from the trunk of a sapling. I attempted to rouse him to a recital of his war experiences, but he scowled at my first hint and preserved a moody silence. A much older man, tending his fat cattle a mile beyond, was, on the contrary, eager to "fight the war over again." It suggested to him none of the bitter memories that assailed the one-legged shepherd. He had been too old to serve, and his two sons, cultivating a field across the way, had returned in full health. He expressed a mild thankfulness that it was over, however, because of the restrictions it had imposed upon the peasants. For every cow he possessed he was obliged to deliver two liters of milk a day. An official milk-gatherer from the town passed each morning. Any cow that habitually fell below the standard set must be reported ready for slaughter. Unproductive hens suffered the same fate. He owned ten *Stück* of them, a hundred and fifty in all, with four roosters to keep them company, and was forced to contribute four hundred and fifty eggs a week to the town larder. At good prices? Oh yes, the prices were not bad—three times those of before the war, but by no means what the "hamsterers" would gladly pay. Of course, he smiled contentedly, there were still milk and eggs left over for his own use. The country people did not suffer from hunger. They could not afford to, with their constant hard labor. It was different with the city folks, who put in short hours and sat down much of the time. He had heard that all the war restrictions would be over in August. He certainly hoped so, for life was growing very tiresome with all these regulations.

Every one of his half-hundred cows wore about its neck a broad board, decorated in colors with fantastic figures, from which hung a large bell. Each of the latter was distinct in timbre and all of fine tone. The chimes produced by the grazing herd was a real music that the breeze wafted to my ears until I had passed the crest of the next hillock. How so much metal suitable for cannon-making had escaped the Kaiser's brass-gatherers was a mystery which the extraordinary influence of the peasant class only partly explained.

Beyond the medieval ruin of Hohenstein, which had served me for half the afternoon as a lighthouse does the mariner, the narrow road led gradually downward and brought me once more toward sunset, to the river valley. The railway followed the stream closely, piercing the many towering crags with its tunnels. But the broad highroad wound in great curves that almost doubled the distance, avoiding every slightest ridge, as if the road-builders of centuries ago had been bent on making the journey through this charming region as long as possible.

Velden, claiming the title of "city," was as unprogressive and as nearly unclean as any town I ever saw in Bavaria. A half-dozen inns flashed signs of welcome in the stranger's face, yet declined to furnish the hospitality they seemed to offer. I canvassed them all, only to be as many times turned away by females almost as slatternly in appearance and as resentful of would-be guests as the Indians of the Andes. One might have fancied the hookworm had invaded the town, so un-Bavarian was the ambitionless manner of its inhabitants and the disheveled aspect of its clientless public-houses. Only one of the latter consented even to lodge me, and that with a bad grace that was colder than indifference. None of them would so much as listen when I broached the question of food.

The shopkeepers treated me with equal scorn. One after another they asserted that they had not a scrap of *Lebensmittel* of any species to sell. Three times, however, they directed me to the *Gasthaus* that had been most decided in proclaiming its inability to supply my wants, assuring me that the proprietor was a farmer and stock-breeder who had "more than enough of everything, if the truth were known." But a second visit to the alleged food-hoarder merely aroused the assertion that his fellow-townsmen were prevaricators striving to cover up their own faults by slandering a poor, hard-working neighbor.

Apparently Velden had developed a case of nerves on the food question. This was natural from its size and situation—it was large enough to feel something of the pinch that the blockade had brought to every German city, yet nearly enough peasant-like in character to make hoarding possible. I did not propose, however, to let an excusable selfishness deprive me of my evening meal. When it became certain that voluntary accommodations were not to be had, I took a leaf from my South American note-book and appealed my case to the local authorities.

The Bürgermeister was a miller on the river-bank at the edge of town. He received me as coldly as I had expected, and continued to discuss with an aged assistant the action to be taken on certain documents which my arrival had found them studying. I did not press matters, well knowing that I could gain full attention when I chose and being interested in examining the town headquarters. It was a high, time-smudged room of the old stone mill, with great beams across its ceiling and crude pigeonholes stuffed with musty, age-yellowed official papers along its walls. Now and again a local citizen knocked timidly at the door and entered, hat in hand, to make some request of the town's chief authority, his apologetic air an amusing contrast to the commanding tone with which the Bürgermeister's wife bade him, from the opposite entrance, come to supper.

He was on the point of obeying this summons when I drew forth my impressive papers and stated my case. The mayor and his assistant quickly lost their supercilious attitude. The former even gave my demands precedence over those of his wife. He slapped a hat on his head and, leaving two or three fellow-citizens standing uncovered where the new turn of events had found them, set out with me for the center of town. There he confirmed the assertions of the "prevaricators" by marching unhesitatingly into the same *Gasthaus*, to "The Black Bear" that had twice turned me away. Bidding me take seat at a table, he disappeared into the kitchen. Several moments later he returned, smiling encouragingly, and sat down opposite me with the information that "everything had been arranged." Behind him came the landlady who had so forcibly denied the existence of food on her premises a half-hour before, smirking hospitality now and bearing in either hand a mug of beer. Before we had emptied these she set before me a heaping plateful of steaming potatoes, boiled in their jackets, enough cold ham to have satisfied even a tramp's appetite several times over, and a loaf of good peasant's bread of the size and shape of a grindstone.

The Bürgermeister remained with me to the end of his second mug of beer, declining to eat for reason of the supper that was awaiting him at home, but answering my questions with the over-courteous deliberation that befitted the official part I was playing. When he left, the *Wirt* seemed to feel it his duty to give as constant attention as possible to so important a guest. He sat down in the vacated chair opposite and, except when his beer-serving duties required him to absent himself momentarily, remained there all the evening. He was of the heavy, stolid type of most of his class, a peasant by day and the chief assistant of his inn-keeping spouse during the evening. For fully a half-hour he stared at me unbrokenly, watching my every slightest movement as an inventor might the actions of his latest contraption. A group of his fellow-townsmen, sipping their beer at another table, kept similar vigil, never once taking their eyes off me, uttering not a sound, sitting as motionless as the old stone statues they somehow resembled, except now and then to raise their mugs to their lips and set them noiselessly down again. The rather slatternly spouse and her brood of unkempt urchins surrounded still another table, eying me as fixedly as the rest. I attempted several times to break the ice, with no other success than to evoke a guttural monosyllable from the staring landlord. The entire assembly seemed to be *dumm* beyond recovery, to be stupidity personified. Unable to force oneself upon them, one could only sit and wonder what was taking place inside their thick skulls. Their vacant faces gave not an inkling of thought. Whenever I exploded a question in the oppressive silence the *Wirt* answered it like a school-boy reciting some reply learned by heart from his books. The stone-headed group listened motionless until long after his voice had died away, and drifted back into their silent, automatic beer-drinking.

It was, of course, as much bashfulness as stupidity that held them dumb. Peasants the world over are more or less chary of expressing themselves before strangers, before "city people," particularly when their dialect differs considerably from the cultured form of their language. But what seemed queerest in such groups as these was their utter lack of curiosity, their apparently complete want of interest in anything beyond their own narrow sphere. They knew I was an American, they knew I had seen much of the other side of the struggle that had oppressed them for nearly five years and brought their once powerful Fatherland close to annihilation. Yet they had not a question to ask. It was as if they had grown accustomed through generations of training to having their information delivered to them in packages bearing the seal of their overlords, and considered it neither advantageous nor seemly to tap any other sources they came upon in their life's journey.

Very gradually, as the evening wore on, the landlord's replies to my queries reached the length of being informative. Velden, he asserted, was a Protestant community; there was not a Catholic in town, nor a Jew. On the other hand, Neuhaus, a few miles beyond, paid universal homage to Rome. With a population of one hundred and seventy families, averaging four to five each now, or a total of eight hundred, Velden had lost thirty-seven men in the war, besides three times that many being seriously wounded, nearly half of them more or less crippled for life. Then there were some fifty prisoners in France, whom they never expected to return. The Allies would keep them to rebuild the cities the Germans had destroyed—and those the Allied artillery had ruined, too; that was the especially unfair side of it. No, he had not been a soldier himself—he was barely forty and to all appearances as powerful as an ox—because he had been more useful at home. His family had not exactly suffered, though the schools had become almost a farce, with all the teachers at war. Women? Faugh! How can women teach boys? They grow up altogether too soft even under the *strengest* of masters. As to food; well, being mostly peasants, they probably had about a hundred pounds of fat or meat where two hundred or so were needed. But it was a constant struggle to keep the "hamsterers" from carrying off what the town required for its own use.

That the struggle had been won was evident from the quantities of ham, beef, potatoes, and bread which his wife served her habitual clients in the course of the evening. She seemed to have food hidden away in every nook and cranny of the house, like a miser his gold, and acknowledged its existence with the canniness of the South American Indian. As she lighted me to a comfortable bedchamber above, as clean as the lower story was disorderly, she remarked, apologetically:

"If I had known in what purpose you were here I would not have sent you away when you first came. But another American food commissioner was in Velden just two days ago, a major who has his headquarters in Nürnberg. He came with a German captain, and they went fishing on the river."

In the morning she served me real coffee, with milk and white loaf sugar, two eggs, appealingly fresh, bread and butter, and an excellent cake—and her bill for everything, including the lodging, was six marks. In Berlin or Munich the food alone, had it been attainable, would have cost thirty to forty marks. Plainly it was advantageous to Velden to pose as suffering from food scarcity.

The same species of selfishness was in evidence in the region round about. Not one of the several villages tucked away in the great evergreen forests of the "Fränkische Schweitz" through which my route wound that day would exchange foodstuffs of any species for mere money. When noon lay so far behind me that I was tempted to use physical force to satisfy my appetite, I entered the crude *Gasthaus* of a little woodcutters' hamlet. A family of nearly a dozen sat at a table occupying half the room, wolfing a dinner that gave little evidence of war-time scarcity. Here, too, there was an abundance of meat, potatoes, bread, and several other appetizing things. But strangers were welcome only to beer. Could one live on that, there would never be any excuse for going hungry in Bavaria. When I asked for food also the coarse-featured, bedraggled female who had filled my mug snarled like a dog over a bone and sat down with her family again, heaping her plate high with a steaming stew. I persisted, and she rose at last with a growl and served me a bowl of some kind of oatmeal gruel, liquid with milk. For this she demanded ten pfennigs, or nearly three-fourths of a cent. But if it was cheap, nothing could induce her to sell more of it. My loudest appeals for a second helping, for anything else, even for a slice of the immense loaf of bread from which each member of the gorging family slashed himself a generous portion at frequent intervals, were treated with the scornful silence with which the police sergeant might ignore the shouts of a drunken prisoner.

Birds sang a bit dolefully in the immense forest that stretched for miles beyond. Peasants were scraping up the mosslike growth that covered the ground and piling it in heaps near the road, whence it was hauled away in wagons so low on their wheels that they suggested dachshunds. The stuff served as bedding for cattle, sometimes for fertilizer, and now and then, during the past year or two, as fodder. The tops of all trees felled were carried away and made use of in the same manner. A dozen times a day, through all this region of Bavaria, I passed women, singly or in groups, in the villages, laboriously chopping up the tops and branches of evergreens on broad wooden blocks, with a tool resembling a heavy meat-cleaver. Hundreds of the larger trees had been tapped for their pitch, used in the making of turpentine, the trunks being scarred with a dozen large V-shaped gashes joined together by a single line ending at a receptacle of the form of a sea-shell. Horses were almost never seen along the roads, and seldom in the fields. The draught animals were oxen, or, still more often, cows, gaunt and languid from their double contribution to man's requirements. At the rare blacksmith shops the combined force of two or three workmen was more likely to be found shoeing a cow than anything else. Of all the signs of the paternal care the Kaiser's government took of its people, none, perhaps, was more amusing than the *Hemmstelle* along the way. At the top of every grade stood a post with a cast-iron rectangle bearing that word—German for "braking-place"—and, for the benefit of the illiterate, an image of the old-fashioned wagon-brake—a species of iron shoe to be placed under the hind wheel—that is still widely used in the region. Evidently the fatherly government could not even trust its simple subjects to recognize a hill when they saw one.

Pegnitz, though not much larger, was a much more progressive town than Velden. Its principal *Gasthaus* was just enough unlike a city hotel to retain all the charm of a country inn, while boasting such improvements as tablecloths and electric buttons that actually brought a servant to the same room as that occupied by the guest who pressed them. Yet it retained an innlike modesty of price. My full day's accommodation there cost no more than had my night in Velden—or would not have had I had the courage to refuse the mugs of beer that were instantly forthcoming as often as I sat down at the guest-room table. To be sure, no meat was served, being replaced by fish. The day was Tuesday and for some reason Pegnitz obeyed the law commanding all Germany to go meatless twice a week. Apparently it was alone among the Bavarian towns in observing this regulation. I remember no other day without meat in all my tramp northward from Munich, even though Friday always caught me in a Catholic section. Usually I had meat twice a day, often three times, and, on one glorious occasion, four.

An afternoon downpour held me for a day in Pegnitz. I improved the time by visiting most of the merchants in town, in my pseudo-official capacity. Of the three grocers, two were completely out of foodstuffs, the other fairly well supplied. They took turns in stocking up with everything available, so that each became the town grocer every third month and contented himself with dispensing a few non-edible articles during the intervening sixty days. The baker, who looked so much like a heavy-weight pugilist that even the huge grindstone loaves seemed delicate in his massive hands, was stoking his oven with rubbish from the surrounding forest, mixed with charcoal, when I found him. Fuel, he complained, had become such a problem that it would have kept him awake nights, if a baker ever had any time to sleep. Before the war the rest of the town burned coal; now he had to compete with every one for his wood and charcoal. His oven was an immense affair of stone and brick, quite like the outdoor bake-huts one finds through all Bavaria, but set down into the cellar at the back of his shop and reaching to the roof. He opened a sack of flour and spread some of it out before me. It looked like a very coarse bran. Yet it was twice as expensive as the fine white flour of pre-war days, he growled. Bread prices in Pegnitz had a bit more than doubled. He had no more say in setting the price than any other citizen; the Municipal Council had assumed that responsibility. Women, children, and men in poor health suffered from the stuff. Some had ruined their stomachs entirely with it. Yet Pegnitz bread had never been made of anything but wheat. In Munich the bakers used potato flour and worse; he had seen some of the rascals put in sawdust. He had heard that America was sending white flour to Germany, but certainly none of it had ever reached Pegnitz.

The village milk-dealer was more incensed on this subject of bread than on the scarcity of his own stock. Or perhaps a milder verb would more exactly picture his attitude; he was too anemic and lifeless to be incensed at anything. His cadaverous form gave him the appearance of an undernourished child, compared to the brawny baker, and anger was too strong an emotion for his weakened state. Misfortune merely left him sad and increased the hopeless look in his watery eyes, deep sunken in their wide frame of blue flesh-rings. He had spent two years in the trenches and returned home so far gone in health that he could not even endure the war-bread his wife and five small children had grown so thin on during his absence. Before the war he could carry a canful of milk the entire length of the shop without the least difficulty. Now if he merely attempted to lift one his head swam for an hour afterward. People were not exactly starved to death, he said, but they were so run down that if they caught anything, even the minor ills no one had paid any attention to before the war, they were more apt to die than to get well. Pegnitz had lost more of its inhabitants at home in that way than had been killed in the war.

One hundred and forty liters of milk was the daily supply for a population of three thousand now. The town had consumed about five hundred before the war. Children under two were entitled to a liter a day, but only those whose parents were first to arrive when the daily supply came in got that amount. My visit was well timed, for customers were already forming a line at the door, each carrying a small pail or pitcher and clutching in one hand his precious yellow milk-sheet. It was five in the afternoon. The town milk-gatherer drew up before the door in an ancient "Dachshund" wagon drawn by two emaciated horses, and carried his four cans inside. The dispenser introduced me to him and turned to help his wife dole out the precious liquid. They knew, of course, the family conditions of every customer and, in consequence, the amount to which each was entitled, and clipped the corresponding coupons from the yellow sheets without so much as glancing at them. Some received as little as a small cupful; the majority took a half-liter. In ten minutes the four cans stood empty and the shopkeeper slouched out to join us again.

"You see that woman?" he asked, pointing after the retreating figure of his last customer. "She looks about sixty, *nicht wahr?* She is really thirty-six. Her husband was killed at Verdun. She has four small children and is entitled to two full liters. But she can only afford to buy a half-liter a day—milk has doubled in price in the past four years; thirty-two pfennigs a liter now—so she always comes near the end when there is not two liters left, because she is ashamed to say she cannot buy her full allowance. We always save a half-liter for her, and if some one else comes first we tell them the cans are *ausgepumpt*. There are many like her in Pegnitz—unable to pay for as much as their tickets allow them. That is lucky, too, for there would not be half enough to go round. If I were not in the milk business myself I don't know what *I* should do, either, with our five children. About all the profit we get out of the business now is our own three liters."

The milk-gatherer was of a jolly temperament. His smile disclosed every few seconds the two lonely yellow fangs that decorated his upper jaw. Perhaps no other one thing so strikingly illustrates the deterioration which the war has brought the German physique as the condition of the teeth. In my former visits to the Empire I had constantly admired the splendid, strong white teeth of all classes. To-day it is almost rare to find an adult with a full set. The majority are as unsightly in this respect as the lower classes of England. When the prisoners who poured in upon us during the last drives of the war first called attention to this change for the worse, I set it down as the result of life in the trenches. Back of the lines, however, *Ersatz* food and under-nourishment seem to have had as deleterious an effect.

Milk, said the man who had brought Pegnitz its supply for years, was by no means as rich as it used to be. Fodder was scarce, and every one used his milch cow as oxen now, far more than formerly. He set out at four every morning of his life, covered twenty miles, or more than twice what he had before the war, and sometimes could not fill his four cans at that. Up to a few months before he had had an assistant—an English prisoner. He never tired of singing the praises of "my Englishman," as he called him. He worked some reference to him into every sentence, each time displaying his fangs in his pleasure at the recollection. "My Englishman" had come to him in 1915. He was a bank clerk at home and knew no more of farming than a child. But he had learned quickly, and to speak German as well—a sad German it must have been indeed if he had copied from the dialect of the region. For months at a time "my Englishman" had driven the milk route alone, while *he* remained at home to work in the fields. Run away! Nonsense! He had told people he had never enjoyed himself half so much in London. He had promised to come back after peace. He stayed until two months after the armistice. His last words were that he knew he could never endure it to sit all day on a stool, in a stuffy office, after roaming the hills of Bavaria nearly four years. On Sundays he went miles away to visit other Englishmen. French prisoners went where they liked, too; no one ever bothered them. They had all left in January, in a special train. Yes, most of them had been good workmen, "my Englishman" especially. They had labored with the women in the fields when the men were away, and helped them about the house. They had always been friendly, sometimes *too* friendly. Did I see that little boy across the street, there in front of the widow's cloth-shop? Every one knew he was English. But what could you expect, with husbands away sometimes for years at a time?

WOMEN AND OXEN—OR COWS—WERE MORE NUMEROUS THAN MEN AND HORSES IN THE FIELDS

THE BAVARIAN PEASANT DOES HIS BAKING IN AN OUTDOOR OVEN

WOMEN CHOPPING UP THE TOPS OF EVERGREEN TREES FOR
FUEL AND FODDER

THE GREAT BREWERIES OF KULMBACH NEARLY ALL STOOD
IDLE

Pegnitz boasted a large iron-foundry and a considerable population of factory hands. Rumor had it that this class held more enmity toward citizens of the Allied powers than the rural population, that it would even be dangerous for me to mix with them. I took pains, therefore, to stroll toward the foundry gate as the workmen were leaving, at six. They toiled eight hours a day, like all their class throughout Germany now, but took advantage of the change to sleep late, "like the capitalists," beginning their labors at eight and taking two hours off at noon. I picked out an intelligent-looking workman and fell into conversation with him, deliberately emphasizing the fact that I was an American. A considerable group of his fellows crowded around us, and several joined in the conversation. But though two or three scowled a bit when my nationality was whispered through the gathering, it was evidently merely a sign that they were puzzling to know how I had come so far afield so soon after the signing of the armistice. Far from showing any enmity, they evinced a most friendly curiosity, tinged only once or twice with a mild and crude attempt at sarcasm which the others at once scowled down. Several wished to know how wages were in their line in America, particularly whether our workmen had forced "the capitalists" to grant the eight-hour day, and several inquired how soon I thought it would be possible to emigrate—how soon, that is, that enough ships would be released from military service to bring fares down within reach of a working-man's purse. Not one of them seemed to suspect that there might be other difficulties than financial ones. Then, of course, the majority deluged me with questions as to when America would actually begin to send fats and foodstuffs and raw materials for their factories and—and tobacco. There was little suggestion of under-nourishment in this gathering, though, to be sure, none of them seemed overfed. They looked hardy and fit; the faces under the red-banded, visorless caps that covered a majority of the heads showed few signs of ill health. It is not so much the factory hands themselves, with their out-of-work pensions even when labor is lacking, who suffer from the stagnation of Germany's industries, as the hangers-on of the factory class—the busy-time helpers, the unprovided women and children, the small shopkeepers who depend on this class for their clientèle.

XV
MUSIC STILL HAS CHARMS

A broad highway offering several fine vistas brought me at noon to Bayreuth. The street that led me to the central square was called Wagnerstrasse and passed directly by the last home of the famous composer. As soon as a frock-tailed hotel force had ministered to my immediate necessities I strolled back to visit the place. Somewhere I had picked up the impression that it had been turned into a museum, like the former residences of Goethe and Schiller. Nearly a year before, I recalled the Paris papers had announced the death of Frau Wagner, and certainly the Germans would not allow the home of their great musician to fall into other hands. I turned in at the tall grilled gate, fastened only with a latch, and sauntered along the broad driveway, shaded by magnificent trees that half hid the wide house at the end of it. This was a two-story building in reddish-yellow brick, rectangular of façade under its almost flat roof, the door gained by a balustraded stone veranda without covering and with steps at either end. A large bust, not of the composer, as I had fancied at a distance, but of his royal companion, Ludwig, stared down the driveway at my approach. As I paused to look at this the only person in sight glanced up at me with what seemed an air between anger and surprise. He was an aged gardener, shriveled in form and face, who was engaged in watering the masses of flowers of many species that surrounded the house on every side. Something in his manner, as he set down his watering-pot and shuffled toward me, plus the absence of any of the outward signs of a public place of pilgrimage, suggested that I was in the wrong pew.

"Does some one *live* here?" I hazarded, lamely.

"Certainly, the Wagner family," he replied, sharply, glaring at me under bushy eyebrows.

"But—er—Frau Wagner being dead, I thought...."

"Frau Wagner is as alive as you or I," he retorted, staring as if he suspected me of being some harmless species of maniac.

"Frau Cosima Wagner, wife of the composer?" I persisted, smiling at what seemed to be the forgetfulness of an old man; "why, my dear fellow, her death was in the papers a year ago...."

"*Frau Cosima Wagner, jawohl, mein Herr,*" he retorted. "As I cut flowers for her room every morning and see her every afternoon, I suppose I know as much about it as the papers. It was quite another Frau Wagner who died last year; and the fool newspapers seldom know what they are talking about, anyway. Then there is...."

His voice had dropped to a whisper and I followed the gaze he had turned into the house. Over the veranda balustrade a bareheaded man stared down at us like one who had been disturbed from mental labors, or an afternoon nap, by our chatter. He was short and slight, yet rather strongly built, too, with iron-gray hair and a smooth-shaven face. A photograph I had seen somewhere suddenly rose to the surface of my memory and I recognized Siegfried Wagner, son of the musician, whose existence I had for the moment forgotten. Having glared us into silence, he turned abruptly and re-entered the house.

"Herr Siegfried and his wife and his two children live here also," went on the gardener, in a whisper that was still harsh and uninviting, "and...."

But I was already beating a discreet retreat, resolved to make sure of my ground before I marched in upon another "museum."

I turned down the next side-street, passing on the corner the house of Herr Chamberlain, the Englishman who married Frau Wagner's daughter, and, farther on, the former home of Liszt, not the least of the old lady's acquaintances, then unexpectedly found myself again looking in upon the Wagner residence. The high brick wall had suddenly ended and the iron-grilled fence that followed it disclosed flower-gardens and house in their entirety. It was an agreeable dwelling-place, certainly, flanked front and rear with forest-like parks in which birds sang constantly, and set far enough back from the main street so that its noises blended together into what, no doubt, the composer would have recognized as music.

But I had no intention of spying upon a private residence. I turned my face sternly to the front and hurried on—until a sound between a cough and a hiss, twice repeated, called my attention once more to the flower-plots behind the grill. The aged gardener was worming his way hurriedly toward me and beckoning me to wait. When only an upright iron bar separated us he whispered hoarsely, still in his curiously unwelcoming tone:

"If you wish to see the Wagner grave, turn down that next opening into the park and come back this way through it. I will be at the gate to let you in."

He had the back entrance to the Wagner estate unlocked when I reached it and led the way around a mass of flowering bushes to the plain flat slab of marble without inscription under which the composer lies buried in his own back yard. But for the house fifty yards away it would have been easy to imagine oneself in the depth of a forest. The old gardener considered his fee earned when he had showed me the grave, and he answered my questions with cold brevity. He had held his present position for thirty-eight years. Of course he had known Herr Richard. Hadn't he seen and talked with him every day for many years? No, there was nothing unusual about him. He was like any other rich man, except that he was always making music. It was plain that the gardener thought this a rather foolish hobby. He spoke of his former master with that slight tinge of scorn, mingled with considerable pride at the importance of his own position, which servants so often show in discussing employers whom the world considers famous, and changed the subject as soon as possible to the all-engrossing scarcity of food. Even Herr Siegfried and his family suffered from that, he asserted. He was still grumbling hungrily when he pocketed what pewter coins I had left and, locking the gate, shuffled back to his watering-pots.

The outwardly ugly Wagner opera-house on a hillock at the farther end of town was as dismal in its abandonment as most cheap structures become that have stood five years unoccupied and unrepaired. There was nothing to recall the famous singers and the international throngs from kings to scrimping schoolma'ams from overseas, who had so often gathered here for the annual Wagner festival. A few convalescing soldiers lounged under the surrounding trees; from the graveled terrace one had an all-embracing view of Bayreuth and the rolling hills about it. But only a few twittering birds broke the silence of a spot that had so often echoed with the strident strains of all the musical instruments known to mankind.

The change from a country town of three thousand to a city of thirty thousand emphasized once more the disadvantage, in the matter of food, of the urban dweller. The hotel that housed me in Bayreuth swarmed with waiters in evening dress and with a host of useless flunkies, but its dining-room was no place for a tramp's appetite. The scarcity was made all the more oppressive by the counting of crumbs and laboriously entering them in a ledger, which occupied an imposing personage at the door, after the fashion of Europe's more expensive establishments. In a Bavarian *Gasthaus* a dinner of meat, potatoes, bread, and perhaps a soup left the most robust guest at peace with the world for hours afterward. I ordered the same here, but when I had seen the "meat" I quickly concluded not to skip the fish course, and the sight of that turned my attention once more to the menu-card. When I had made way with all it had to offer, from top to bottom, I rose with a strong desire to go somewhere and get something to eat. It would probably have been a vain quest, in Bayreuth. Yet my bill was more than one-fourth as much as the one hundred and twenty-four marks I had squandered during my first week on the road in Bavaria.

The hotel personnel was vastly excited at the announcement of my nationality. To them it seemed to augur the arrival of more of my fellow-countrymen, with their well-filled purses, to be the rebeginning of the good old days when tips showered upon them. Moreover, it gave them an opportunity to air their opinions on the "peace of violence" and the Allied world in general. They were typically German opinions, all carefully tabulated under the customary headings. The very errand-boys bubbled over with impressions on those unescapable Fourteen Points; they knew by heart the reasons why the proposed treaty was "inacceptable" and "unfulfillable." But the final attitude of all was, "Let's stop this foolish fighting and get back to the times of the annual festival and its flocks of tourists."

The Royal Opera House next door announced a gala performance that evening. I got my ticket early, fearful of being crowded away from what promised to be my first artistic treat in a fortnight. I took pains to choose a seat near enough the front to catch each detail, yet far enough away from the orchestra not to be deafened by its Wagnerian roar—and when I arrived the orchestra seemed to have been dead for years! The place it should have occupied was filled with broken chairs and music-racks black with age, and resembled nothing so much as grandfather's garret. A single light, somewhat more powerful than a candle, burned high up under the dome of the house and cast faint, weird flickers over its dusty regal splendor. For some reason the place was cold as an ice-house, though the weather outside was comfortable, and the scattered audience shivered audibly in its scanty *Ersatz* garments. It was without doubt the most poorly dressed, unprepossessing little collection of hearers that I had ever seen gathered together in such an edifice. One was reminded not merely that the textile-mills of Bayreuth had only paper to work with now, but that soap had become an unattainable luxury in Germany. Plainly *das Volk* had taken over the exiled king's playhouse for itself. Even the ornate old royal loge was occupied by a few patched soldiers and giggling girls of the appearance of waitresses. But to what purpose? Surely such an audience as this could not find entertainment in one of Germany's classics! Alas! it was I who had been led astray! The promising title of the play announced was mere camouflage. Who perpetrated the incomprehensible, inane rubbish on which the curtain finally rose, and why, are questions I willingly left to the howling audience, which dodged back and forth, utterly oblivious of the fact that the Royal Opera House had been erected before theater-builders discovered that it was easier to see between two heads than through one. Surely German *Kultur*, theatrically at least, was on the down-grade in Bayreuth.

A few miles out along a highway framed in apple blossoms next morning I overtook a group of some twenty persons. The knapsacks on their backs suggested a party of "hamsterers," but as I drew nearer I noted that each carried some species of musical instrument. Now and again the whole group fell to singing and playing as they marched, oblivious to the stares of the peasants along the way. I concluded that it was my duty to satisfy my curiosity by joining them, and did so by a simple little ruse, plus the assistance of my kodak. They were a *Sängerverein* from Bayreuth. Each holiday they celebrated by an excursion to some neighboring town, and this was *Himmelsfahrt*, or

Assumption Day. The members ranged from shy little girls of twelve to stodgy men and women of fifty. The leader was a blind man, a veteran of the trenches, who not only directed the playing and singing, with his cane as a baton, but marched briskly along the snaky highway without a hint of assistance.

There were a half-dozen discharged soldiers in the glee club, but if anything this increased the eagerness with which I was welcomed. Their attitude was almost exactly what would be that of a football team which chanced to meet a rival player a year or so after disbanding—they were glad to compare notes and to amuse themselves by living over old times again. For a while I deliberately tried to stir up some sign of anger or resentment among them; if they had any personal feelings during the contest they had now completely faded out of existence. One dwarfish, insignificant, whole-hearted little fellow, a mill-hand on week-days, had been in the same sector as I during the reduction of the St.-Mihiel salient. Unless we misunderstood each other's description of it, I had entered the dugout he had lived in for months a few hours after he so hastily abandoned it. He laughed heartily at my description of the food we had found still on the stove; he had been cook himself that morning. Every one knew, he asserted, that the St.-Mihiel attack was coming, two weeks before it started, but no one had expected it that cold, rainy morning. On the strength of the coincidence we had discovered, he proposed me as an honorary member of the *Verein* for the day, and the nomination was quickly and unanimously accepted.

We loafed on through the perfect early-summer morning, a soloist striking up on voice and instrument now and then, the whole club joining frequently in some old German song proposed by the blind leader, halting here and there to sit in the shade of a grassy slope, pouring pellmell every mile or two into a *Gasthaus*, where even the shy little girls emptied their half-liter mugs of beer without an effort. One of the ex-soldiers enlivened the stroll by giving me his unexpurgated opinion of the Prussians. They "hogged" everything they could lay their hands on, he grumbled. Prussian wounded sent to Bavaria had been fed like princes; Bavarians who were so unfortunate as to be assigned to hospitals in Prussia—he had suffered that misfortune himself—had been treated like cattle and robbed even of the food sent them from home. He "had no use for" *die verdammten Preussen*, from any viewpoint; it was their "big men" who had started the war in the first place, but.... No, indeed, Bavaria could not afford to separate from Prussia. She had no coal of her own and she had no seaport. Business interests were too closely linked together through all the Empire to make separation possible. It would be cutting their own throats.

Toward noon we reached the village of Neudrossenfeld, where the *Verein* had engaged for the day a rambling old country inn, with a spacious dance-hall above an outdoor *Kegelbahn* for those who bowled, and a shady arbor overlooking a vast stretch of rolling summer landscape for those who did not, in the garden at the rear. Other glee clubs, from Kulmbach and another neighboring city, had occupied the other two *Gasthäuser* and every even semi-public establishment. The town resounded from one end to the other with singing and playing, with laughter and dancing, with the clatter of ninepins and the rattle of table utensils. A lone stranger without glee-club standing would have been forced to plod on, hungry and thirsty. I spent half the afternoon in the shady arbor. Several of the girls were well worth looking at; the music, not being over-ambitious, added just the needed touch to the languid, sun-flooded day. One could not but be struck by the innocence of these typically Bavarian pleasures. Not a suggestion of rowdyism, none of the questionable antics of similar gatherings in some other lands, marred the amusements of these childlike holiday-makers. They were as gentle-mannered as the tones of the guitars, zithers, and mandolins they thrummed so diligently, with never a rude word or act even toward hangers-on like myself. Yet there was a bit less gaiety than one would have expected. Even the youthful drifted now and then into moods of sadness—or was it mere apathy due to their long lack of abundant wholesome food?

The philosophical old landlord brought us a word of wisdom with each double-handful of overflowing beer-mugs. "If ever the world gets reasonable again," he mused, "the good old times will come back—and we shall be able to serve real beer at the proper price. But what ideas people get into their *Schädels* nowadays! They can never let well enough alone. The moment man gets contented, the moment he has everything as it should be, he must go and start something and tumble it all into a heap again."

A rumor broke out that cookies were being sold across the street. I joined the foraging-party that quickly fled from the arbor. When we reached the house of the enterprising old lady who had mothered this brilliant idea it was packed with clamoring humanity like the scene of the latest crime of violence. At intervals a glee-clubber catapulted out of the mob, grinning gleefully and tenaciously clutching in one hand a paper sack containing three of the precious *Kuchen*, but even with so low a ration the producer could not begin to make headway against the feverish demands. I decided that I could not justly add my extraneous competition in a contest that meant so much more to others and, taking my leave of the *Sängerverein*, struck off again to the north.

A middle-aged baker from Kulmbach, who had been "hamstering" all day, with slight success, fell in with me. He had that pathetic, uncomplaining manner of so many of his class, seeming to lay his misfortunes at the door of some power too high to be reached by mere human protest. The war had left him one eye and a weakened physique. Two *Ersatz* teeth gleamed at me dully whenever his wan smile disclosed them. He worked nights, and earned forty-eight marks a week. That was eighteen more than he had been paid before the war, to be sure, and the hours were a bit shorter. But how was a man to feed a wife and three children on forty-eight marks, with present prices; would I tell him that? He walked his legs off during the hours he wished to be sleeping, and often came home without so much as a potato. There were a dozen or so in his rucksack now, and he had tramped more than thirty kilometers. I suggested that the apples would be large enough on the trees that bordered our route to be worth picking in a couple of months. He gave me a startled glance, as if I had proposed that we rob a bank together. The apples along public highways, he explained patiently, were property of the state. No one but those the government sent to pick them could touch them. True, hunger was driving people to strange doings these days. Guards patrolled the roads now when the apples began to get ripe. Peasants had to protect their potato-fields in the same manner. He, however, would remain an honest man, no matter what happened to him or to his wife and his three children. The apparently complete absence of country police was one of the things I had often wondered at during my tramp. The baker assured me that none were needed, except in harvest time. He had never seen a kodak in action. He would not at first believe that it could catch a picture in an instant. Surely it would need a half-hour or so to get down all the details! Queer people Americans must be, to send men out through the world just to get pictures of simple country people. Still he wouldn't mind having a trade like that himself—if it were not for his wife and his three children.

Kulmbach, noted the world over for its beer, is surrounded with immense breweries as with a medieval city wall. But the majority of them stood idle. The beverages to be had in its *Gasthäuser*, too, bore little resemblance to the rich Kulmbacher of pre-war days. Thanks perhaps to its industrial character, the city of breweries seemed to be even shorter of food than Bayreuth; or it may be that its customary supply had disappeared during the celebration of Assumption Day. The meat-tickets I had carried all the way from Munich were required here for the first time. Some very appetizing little rolls were displayed in several shop-windows, but when I attempted to stock up on them I found they were to be had in exchange for special *Marken*, issued to Kulmbachers only. There was a more sinister, a more surly air about Kulmbach, with its garrison of Prussian-mannered soldiers housed in a great fortress on a hill towering high above the town, than I had thus far found in Bavaria.

As I sat down to an alleged dinner in a self-styled hotel, my attention was drawn to a noisy group at a neighboring table. I stared in amazement, not so much because the five men opposite were Italian soldiers in the uniform with which I had grown so familiar during my service on the Padovan plains the summer before, but because of the astonishing contrast between them and the pale, thin Germans about me. The traveler grows quickly accustomed to any abnormality of type of the people among whom he is living. He soon forgets that they look different from other people—until suddenly the appearance of some really normal being in their midst brings his judgment back with a jerk to his customary standards. I had grown to think of the Germans, particularly the Bavarians, as looking quite fit, a trifle under weight perhaps, but healthy and strong. Now all at once, in comparison with these ruddy, plump, animated Italians, they seemed a nation of invalids. The energetic chatter of the visitors brought out in striking relief the listless taciturnity of the natives; they talked more in an hour than I had ever heard all Germany do in a day. Meanwhile they made way with an immense bowlful of—well, what would you expect Italians to be eating? Macaroni, of course, and with it heaping plates of meat, vegetables, and white hard-bread that made the scant fare before me look like a phantom meal. I called the landlady aside and asked if I might not be served macaroni also. She gave me a disgusted look and informed me that she would be glad to do so—if I would bring it with me, as the Italians had. When I had paid my absurd bill I broke in upon the garrulous southerners. They greeted my use of their tongue with a lingual uproar, particularly after I had mentioned my nationality, but quickly cooled again with a reference to Fiume, and satisfied my curiosity only to the extent of stating that they were billeted in Kulmbach "on official business."

I sought to replenish my food-tickets before setting out again next morning, but found the municipal *Lebensmittelversorgung* packed ten rows deep with disheveled housewives. Scientists have figured it out that the human body loses twice as much fat standing in line the four or five hours necessary to obtain the few ounces of grease-products issued weekly on the German food ration as the applicant receives for his trouble. The housewife, they assert, who remains in bed instead of entering the contest gains materially by her conservation of energy. In other words, apparently, it would have been better for the Fatherland—to say nothing of the rest of the world—had the entire nation insisted on sleeping during the five years that turned humanity topsy-turvy. Millions agree with them. But for once the German populace declines to accept the assertions of higher authorities and persists in wearing itself out by its struggles to obtain food. However short-sighted this policy may be on the part of the natives, it is certain that the tail-end of a multitude besieging a food-ticket dispensary is no place for a traveler gifted with scant patience and a tendency to profanity, and I left Kulmbach behind hours before I could have hoped to reach the laborious officials who dealt out legal permission to eat.

A General Staff map in several sheets, openly sold in the shops and giving every cowpath of the region, made it possible for me to set a course due north by compass over the almost mountainous region beyond. "Roads" little more deserving the name than those of the Andes led me up and down across fertile fields, through deep-wooded valleys, and into cozy little country villages tucked away in delightful corners of the landscape. Even in these the peasant inhabitants complained of the scarcity of food, and for the most part declined to sell anything. They recalled the South American Indian again in their transparent ruses to explain the visible presence of foodstuffs. Ducks, geese, and chickens, here and there guinea-fowls, peacocks, rabbits, not to mention pigs, sheep, and cattle, enlivened the village lanes and the surrounding meadows, but every suggestion of meat brought from innkeepers and shopkeepers clumsy, non-committal replies. At one *Gasthaus* where I had been refused anything but beer I opened by design the wrong door at my exit, and stared with amazement at four heaping bushel baskets of eggs, a score of grindstone-shaped cheeses, and an abundant supply of other local products that all but completely filled what I had correctly surmised was the family storeroom. "They are not ours," exclaimed the landlady, hastily; "they belong to others, who will not permit us to sell anything." Her competitor across the street was more hospitable, but the anticipations I unwisely permitted his honeyed words to arouse were sadly wrecked when the "dinner" he promised stopped abruptly at a watery soup, with a meager serving of real bread and butter. Another village astonished me by yielding a whole half-pound of cheese; it boasted a *Kuhkäserei*—what we might call a "cow cheesery"—that was fortunately out of proportion to its transportation facilities. Rodach, at the bottom of a deep cleft in the hills where my route crossed the main railway line to the south, had several by no means empty shops. I canvassed them all without reward, except that one less hard-hearted soul granted me a scoopful of the mysterious purple "marmalade" which, with the possible exception of turnips, seemed to be the only plentiful foodstuff in Germany. But has the reader ever carried a pint of marmalade, wrapped in a sheet of porous paper, over ten miles of mountainous byways on a warm summer afternoon? If not, may I not be permitted to insist, out of the fullness of experience, that it is far wiser to swallow the sickly stuff on the spot, without hoping in vain to find bread to accompany it, or, indeed, to smear it on some convenient house-wall, than to undertake that hazardous feat?

In short, my travels were growing more and more a constant foraging expedition, with success never quite overhauling appetite. The country, indeed, was changing in character, and with it the inhabitants. I had entered a region noted for its slate quarries, and in place of the attractive little villages, with their red-tile roofs and masses of flowering bushes, there came dismal, slate-built black hamlets, almost treeless in setting and peopled by less progressive, more slovenly citizens. The only public hostess of Lahm refused to take me in for the night because her husband was not at home, a circumstance for which I was duly thankful after one glimpse of her slatternly household. A mile or more farther on my eyes were drawn to an unusual sight. An immense rounded hillock ahead stood forth in the sunset like an enameled landscape painted in daring lilac-purple hues. When I reached it I found acres upon acres closely grown with that species of wild pansy which American children call "snap-heads." Similar fields followed, until the entire country-side had taken on the-same curious color, and the breeze blowing across it carried to the nostrils a perfume almost overpowering in its intensity. They were not, as I supposed, meadows lying fallow and overrun with a useless, if attractive, weed, but another example of the German's genius for discovering *Ersatz* species of nourishment. Sown like wheat in the spring, the flowers were harvested, stem and all, in the autumn, and sent to Hamburg to be made into "tea."

Effelter was as black as any African tribe, but its *Gasthaus* was homelike enough within. By the time darkness had thoroughly fallen its every table was closely surrounded by oxlike, hob-nailed countrymen who had stamped in, singly or in small groups, as the last daylight faded away. The innkeeper and his family strove in vain to keep every mug filled, and sprinkled the floor from end to end with drippings of beer. The town was Catholic. While the church-bell tolled the end of evening vespers, the entire gathering sat silently, with bared heads, as is the Bavarian custom, but once the tolling had ceased they did not resume their interrupted conversation. Instead they rose as one man and, each carrying his beer-mug, filed solemnly across the hallway into an adjoining room. The landlord disappeared with them, and I was left entirely alone, except for one horny-handed man of fifty at my own table. He slid bit by bit along the bench on which we both sat, until his elbow touched mine, and entered into conversation by proffering some remark in the crippled dialect of the region about the close connection between crops and weather.

From the adjoining room rose sounds of untrained oratory, mingled with the dull clinking of beer-mugs. The innkeeper and his family had by no means abandoned their service of supply; they had merely laid out a new line of communication between spigots and consumers. Gradually the orderly discussion became a dispute, then an uproar in which a score of raucous voices joined. I looked questioningly at my companion.

"They are electing a new Bürgemeister," he explained, interrupting a question he was asking about the "peasants" of America. "It is always a fight between the *Bürger* and the *Arbeiter*—the citizens and the workers—in which the workers always win in the end."

One could easily surmise in which class he claimed membership by the scornful tone in which he pronounced the word "citizen."

"I live in another town," he added, when I expressed surprise that he remained with me in the unlighted *Gastzimmer* instead of joining his fellows.

I slipped out into the hallway and glanced in upon the disputants. A powerful young peasant stood in an open space between the tables, waving his beer-mug over his head with a gesture worthy of the Latin race, at the same time shouting some tirade against the "citizens." An older man, somewhat better dressed, pounded the table with his empty glass and bellowed repeatedly: *"Na, da' is' giene Wahrhied! Da' is' giene Wahrhied, na!"* The other twoscore electors sipped their beer placidly and added new clouds to the blue haze of tobacco smoke that already half hid the gathering, only now and then adding their voices to the dispute. It was evident that the youthful *Arbeiter* had the great majority with him. As I turned away, my eyes caught a detail of the election that had so far escaped my attention. In a corner of the hallway, huddled closely together, stood a score or more of women, dressed in the gloomy all-black of church service, peering curiously into the room where their husbands smoked, drank, and disputed, and preserving the most absolute silence.

I mentioned the detail to my companion of the guest-room, recalling frequent assertions by Germans in a position to know that the women had been quick to take advantage of the granting of equal suffrage to both sexes by the new "republican" government.

"Certainly," he replied, "they have the *right* to vote, but the German *Frau* has not lost her character. She is still satisfied to let her man speak for her. Oh yes, to be sure, in the large cities there are women who insist on voting for themselves. But then, in the cities there are women who insist on smoking cigarettes!"

In contrast with this conservative, rural viewpoint I have been assured by persons worthy of credence that in the more populous centers some 80 per cent. of the women flocked to the polls for the first election in which suffrage was granted them.

An *Arbeiter* was eventually elected burgmaster of Effelter, as the non-resident had prophesied, but not until long after I had retired to a bedroom above the place of meeting. The vocal uproar intruded for some time upon my dreams and mingled fantastically with them. From the dull clinking of mugs that continued far into the night it was easy to surmise that the evening election turned out to the complete satisfaction, at least, of the innkeeper and his family.

My route next morning lay along the top of a high plateau, wooded in places, but by no means such an Andean wilderness of forest and mountain as that which spread away to the horizon on the left, across a great chasm, in the direction of Teuschnitz. Black hills of slate stood here and there tumbled together in disorderly heaps. Tschirn, the last town of Bavaria, laid out on a bare sloping hillside as if on display as a curiosity in the world's museum, was jet-black from end to end. Not merely were its walls and roofs covered with slate, but its very foundations and cobblestones, even the miniature lake in its outskirts, were slate-black in color.

It was in Tschirn that I discovered I had been "overlooking a bet" on the food question—experience, alas! so often arrives too late to be of value! The innkeepess to whom I murmured some hint about lunch shook her head without looking up from her ironing, but a moment later she added, casually:

"You passed the butcher's house a few yards down the hill, and to-day is Saturday."

The last day of the week, I had been slow in discovering, was meat day in most of the smaller towns of Germany. I grasped at the hint and hastened down to the slate-faced *Metzgerei*. As I thrust my head in at the door, the Falstaffian butcher paused with his cleaver in the air and rumbled, "Ha! *Ein ganz Fremder!*" ("A total stranger"). The carcass of a single steer was rapidly disappearing under his experienced hands into the baskets of the citizens who formed a line at the home-made counter. As each received his portion and added his meat-tickets to the heap that already overflowed a cigar-box, the butcher marked a name off the list that lay before him. I drew out the *Anmeldungskarte* I had received in Berlin, by no means hopeful that it would be honored in a Bavarian mountain village. The butcher glanced at it, read the penciled "*Dauernd auf Reise*" ("Always traveling") at the top, and handed it back to me. The regulations required that I present the document to the Bürgermeister, who would issue me meat-tickets to be in turn handed to the butcher; but it happened that the Bürgermeister and butcher of Tschirn were one and the same person.

"*Amerikaner*, eh!" he cried, hospitably, at once giving me precedence over his fellow-townsmen, whose stares had doubled at the revelation of my nationality. "*Na*, they say it is always meat day in America!"

He carefully selected the best portion of the carcass, cut it through the center to get the choicest morsel, and slashed off an appetizing tenderloin that represented the two hundred grams of the weekly meat ration of Tschirn so exactly that the scales teetered for several seconds. Then he added another slice that brought the weight up to a generous half-pound and threw in a nubbin of suet for good measure.

"Making just two marks," he announced, wrapping it up in a sheet of the local newspaper. "That will put kick in your legs for a day or two—if you watch the cook that prepares it for you."

There was nothing to indicate where Bavaria ended and Saxe-Weimar began, except the sudden appearance of blue post-boxes instead of yellow, and the change in beer. This jumped all at once from sixteen pfennigs a mug to twenty-five, thirty, and, before the day was done, to forty, at the same time deteriorating in size and quality so rapidly that I took to patronizing hillside springs instead of wayside taverns. At the first town over the border I found the municipal ration official at leisure and laid in a new supply of food-tickets. My week's allowance of butter, sugar, and lard I bought on the spot, since those particular *Marken* were good only in specified local shops. The purchases did not add materially to the weight of my knapsack. I confess to having cheated the authorities a bit, too, for I had suddenly discovered a loophole in the iron-clad German rationing system. The jolly butcher-mayor of Tschirn had neglected to note on my "travel-sheet" the tenderloin he had issued me. Meat-tickets were therefore furnished with the rest—and I accepted them without protest. Had all officials been as obliging as he I might have played the same passive trick in every town I passed. But the clerks of the Saxe-Weimar municipality decorated my precious document in a thoroughly German manner with the information that I had been supplied all the tickets to which I was entitled for the ensuing week. That Saturday, however, was a Gargantuan period, and a vivid contrast to the hungry day before; for barely had I received this new collection of *Marken* when an innkeeper served me a generous meat dinner without demanding any of them.

A tramp through the Thuringian highlands, with their deep, black-wooded valleys and glorious hilltops bathed in the cloudless sunshine of early summer, their flower-scented breezes and pine-perfumed woodlands, would convert to pedestrianism the most sedentary of mortals. Laasen was still slate-black, like a village in deep mourning, but the next town, seen far off across a valley in its forest frame, was gay again under the familiar red-tile roofs. With sunset I reached Saalfeld, a considerable city in a broad lowland, boasting a certain grimy industrial progress and long accustomed to batten on tourists. In these untraveled days it was sadly down at heel, and had a grasping disposition that made it far less agreeable than the simple little towns behind that earn their own honest living. Food, of course, was scarce and poor, and, as is always the case, the more one paid for it the more exacting was the demand for tickets. A hawk-faced hostess charged me twice as much for boiling the meat I had brought with me as I had paid for it in Tschirn.

Sunday had come again. The cities, therefore, were all but forsaken and my hob-nails echoed resoundingly through the stone-paved streets. Their inhabitants one found miles beyond, "hamstering" the country-side or holidaying with song, dancing, and beer in the little villages higher up among the hills. The habitual tramp, however, was nowhere to be seen; the Great

War has driven him from the highways of Europe. An occasional band of gipsies, idling about their little houses on wheels, in some shaded glen, or peering out through their white-curtained windows, were the only fellow-vagabonds I met during all my German tramp. I talked with several of them, but they were unusually wary of tongue, taking me perhaps for a government spy; hence there was no way of knowing whether their fiery-eyed assertion of patriotism was truth or pretense.

My last village host was a man of far more culture than the average peasant innkeeper. In his youth he had attended the *Realschule* of Weimar. But Germany is not America in its opportunity to climb the ladder of success irrespective of caste and origin, and he had drifted back to his turnip-fields and a slattern household strangely out of keeping with his clear-thinking mental equipment. He had gone through the entire war as a private, which fact of itself was a striking commentary on the depressing caste system of the German army. Yet there was not the slightest hint in his speech or manner to suggest that he resented what would have been branded a crying injustice in a more democratic land. A society of solidified strata he seemed to find natural and unavoidable. The goddess of chance had been more kind to him than had his fellow-men. Four unbroken years he had served in the trenches, on every front, yet though he towered 1.87 meters aloft, or an inch above the regulation German parapet, his only wound was a tiny nick in the lobe of an ear. Gas, however, had left him hollow-chested and given him, during his frequent spasms of coughing, a curious resemblance to a shepherd's crook.

The thoroughness with which Germany utilized her man-power during the war was personified in this human pine-tree of the Weimar hills. He had been granted just two furloughs—of six and fourteen days, respectively. Both of them he had spent in his fields, laboring from dawn to dark, for, as he put it, "the women were never able to keep up with the crops." His only grievance against fate, however, was the setback it had given the education of his children. Since 1914 his boys had received only four hours of schooling a week—as to the girls he said nothing, as if they did not matter. The teachers had all gone to war; the village pastor had done his best to take the place of six of them. Women, he admitted, might have made tolerable substitutes, but in Germany that was not the custom and they had never been prepared to teach. The optimistic American attitude of overlooking the lack of specific preparation when occasion demanded has no champions in the Fatherland, where professions, as well as trades, are taken with racial seriousness. The end of the war, he complained, with the only suggestion of bitterness he displayed during a long evening, had found him with a son "going on twelve" who could barely spell out the simplest words and could not reckon up the cost of a few mugs of beer without using his fingers.

XVI
FLYING HOMEWARD

The next afternoon found me descending the great avenue of chestnuts, white then with blossoms, that leads from the Belvedere into the city of Weimar. The period was that between two sittings of the National Assembly in this temporary capital of the new German *Volksreich*, and the last residence of Goethe, had sunk again into its normal state—that of a leisurely, dignified, old provincial town, more engrossed with its local cares than with problems of world-wide significance. Self-seeking "representatives of the people," frock-tailed bureaucrats, scurrying correspondents from the four comers of the earth and the flocks of hangers-on which these unavoidable appendages of modern society inevitably bring in their train, had all fled Berlinward. Weimar had been restored to her own simple people, except that one of her squares swarmed with the Jews of Leipzig, who had set up here their booths for an annual fair and awakened all the surrounding echoes with their strident bargainings.

The waiter who served me in a hotel which the fleeing Assembly had left forlorn and gloomy was a veteran *Feldwebel* and a radical Socialist. The combination gave his point of view curious twists. He raged fiercely against the lack of discipline of the new German army of volunteers. The damage they had done to billets they had recently abandoned he pictured to me with tears in his watery eyes. Did I imagine the men who served under *him* had ever dared commit such depredations? Could I believe for an instant that *his* soldiers had ever passed an officer without saluting him? *Ausgeschlossen!* He would have felled the entire company, like cattle in a slaughter-house! Yet in the same breath he gave vent to Utopian theories that implied a human perfection fit for thrumming harps on the golden stairs of the dreary after-world of the theologians. Man in the mass, he asserted, was orderly and obedient, ready to make his desires subservient to the welfare of society. It was only the few evil spirits in each gathering who stirred up the rest to deeds of communal misfortune. The mass of workmen wished only to pursue their labors in peace; but the evil spirits forced them to strike. Soldiers, even the volunteer soldiers of the new order of things that was breaking upon the world, wished nothing so much as to be real soldiers; but they were led astray by the fiends in human form among them. These latter must be segregated and destroyed, root and branch.

I broke in upon his dreams to ask if he could not, perhaps, round up a pair of eggs somewhere.

"Eggs, my dear sir!" he cried, raising both arms aloft and dropping them inertly at his sides. "Before the National Assembly came to Weimar we bought them anywhere for thirty pfennigs, or at most thirty-five. Then came the swarms of politicians and bureaucrats—it is the same old capitalistic government, for all its change of coat—every last little one of them with an allowance of thirty marks a day for expenses, on top of their generous salaries. It is a lucky man who finds an egg in the whole dukedom now, even if he pays two marks for it."

My German tramp ended at Weimar. Circumstances required that I catch a steamer leaving Rotterdam for the famous port of Hoboken three days later, and to accomplish that feat meant swift movement and close connections. The most rapid, if not the most direct, route lay through Berlin. Trains are never too certain in war-time, however, and I concluded to leave the delay-provoking earth and take to the air.

There was a regular airplane mail service between Weimar and Berlin, three times a day in each direction, with room for a passenger or two on each trip. The German may not forgive his enemies, but he is quite ready to do business with them, to clothe them or to fly them, to meet any demand of a possible customer, whatever his origin. He still tempers his manners to outward appearances, however, for the great leaden god of caste sits heavily upon him, in spite of his sudden conversion to democracy. Turn up at his office in tramping garb and you are sure to be received like the beggar at the gate. Whisper in his ear that you are prepared to pay four hundred and fifty marks for the privilege of sitting two hours in his airplane express and he grovels at your feet.

The price was high, but it would have been several times more so for those unable to buy their marks at the foreign rate of exchange. A swift military automobile called for me at the hotel next morning, picking up a captain in mufti next door, who welcomed me in a manner befitting the ostensible fatness of my purse. On the way to the flying-field, several miles out, we gathered two youthful lieutenants in civilian garb and slouchy caps, commonplace in appearance as professional truck-drivers. The captain introduced me to them, emphasizing my nationality, and stating that they were the pilot and pathfinder, respectively, who were to accompany me on my journey. They raised their caps and bowed ceremoniously. The pilot had taken part in seven raids on Paris and four on London, but the biplane that was already fanning the air in its eagerness to be off had seen service only on the eastern front. It still bore all the military markings and a dozen patched bullet-holes in wings and tail. The captain turned me over to a middle-aged woman in an anteroom of the hangar, who tucked me solicitously into a flying-suit, that service being included in the price of the trip.

Flying had become so commonplace an experience that this simple journey warrants perhaps no more space than a train-ride. Being my own first departure from the solid earth, however, it took on a personal interest that was enhanced by the ruthlessness with which my layman impressions were shattered. I had always supposed, for instance, that passengers of the air were tucked snugly into upholstered seats and secured from individual mishap by some species of leather harness. Not at all! When my knapsack had been tossed into the cockpit—where there was room for a steamer-trunk or two—the pathfinder motioned to me to climb in after it. I did so, and gazed about me in amazement. Upholstered seats indeed! Two loose boards, a foot wide and rudely gnawed off on the ends by some species of *Ersatz* saw, teetered insecurely on the two frail strips of wood that half concealed the steering-wires. Now and then, during the journey, they slipped off at one end or the other, giving the ride an annoying resemblance to a jolting over country roads in a farm wagon. One might at least have been furnished a cushion, at two hundred and twenty-five marks an hour!

The pathfinder took his seat on one of the boards and I on the other. Behind me was a stout strap, attached to the framework of the machine.

"I suppose I am to put this around me?" I remarked, as casually as possible, picking up the dangling strip of leather.

"Oh no, you won't need that," replied my companion of the cockpit, absently. "We are not going high; not over a thousand meters or so." He spoke as if a little drop of that much would do no one any harm.

The silly notion flashed through my head that perhaps these wicked Huns were planning to flip me out somewhere along the way, an absurdity which a second glance at the pathfinder's seat, as insecure as my own, smothered in ridicule. There was no mail and no other passenger than myself that morning. *Regular* service means just that, with the German, and the flight would have started promptly at nine even had I not been there to offset the cost of gasolene at two dollars a quart. We roared deafeningly, crawled a few yards, sped faster and faster across a long field, the tall grass bowing prostrate as we passed, rose imperceptibly into the air and, circling completely around, sailed majestically over a tiny toy house that had been a huge hangar a moment before, and were away into the north.

Like all long-imagined experiences this one was far less exciting in realization than in anticipation. At the start I felt a slight tremor, about equal to the sensation of turning a corner a bit too swiftly in an automobile. Now and then, as I peered over the side at the shrunken earth, the reflection flashed upon me that there was nothing but air for thousands of feet beneath us; but the thought was no more terrifying than the average person feels toward water when he first sails out to sea. By the time Weimar had disappeared I felt as comfortably at home as if I had been seated on the floor of a jolting box-car—the parallel is chosen advisedly. I glanced through the morning paper, scribbled a few belated notes, and exchanged casual remarks in sign language with my companion.

The roar of the machine made conversation impossible. Whenever a new town of any importance appeared on the animated relief map far below us, the pathfinder thrust a thumb downward at it and pointed the place out on the more articulate paper map in his hands. The view was much the same as that from the brow of a high mountain. I knew a dozen headlands in the Andes below which the world spread out in this same entrancing entirety, except that here the performance was continuous rather than stationary, as a cinema film is different from a "still" picture. To say that the earth lay like a carpet beneath would be no trite comparison. It resembled nothing so much as that—a rich Persian carpet worked with all manner of fantastic figures; unless it more exactly imitated the "crazy-quilt" of our grandmothers' day, with the same curiously shaped patches of every conceivable form and almost every known color. Here were long narrow strips of brilliant green; there, irregular squares of flowery purple-red; beyond, mustard-yellow insets of ridiculously misshapen outlines; farther off, scraps of daisy-white, and between them all velvety brown patches that only experience could have recognized as plowed fields. I caught myself musing as to how long it would be before enterprising mankind took to shaping the surface of the earth to commercial purposes, advising the airmen by the form of the meadows to "Stop at Müller's for gas and oil," or to "See Smith for wings and propellers." All the scraps of the rag-bag had been utilized by the thrifty quilt-maker. Corn-fields looked like stray bits of green corduroy cloth; wheat-fields like the remnants of an old khaki uniform; the countless forests like scattered pieces of the somber garb cast off after the period of family mourning was over; rivers like sections of narrow, faded-black tape woven fantastically through the pattern in ridiculously snaky attempts at decorative effect. Here and there the carpet was moth-eaten—where a crop of hay had recently been gathered. A forest that had lately been turned into telegraph poles seemed a handful of matches spilled by some careless smoker; ponds and small lakes, the holes burned by the sparks from his pipe.

We had taken a rough road. Like all those inexperienced with the element, I suppose, I had always thought that flying through the air would be smoother than sailing the calmest sea known to the tropical doldrums.

Experience left another illusion ruthlessly shattered. It was a fitful, blustery day, with a high wind that rocked and tossed us about like a dory on a heavy sea; moreover, at irregular intervals averaging perhaps a minute apart the machine struck an air current that bounced us high off our precarious perches in the cockpit as a "thank-you-ma'am" tosses into one another's laps the back-seat passengers in an automobile. The sickening drop just beyond each such ridge in the air road gave one the same unpleasant sensation of vacancy in the middle of the body that comes with the too sudden descent of an elevator. Particularly was this true when the pilot, in jockeying with the playful air waves, shut off his motor until he had regained his chosen altitude. There may be nothing more serious about a faulty carburetor a thousand yards aloft than on the ground, but the novice in aerial navigation is apt to listen with rapt attention to anything that ever so briefly suggests engine trouble.

Yet none of these little starts reached the height of fear. There was something efficient about the ex-raider who sat at the controls with all the assurance of a long-experienced chauffeur that would have made fright seem absurd. I did get cold feet, it is true, but in the literal rather than the figurative sense. After a May of unbroken sunshine, early June had turned almost bitter cold, and the thin board floor of the cockpit was but slight protection against the wintry blasts. Every now and then we ran through a rain-storm, but so swiftly that barely a drop touched us. Between them the sun occasionally flashed forth and mottled the earth-carpet beneath with fleeing cloud shadows. Now the clouds charged past close over our heads, now we dived headlong into them; when we were clear of them they moved as does a landscape seen from a swift train—those near at hand sped swiftly to the rear, those farther off rode slowly forward, seeming to keep pace with us. Villages by the score were almost constantly visible, reddish-gray specks like rosettes embroidered at irregular intervals into the carpet pattern. It made one feel like a "Peeping Tom" to look down into their domestic activities from aloft. The highways between them seemed even more erratic in their courses than on the ground, and aroused still more wonder than the pedestrian would have felt as to what excuse they found for their strange deviations. Gnatlike men and women were everywhere toiling in the fields and only rarely ceased their labors to glance upward as we droned by overhead. Many enticing subjects for my kodak rode tantalizingly southward into the past, emphasizing at least one advantage of the tramp over the passenger of the air.

We landed at Leipzig, girdled by its wide belt of "arbor gardens," theoretically to leave and pick up mail. But as there was none in either direction that morning, the halt was really made only to give the pilot time to smoke a cigarette. That finished, we were off again, rolling for miles across a wheat-field, then leaving the earth as swiftly as it had risen up to meet us ten minutes before. Landing and departure seem to be the most serious and time-losing tasks of the airman, and, once more aloft, the pilot settled down with the contentment of a being returned again to its native element. As we neared Berlin the scene below turned chiefly to sand and forest, with only rare, small villages. One broad strip that had been an artillery proving-ground was pitted for miles as with the smallpox. To my disappointment, we did not fly over the capital, but came to earth on the arid plain of Johannesthal, in the southernmost suburbs, the sand cutting into our faces like stinging gnats as we snorted across it to the cluster of massive hangars which the machine seemed to recognize as home. My companions took their leave courteously but quickly and disappeared within their billets. Another middle-aged woman despoiled me of my flying-togs, requested me to sign a receipt that I had been duly delivered according to the terms of the contract, and a swift automobile set me down, still half deaf from the roar of the airplane, at the corner of Friedrichstrasse and Unter den Linden—as it would have at any other part of Berlin I might have chosen—just three hours from the time I had been picked up at my hotel in Weimar.

The capital was still plodding along with that hungry placidity which I had always found there. Surely it is the least exciting city of its size in the world, even in the midst of wars and revolutions! My total expenses during thirty-five days within unoccupied Germany summed up to three thousand marks, a less appalling amount than it would have been to a German, since the low rate of exchange reduced it to barely two hundred and fifty dollars. Of this— and the difference is worthy of comment—eighty dollars had been spent for food and only sixteen dollars for lodging. Transportation had cost me seventy dollars and the rest had gone for theater-tickets, photographic supplies, and the odds and ends that the traveler customarily picks up along the way more or less necessarily. There remained in my purse some five hundred marks in war-time "shin-plasters," of scant value in the world ahead even were I permitted to carry them over the border. Unfortunately the best bargains in the Germany of 1919 were just those things that cannot be carried away—hotel rooms, railway and street-car tickets, public baths, cab and taxi rides, theater and opera seats and a few bulky commodities such as paper or books. Perhaps a connoisseur might have picked up advantageously art treasures, jewels, or the curiosities of medieval households, but for one without that training there was little choice but to follow the lead of all Allied officers leaving the capital and invest in a pair of field-glasses. The lenses for which Germany is famous had greatly risen in price, but by no means as much as the mark had fallen in foreign exchange.

Only one episode broke the monotony of the swift express journey to the Holland border. I gained a seat in the dining-car at last, only to discover that the one possibly edible dish on the bill of fare cost two marks more than the few I had kept in German currency. To change a French or Dutch banknote would have meant to load myself down again with useless Boche paper money. Suddenly a brilliant idea burst upon me. In my bag there was still a block or two of the French chocolate which I had wheedled out of the American commissary in Berlin. I dug it up, broke off two inch-wide sections, and held them out toward a cheerful-looking young man seated on the floor of the corridor.

"Would that be worth two marks to you?" I asked.

"Two marks!" he shouted, snatching at the chocolate with one hand while the other dived for his purse. "Have you any more of it to sell?"

At least a dozen persons of both sexes came to ask me the same question before my brief dinner was over. Their eagerness aroused a curiosity to know just how much they would be willing to pay for so rare a delicacy. I opened my bag once more and, taking out the unopened half-pound that remained, laid it tantalizingly on the corner of my table. If eyes could have eaten, it would have disappeared more quickly than a scrap thrown among a flock of seagulls. When the likelihood of becoming the center of a riot seemed imminent, I rose to my feet.

"*Meine Herrschaften*," I began, teasingly, "in a few hours I shall be in Holland, where chocolate can be had in abundance. It would be a shame to take this last bar out of a country where it is so scarce. It is genuine French chocolate, no 'war wares,' So many of you have wished to buy it that I see no just way of disposing of it except to put it up at auction."

"Ah, the true American spirit!" sneered at least a half-dozen in the same breath. "Always looking for a chance to make money."

I ignored the sarcastic sallies and asked for bids. The offers began at ten marks, rose swiftly, and stopped a moment later at twenty-five. To a German that was still the equivalent of ten dollars. I regret to report that the successful bidder was a disgustingly fat Jewess who seemed least in need of nourishment of the entire carload. The cheerful-looking young man who had bought the first morsels had been eager to carry this prize to the fiancée he was soon to see for the first time since demobilization, but he had abandoned the race at twenty marks.

"Now then, *meine Damen und Herren*," I went on, haughtily, when the purchaser had tucked the chocolate into her jeweled arm-bag with a sybaritic leer and laid the specified sum before me, "I am no war-profiteer, nor have I the soul of a merchant. These twenty-five marks I shall hand to this gentleman opposite"—he had the appearance of one who could safely be intrusted with that amount—"with the understanding that he give it to the first *grand blessé* he meets—the first soldier who has lost an arm, a leg, or an eye."

The expressions of praise that arose on all sides grew maudlin. The trustee I had chosen ceremoniously wrote his address on a visiting-card and handed it to the Jewess, requesting hers in return, and promising to forward a receipt signed by the recipient of the "noble American benefaction." Then he fell into conversation with me, learned the purpose that had brought me to Germany, and implored me to continue to Essen with him, where he was connected with the Krupp factories. He would see to it that I was received by Herr von Krupp-Bohlen himself—the husband of Frau Bertha whom the Kaiser had permitted to saddle himself with the glorious family name—and that I be conducted into every corner of the plant, a privilege which had been accorded no Allied correspondent since the war began. His pleas grew almost tearful in spite of my reminder that time and transatlantic steamers wait for no man. The world, he blubbered, had a wholly false notion of the great Krupps of Essen. They were really overflowing with charity. Were they not paying regular wages to almost their war-time force of workmen, though there was employment for only a small fraction of them? It was high time a fair-minded report wiped out the slanders that had been heaped upon a noble family and establishment by the wicked Allied propagandists. Essen at least would never be troubled with labor agitators and Sparticist uprisings....

We reached Bentheim on the frontier at four. Most of my companions of the chocolate episode had been left behind with the change of cars at Löhne, and the coaches now disgorged a throng of fat, prosperous-looking Hollanders. War and suffering, after all, are good for the soul, one could not but reflect, at the sudden change from the adversity-tamed Germans to these gross, red-faced, paunchy, overfed Dutchmen, who, though it be something approaching heresy to say so, perhaps, were far less agreeable to every sense, who had something in their manner that suggested that their acquaintance was not worth cultivating. My last chance for a German adventure had come. Unless the frontier officials at Bentheim visited their wrath upon me in some form or other, my journey through the Fatherland would forever remain like the memory of a Sunday-school picnic in the crater of an extinct volcano— a picnic to which most of the party had neglected to bring their lunch-baskets, and where the rest had spilled their scant fare several times in the sand and ashes along the way.

The same dapper young lieutenant and grizzled old sergeant of five weeks before still held the station gate. Apparently neither of them recognized me as a former acquaintance. At any rate, they showed no curiosity to know how I had managed to spend that length of time on a little journey to Hamburg. Perhaps the stamp of the Foreign Office on my passport left them no choice but to hold their peace. The customs inspector was a bit more inquisitive. He rummaged through my hamper with the manner of one accustomed to do his duty to the letter, at the same time desiring to know how much German money the gentleman was carrying with him. A placard on the wall warned travelers that no gold, only three marks in silver, and not more than fifty marks in paper could be taken out of the country. Those who had more than that amount were the losers, for though the frontier guards gave French or Dutch paper in return for what they took away, it was at a far less advantageous rate of exchange than that in the open market. The inspector accepted my assertion of marklessness without question, but in the mean time he had brought to light the spiked helmet that had been given me in Schwerin. His face took on an expression of puzzled amusement.

"*So!* You are taking it with you?" he chuckled, in a tone implying the belief that it had decorated my own head during the war.

"It was given me as a souvenir," I replied. "I am an American."

"*So!*" he rumbled again, looking up at me with an air of surprise— "American!"

He turned the helmet over several times in his hands, apparently deep in thought, then tucked it down into the hamper again and closed the lid.

"We-ell," he said, slowly, "take it along. We don't need them any more."

There was but one barrier left between me and freedom. Judging from the disheveled appearance of the fat Hollanders who emerged, after long delay in every case, from the little wooden booths along the wall, the personal search that awaited me would be exacting and thorough. One could not expect them to take my word for it that I had no German money or other forbidden valuables concealed about my person. Yet that was exactly what they did. True, five weeks of knocking about in a "hand-me-down" that had been no fit costume for attending a court function in the first place had not left me the appearance of a walking treasury. But frontier officials commonly put less faith in the outward aspect of their victims than did the courteous German soldier who dropped his hands at his sides as I mentioned my nationality and opened the door again without laying a finger upon me.

"Happy journey," he smiled, as I turned away, "and—and when you get back to America tell them to send us more food."

My last hope of adventure had faded away, and Germany lay behind me. At Oldenzaal the Dutch were more exacting in their formalities than their neighbors had been, but they admitted me without any other opposition than the racial leisureliness that caused me to miss the evening train. A stroll through the frontier village was like walking through a teeming market-place after escape from a desert island. The shop-windows bulged with every conceivable species of foodstuffs—heaps of immense fat sausages, suspended carcasses of well-fed cattle, calves, sheep, and hogs, huge wooden pails of butter, overflowing baskets of eggs, hillocks of chocolate and sweets of every description, countless cans of cocoa.... I had almost forgotten that nature, abetted by industry, supplied mankind with such abundance and variety of appetizing things. I restrained with difficulty my impulse to buy of everything in sight.

At the hotel that evening the steak that was casually set before me would have instigated a riot in Berlin. Moreover, it was surrounded by a sea of succulent gravy. I could not recall ever having seen a drop of gravy in all Germany. When I paid my bill, bright silver coins were handed me as change. A workman across the room lighted a fat cigar as nonchalantly as if they grew on the trees outside the window. Luxurious private automobiles rolled past on noiseless rubber tires.

In the train next morning the eye was instantly attracted to the window-straps of real leather, to the perfect condition of the seat-cushions. A German returning to his pre-war residence in Buenos Aires with his Argentine wife and two attractive daughters, whom I had met at table the evening before, insisted that I share his compartment with them. He had spent three months and several thousand marks to obtain his passports, and the authorities at the border had forced him to leave behind all but the amount barely sufficient to pay his expenses to his destination. The transplanted wife was far more pro-German in her utterances than her husband, and flayed the "wicked Allies" ceaselessly in her fiery native tongue. During all the journey the youngest daughter, a girl of sixteen whose unqualified beauty highly sanctioned this particular mixture of races, sat huddled together in her corner like a statue of bodily suffering. Only once that morning did she open her faultless lips. At my expression of solicitude she turned her breath-taking countenance toward me and murmured in a tone that made even German sound musical:

"You see, we have not been used to rich food in Germany since I was a child, and—and last night I ate *so* much!"

The stern days of the Kaiser's régime, with their depressing submergence of personal liberty, would seem to have faded away. During all my weeks of wandering at large throughout the Fatherland not once did a guardian of the law so much as whisper in my ear. In contrast, during twenty-four hours in Holland I was twice taken in charge by detectives—it seems they were looking for a "bird" named Vogel—once in the streets of Oldenzaal and again as I descended from the train at Rotterdam.

THE END

Milton Keynes UK
Ingram Content Group UK Ltd.
UKHW040831071024
449371UK00007B/718

9 789362 093035